Rethinking Reconciliation and Transitional Justice After Conflict

The concepts of reconciliation and transitional justice are inextricably linked in a new body of normative meta-theory underpinned by claims related to their effects in managing the transformation of deeply divided societies to a more stable and more democratic basis. This edited volume is dedicated to a critical re-examination of the key premises on which the debates in this field pivot. The contributions problematise core concepts, such as victimhood, accountability, justice and reconciliation itself; and provide a comparative perspective on the ethnic, ideological, racial and structural divisions to understand their rootedness in local contexts and to evaluate how they shape and constrain moving beyond conflict. With its systematic empirical analysis of a geographic and historic range of conflicts involving ethnic and racial groups, the volume furthers our grasp of contradictions often involved in transitional justice scholarship and practice and how they may undermine the very goals of peace, stability and reconciliation that they seek to promote.

This book was originally published as a special issue of *Ethnic and Racial Studies*.

James Hughes is a Professor of Comparative Politics in the Department of Government at the London School of Economics and Political Science, UK.

Denisa Kostovicova is an Associate Professor of Global Politics in the Department of Government at the London School of Economics and Political Science, UK. Her research interests include transitional justice and post-conflict reconstruction. She is the author of *Kosovo: The Politics of Identity and Space* (2005).

Ethnic and Racial Studies

Series editors: Martin Bulmer, University of Surrey, UK, and John Solomos, University of Warwick, UK

The journal *Ethnic and Racial Studies* was founded in 1978 by John Stone to provide an international forum for high-quality research on race, ethnicity, nationalism and ethnic conflict. At the time the study of race and ethnicity was still a relatively marginal sub-field of sociology, anthropology and political science. In the intervening period the journal has provided a space for the discussion of core theoretical issues, key developments and trends and for the dissemination of the latest empirical research.

It is now the leading journal in its field and has helped to shape the development of scholarly research agendas. *Ethnic and Racial Studies* attracts submissions from scholars in a diverse range of countries and fields of scholarship, and crosses disciplinary boundaries. It is now available in both printed and electronic form. From 2015 it will publish 15 issues per year, three of which will be dedicated to *Ethnic and Racial Studies Review* offering expert guidance to the latest research through the publication of book reviews, symposia and discussion pieces, including reviews of work in languages other than English.

The *Ethnic and Racial Studies* book series contains a wide range of the journal's special issues. These special issues are an important contribution to the work of the journal, where leading social science academics bring together articles on specific themes and issues that are linked to the broad intellectual concerns of *Ethnic and Racial Studies*. The series editors work closely with the guest editors of the special issues to ensure that they meet the highest-quality standards possible. Through publishing these special issues as a series of books, we hope to allow a wider audience of both scholars and students from across the social science disciplines to engage with the work of *Ethnic and Racial Studies*.

Most recent titles in the series include:

Migrant Mothers' Creative Challenges to Racialized Citizenship
Edited by Umut Erel and Tracey Reynolds

Celebrating 40 Years of Ethnic and Racial Studies
Classic Papers in Context
Edited by Martin Bulmer and John Solomos

Rethinking Reconciliation and Transitional Justice After Conflict
Edited by James Hughes and Denisa Kostovicova

Migration and Race in Europe
Edited by Martin Bulmer and John Solomos

Why Do We Still Talk About Race?
Edited by Martin Bulmer and John Solomos

Race and Crisis
Edited by Suman Gupta and Satnam Virdee

Rethinking Reconciliation and Transitional Justice After Conflict

Edited by
James Hughes and
Denisa Kostovicova

Routledge
Taylor & Francis Group
LONDON AND NEW YORK

ETHNIC AND RACIAL STUDIES

First published 2019
by Routledge
2 Park Square, Milton Park, Abingdon, Oxon, OX14 4RN, UK

and by Routledge
52 Vanderbilt Avenue, New York, NY 10017, USA

First issued in paperback 2020

Routledge is an imprint of the Taylor & Francis Group, an informa business

British Library Cataloguing-in-Publication Data
A catalogue record for this book is available from the British Library

ISBN 13: 978-0-367-58437-5 (pbk)
ISBN 13: 978-1-138-36199-7 (hbk)

Typeset in Myriad Pro
by codeMantra

Publisher's Note
The publisher accepts responsibility for any inconsistencies that may have arisen during the conversion of this book from journal articles to book chapters, namely the possible inclusion of journal terminology.

Contents

Citation Information

The chapters in this book were originally published in the journal *Ethnic and Racial Studies*, volume 41, issue 4 (March 2018). When citing this material, please use the original page numbering for each article, as follows:

Introduction
Rethinking reconciliation and transitional justice after conflict
James Hughes and Denisa Kostovicova
Ethnic and Racial Studies, volume 41, issue 4 (March 2018) pp. 617–623

Chapter 1
Agency versus structure in reconciliation
James Hughes
Ethnic and Racial Studies, volume 41, issue 4 (March 2018) pp. 624–642

Chapter 2
Decolonization as reconciliation: rethinking the national conflict paradigm in the Israeli-Palestinian conflict
Nadim N. Rouhana
Ethnic and Racial Studies, volume 41, issue 4 (March 2018) pp. 643–662

Chapter 3
Transitional justice and political order in Rwanda
Cyanne E. Loyle
Ethnic and Racial Studies, volume 41, issue 4 (March 2018) pp. 663–680

Chapter 4
Norm contestation and reconciliation: evidence from a regional transitional justice process in the Balkans
Denisa Kostovicova and Aude Bicquelet
Ethnic and Racial Studies, volume 41, issue 4 (March 2018) pp. 681–700

Chapter 5

Implementing transformative justice: survivors and ex-combatants at the Comisión de la Verdad y Reconciliación in Peru
Rebekka Friedman
Ethnic and Racial Studies, volume 41, issue 4 (March 2018) pp. 701–720

Chapter 6

Looking beyond the state: transitional justice and the Kurdish issue in Turkey
Joost Jongerden
Ethnic and Racial Studies, volume 41, issue 4 (March 2018) pp. 721–738

Chapter 7

Towards transitional justice? Black reparations and the end of mass incarceration
Desmond S. King and Jennifer M. Page
Ethnic and Racial Studies, volume 41, issue 4 (March 2018) pp. 739–758

Chapter 8

Race, reconciliation, and justice in Australia: from denial to acknowledgment
Mark McMillan and Sophie Rigney
Ethnic and Racial Studies, volume 41, issue 4 (March 2018) pp. 759–777

Notes on Contributors

Aude Bicquelet is the Deputy Head of Policy and Research at Royal Town Planning Institute, London, UK. She was also the Research Director at NatCen Social Research, London, UK, where she designed and managed projects for ministerial departments, regulatory bodies and charities.

Rebekka Friedman is a Senior Lecturer of International Relations in the Department of War Studies at Kings College London, UK. Her research and teaching are at the intersection of reconciliation, transitional justice, collective memory, gender and peace-building.

James Hughes is a Lecturer in the Department of Government at the London School of Economics and Political Science, UK. He is a Professor of Comparative Politics, Convenor of the MSc Conflict Studies and Director of the Conflict Research Group.

Joost Jongerden is an Associate Professor of Do-It-Yourself Development in Rural Sociology at Wageningen University, the Netherlands and a Project Professor at the Asian Platform for Global Sustainability and Transcultural Studies at Kyoto University, Japan.

Desmond S. King is a Professor of American Government in the Department of Politics and International Relations at the University of Oxford, UK.

Denisa Kostovicova is an Associate Professor in Global Politics at the Government Department and a Research Fellow in the Civil Society and Human Security Research Unit in the Department of International Development at the London School of Economics and Political Science, UK.

Cyanne E. Loyle is an Assistant Professor of Political Science at Indiana University, Bloomington, USA. She is an East African specialist and has done field work in Rwanda, Uganda, Burundi and the Democratic Republic of Congo, as well as Nepal, Northern Ireland and Turkey.

Mark McMillan is the Deputy Pro Vice-Chancellor of Indigenous Education and Engagement at RMIT University, Melbourne, Australia. He also held associate and senior professor positions at the University of Melbourne, Australia.

Jennifer M. Page is a Postdoctoral Fellow and Chair of Political Philosophy at the University of Zurich, Switzerland. She was also a Postdoctoral Fellow in the Centre for the Study of Slavery & Justice at Brown University, Providence, USA.

Sophie Rigney joined the University of Dundee, UK as a Lecturer in Law in May 2017. Previously, She had been appointed as a Senior Research Fellow at the Melbourne Law School, Australia and co-appointed as a Visiting Fellow at the Institute of Commonwealth Studies, University of London, UK.

Nadim N. Rouhana is a Professor of International Negotiation and Conflict Studies in The Fletcher School of Law and Diplomacy at Tufts University Massachusetts, Medford, USA and the Founder and General Director of Mada al-Carmel, Arab Center for Applied Social Research, Haifa, Israel.

INTRODUCTION

Rethinking reconciliation and transitional justice after conflict

James Hughes and Denisa Kostovicova

ABSTRACT
The concepts of reconciliation and transitional justice are the foundations for a new body of connected normative meta-theories that address conflict transformation and peace building. The articles in this special issue provide a comparative perspective on the concepts and their implementation. The articles are primarily focused on intra-state conflicts. A range of cases involving different types of conflict are included, including those driven by ethnic, racial, religious and ideological factors, and different regimes from authoritarian to democratic states, and cases where colonial legacies and mentalities endure. The articles offer critical reflections on the contradictory logics between external construction of norms and the efforts at their domestic imposition, adoption, and distortion and obstruction in conflict states and societies. These processes are not linear but vary over time. The ambiguities in the concepts are also often magnified by political considerations, which make the peace processes new stages in the conflict.

Too much and too little memory of the past can both be unhealthy. The idea that social peace requires fixing boundaries to the memory of the past was formulated by Nietzsche, who feared that too much historical memory would be a "gravedigger of the present" ([1874] 2010, 4). This special issue has been developed to focus on critical perspectives on the concepts of reconciliation and transitional justice. These are fields of social science inquiry and policy practice that are pervaded by normative impulses about how to deal with the past. If conflicts are generally rooted in past legacies, and if they are driven by constructed historical narratives, how can a conflictual past be managed to foster peace building in the present and for the future? The articles offer fresh analyses and insights into the questions of how the past is to be dealt with in peace building, i.e. analysing the lived experience from a number of key cases to demonstrate how the past is being managed to achieve peace and reconciliation. The concept of reconciliation has been increasingly used since the 1990s in academic and policy discussions on peace building after violent conflict and about the processes involved in "transitional justice" both during regime transitions and in the aftermath of violent conflict. While studies of reconciliation have multiplied, the concept itself is persistently often identified normatively with highly ambiguous and ill-defined processes and end goals. Yet the enduring quality of the concept is that it continues to be universally promoted as the foundation for a durable peace, and as being essential for the move of any society that has endured a divisive and destructive conflict to a shared and constructive future. Yet it is a contested term with multiple meanings. Is reconciliation about the "self", inter-personal relationships, group relations, or relations to and between states, or all of these things? In thinking about the concept, how much attention should we pay to the future, the present or the past? This special issue is dedicated to a critical reexamination of the key premises on which the debates in this field pivot.

The study of the concepts of reconciliation and transitional justice has expanded greatly since the early 1990s and has become inextricably linked with a new body of normative meta-theory that emerged to account for and to direct, in the main, two types of regime transformation and state-building: firstly, rebuilding society in the aftermath of violent conflicts that are generally fought around some deep cleavage such as ideology, or religious, ethnic and racial identity; and secondly, managing transitions by states from forms of non-democratic rule, where human rights abuses were systemic, to democracy. There are also cases involving colonial legacies which tend to straddle both aspects. These two forms of change are not always contiguous, coincidental or causally connected. In the state of play in the scholarly studies in this field, certain processes have been generally understood to be paramount, whether in practice, or from a normative perspective. Among the most important are that reconciliation has a processual quality, though the precise pattern of the sequence is indeterminate. Generally, it is expected that there will be institutional and society-led mechanisms for dialogue, truth recovery and narrative construction about the past of a conflict, combined with legal processes of settling accounts for past wrongdoings, and civil society-led production of inter-group bonding social capital, which will be often internationally funded and conditioned. The concepts and lived experience of the processes suggest that professional expertise is considered vital in two sectors: the legal aspects of retribution, and the mediation of inter-group contact and peace processes involving elites and society. Successful implementation of reconciliation and transitional justice is assumed almost universally to be a necessary precondition for the consolidation of peace and stability, and for delivering interrelated incentives and benefits, such as democratization, nation-building and post-conflict economic and social reconstruction.

Over time, two critical orientations have become increasingly salient in the field. Firstly, normative claims have been increasingly challenged and tested by a growing body of empirical scholarship on specific conflicts, which has illuminated the complexity and nuances at work. There is by now a sharp contrast between the starkness of decontextualized normative claims about how processes should be conducted and what they should achieve, and the murky realties of the grey zone of context, actual practice and lived experience. Secondly, the study of post-conflict processes of dealing with the past has become a multi-disciplinary exercise, moving far beyond the confines of historical debates about any particular conflict, and outpacing the initial premises of the 1990s that were rooted in a legal preoccupation with human rights abuses. The growth of multi-disciplinary studies of managing post-conflict states and societies has introduced methodological pluralism into the field.

At the minimalist end of the spectrum, studies of reconciliation stress coexistence. At the opposite end are the most deeply normative, where we find approaches are often informed by Christian teachings on the pursuit of salvation through forgiveness, and also by secular recognition of common humanity. Somewhere along that spectrum, we find transitional justice advocates, mainly lawyers, dealing in the pursuit of perpetrators, seeking justice-seeking, concerned with vengeance and reparations, and the stamping out of "impunity". This spectrum is replete with any number of complex questions, including how to eradicate prejudice and discrimination, and how to deal with the legacies of the past conflict, and what are the relative roles of agency and structure in these processes. It is not just the matter of reconciling competing narratives of the past and "truth recovery" (if such is possible), or reparations for "victims" (itself an ill-defined term), but also excavating the structural legacies of a deep past in which the conflict is or was embedded, and in particular in a colonial past, and finding ways to come to terms with the past (what Germans call *vergangenheitsbewältigung*, a term which signifies that this is a process). Most of the studies of post-conflict reconciliation included in this special issue are, in fact, conflicts that have roots in colonial pasts, and the power asymmetries, and prejudices, and structural legacies that have evolved out of colonialism. Challenges posed by historical legacies are further compounded by the contemporary institutional context and conflict resolution fads which set parameters for how reconciliation and transitional justice are supposed to take place. International conflict management theory and practice is overly focused on technocratic statist institutionalism, on top-down approaches such as elite agreements and cooperation to make governance effective, at the expense of thinking about divisions in society and the structural barriers to inter-group reconciliation. Many peace agreements to end conflicts, whether they are shaped mainly by internal parties or are externally imposed, tend to be elite-led and top-down processes.

In some cases, conflicts have ended with a clear victor and that has often been followed by forms of exclusion, "victor's justice", and hegemonic state narratives. In other cases, conflicts have ended messily, with no clear winner, and in these cases often we see institutionalized structural ethnic divisions in forms of power-sharing being pushed on domestic elites by external powers, leading to the embedding of ethnic divisions in political structures. This outcome is usually starkly at odds with efforts aimed at promoting cross-ethnic accommodation at the societal level. Furthermore, while reconciliation and transitional justice as a package has become an unquestioned policy mantra internationally, as well as in most domestic contexts, often at the grassroots level among communities that are supposed to be the object of the process, the very terms reconciliation and justice have become at best sardonic references, and at worst dirty words. This is largely a reaction to the vague use and politicized imposition of the concepts by external peace builders who rigidly adhere to combinations of interests and "global justice" norms detached from local context.

The articles in this special issue provide a comparative perspective on reconciliation in relation to divisive inter-ethnic relations in post-conflict states and societies. The articles are primarily focused on the question of inter-group reconciliation within a state, and this poses a different and more complex set of challenges compared to the question of reconciliation between states. The articles also cover a range of cases involving different types of conflict, including those driven by ethnic, racial, religious and ideological factors, and those where colonial legacies and mentalities endure. A broad range of different cases and approaches to the question of post-conflict reconciliation have been included. The articles offer critical reflections on the logic of external construction of norms that are then diffused into the post-conflict states and societies, often with limited normative resonance, recognition, or acceptance in domestic political and cultural environments. The local scope conditions in each case are analysed, querying the interaction of agency and structure in the processes, the nature and impact of violence, the role played by exclusivist ethnic, racial and other identities, the role of different actors (elites vs. civil society) and the construction of competing narratives about conflict. The articles provide comparative perspectives on the ethnic, ideological, racial and structural divisions and attempt to systematically evaluate and understand their rootedness, and how they shape and constrain moving beyond conflict. Is it possible to have any meaningful reconciliation in a post-conflict society without tearing down some or all of these structural barriers? How would the restructuring of conflict societies be conducted? What is the relationship between societal and institutional/state-level and elite reconciliation? What is the objective in terms of reconstructing identities and narratives? On what basis can reconstruction occur, if it is to occur? What is the role of state power, or international power, or civil society in these processes? The contributions problematize the key concepts with which this field operates, such as dialogue and contact, victimhood, accountability, justice, reparations and reconciliation itself. We aim to critique and redefine the conceptual tools with which this field operates.

In the opening article, James Hughes critically reassesses reconciliation theories, discourses and policy practices, arguing that these have tended to prioritize agency over structure and are grounded in a paradox. Conflicts are generally seen as being driven by structural factors, yet theory and practice in reconciliation is focused on developing inter-personal contact between members of conflictual groups as the crucial tool for changing relationships and building peace. Hughes analyses segregation as a common structural factor in conflict societies that constitutes a block to making contact work in the way envisaged by theory. Nadim Rouhana tackles the hegemonic discourses on reconciliation in the Israeli–Palestinian conflict and argues that thinking about reconciliation in this case requires a paradigmatic shift in conflict analysis. According to him, a new paradigm (in the Kuhnian sense) needs to apply a settler-colonial framework to the conflict while also taking into consideration the national component. He therefore reframes reconciliation as decolonization within a transitional justice framework. Cyanne Loyle develops a theory of transitional justice adoption which focuses on the government use of transitional justice as a tool for establishing and maintaining political order. Within this framework, reconciliation and transitional justice discourse and practices are instrumentalized to advance political interests in meeting security, resource and legitimacy challenges in the post-conflict period rather than to provide truth and reconciliation as is often ascribed. Through an examination of the Gacaca courts, the article explores the way the transitional government in Rwanda has used international and domestic calls for accountability to frame its post-conflict consolidation of power. Denisa Kostovicova and Aude Bicquelet address the question whether contestation over the norm of transitional justice prevents inter-ethnic reconciliation, operationalized by them as reconciliatory discourse. Drawing on empirical evidence from the study of debates conducted by a transnational advocacy network (RECOM), which proposes a regional fact-finding commission in the Balkans, they find reconciliatory discourse in those debates where there is norm contestation. They demonstrate that the spatial scale of a transitional justice process matters, with different patterns of discourse in national and regional debates. Rebekka Friedman investigates a transformative and contextual approach to transitional justice that addresses the root causes of violence in Peru. Focusing on Peru's major transitional justice effort with a truth commission, the *Comisión de la Verdad y Reconciliación*, she argues that more conceptual work is needed to link the drivers of conflict, reconciliation and transitional justice. Joost Jongerden critiques the transitional justice approach for its focus on peace through a strengthening of the democratic rule of law at the expense of investigating the injustices underlying conflict and the structural causes of abuse. His article looks critically at ways in which the state in Turkey applied a transitional justice approach to the Kurdish issue, and argues that the concept of self-administration as it emerged in the course of the struggle of the Kurdish movement may be considered as a form of "do-it-yourself" transitional justice.

Established democracies are not usually incorporated within the reconciliation and transitional justice paradigm, and the special issue concludes with two articles that examine reconciliation and transitional justice in relation to colonial legacies of race relations in developed democracies. Desmond King and Jennifer Page analyse the development of the demand for reparations for enslavement and Jim Crow in the United States as an example of a reparations movement that illustrates the commonalities between the goal of transitional justice and domestic redress movements. They show that a future democratic transition – the end of mass incarceration – could animate a renewed push for reparations and a formal investigation into America's legacy of racial injustice. Mark McMillan and Sophie Rigney argue that it is appropriate to apply transitional justice practices to the relationship between the Australian state and Indigenous peoples. The article discusses the historical denial of the harm that the state of Australia has perpetrated against its indigenous peoples. They argue that a transitional justice framework, if adopted, may allow Indigenous voices to name the harm inflicted on them, and position the state as acknowledging the harm that they have perpetrated – bringing a fundamentally new process of reconciliation between the state and Indigenous peoples.

What emerges from these studies is a complex and diverse picture of how the issues of reconciliation and transitional justice are dealt with, and that even within cases the processes at work vary over time. The articles also illustrate that the use of the concepts spans a spectrum from minimalist to maximalist positions, and that in many cases both the normative scholarship and the lived experience are often contradictory. The ambiguities in the concepts are also often magnified by divergent external and local interpretations. Even if we assume that some form of reconciliation and transitional justice is required between groups after a conflict, violent or other, and the assumption is that these processes will advance the stabilization of political and social relations in post-conflict societies, how exactly should we measure and evaluate the roles of the concepts? In sum, we are questioning the analytical usefulness of the concepts of reconciliation and transitional justice for being normatively too vague and often overly politicized.

Perhaps the most perplexing conundrum about reconciliation and transitional justice in conflictual societies is whether the processes that are envisaged by theory, actually have the purported beneficial effects of promoting stable, peaceful and democratic states. In fact, the processes involved in both theory and practice are so ambivalent and contradictory that they may often undermine the goals of peace and stability that they seek to promote. As Chief Justice Ismail Mahomed put it in his judgement on the test-case challenge to the Amnesty Law for South Africa: "If the Constitution kept alive the prospect of continuous retaliation and revenge, the agreement of those threatened by its implementation might never have been forthcoming" (cited in Tutu 1999, 26). The choice seems to be between a number of poisoned chalices, with no single process delivering a satisfactory outcome even within the parameters set by the normative claims of most scholarship. There is the option of "national amnesia" at one end of the spectrum, and at the other end, there is a corrosive permanent state of contesting the past and prosecuting past behaviour, depending on the political balance of power at any given time. The danger for reconciliation and transitional justice approaches is that they do not help to end a conflict, but rather the processes themselves become instruments to continue the conflict.

Disclosure statement

No potential conflict of interest was reported by the authors.

ORCID

James Hughes http://orcid.org/0000-0002-8516-7402

References

Nietzsche, Friedrich. (1874) 2010. "On the Use and Abuse of History for Life." Translated by Ian Johnston. Nanaimo, BC: Vancouver Island University. https://www.classicalpursuits.com/wp-content/uploads/2014/08/Friedrich-Nietzsche_trans_Johnston.pdf.
Tutu, Desmond. 1999. *No Future Without Forgiveness*. New York City: Doubleday.

Agency versus structure in reconciliation

James Hughes

ABSTRACT
Reconciliation theories, discourses and practices prioritize agency over structure. They suggest that inter-group conflicts involving deep cleavages such as ethnicity, race and religion can be resolved by processes involving interpersonal contacts, and achieving a desired end-state of shared values, narratives and identity. Contact between group members under optimal conditions of parity and trust is viewed as the critical tool for change. By problematizing conflictual identities and social relations as agential and interpersonal, conflicts are decontextualized from their structural environment. Structural segregation provides us with a bridging concept between the agency factors, structural dynamics of conflict, and the obstacles to post-conflict reconciliation. The case of Northern Ireland, often elevated to the status of a model for conflict resolution, is analysed to show how structural segregation is the critical barrier to the optimal group interactions envisaged by agential reconciliation, as it sustains low inter-group trust and political polarization.

Studies of reconciliation during and after conflict attach great importance to the role of individual emotions and behaviour in the fostering of good relations between groups. Much less attention is given to how the relationships between people and space are structured, for example by segregation, and how this impacts upon reconciliation efforts. The concept of reconciliation is used in peace-building discourses in such multiple ways that one wonders whether it is possible to identify a coherent consensus meaning for the term. Broadly, reconciliation encompasses all those mechanisms deployed at different levels (international, state, NGOs and civil society, the low level and personal) which aim to reshape antagonistic identities, values and behaviour that are a source of conflict. There has been a surge in interest and publications on reconciliation since the 1980s. The concept was shaped, to a large extent, by the context of the period of regime transitions in the 1980s and 1990s from authoritarianism to democracy, the global turmoil following the collapse of communism, the surge in violent national and ethnic conflicts, and then concomitant peace processes, peace settlements and the drives for transitional justice and social reconstruction after conflict. While accepting the interconnection between reconciliation and transitional justice my concern here is not with transitional justice mechanisms per se. A process of the commodification of peace-building has ensued since the 1990s. Large sums of money have been poured into these policy areas by states, international organizations and independent foundations, which has fostered professionalization and bred a new caste of "expert" consultant, often advising and mediating between groups.

Although, the general goal of reconciliation is to contrive a continuation of peace through overcoming antagonistic identities and building a "shared society", what this entails precisely is not clearly stated. Studies of reconciliation across many disciplines (including theology, philosophy, psychology, law, history, political science, international relations and sociology), as well as policy practices, have a bias towards some variant of the values of a liberal society (see the interdisciplinary collections of Kymlicka and Bashir 2008; Nadler, Malloy, and Fisher 2008; Hirsch 2012). Reconciliation is therefore a form of normative theory, being bound up with notions of peace-making, positive transformation, toleration, atonement and harmony, that to critique it risks a charge of illiberalism, if not nihilism.

While the concept is generally lauded, the dissensus on its meaning is arrayed along a spectrum of minimalist to maximalist positions, from a pragmatic low-expectation of "peaceful coexistence" of groups to the highest level of "harmony" (Bloomfield 2006). For most liberal peace-building advocates the concept of "coexistence" is viewed negatively, as it implies that groups (and also states) are living more or less separately, in parallel, and not sharing values except perhaps not intending to destroy or seriously harm rivals. Coexistence implicitly assumes group parity, or some symmetry of power, and at the very least the absence of domination, which is what facilitates the coexistence. Yet, as we see in the analysis of segregation later, coexistence usually persists with structural segregation and various elements of asymmetry, from severe inequalities of opportunity, wealth, cultural recognition and prejudice. The assumption in the maximalist reconciliation model is that there is a linear sequence of positive steps for a "healing" reconciliation process leading to a common group think around shared values and identity, involving a combination of institutional and informal measures: from contact and dialogue to truth recovery to justice, with the effect of generating trust, mutual respect, catharsis and closure for victims, leading to reduced prejudice, shared narratives and ultimately to a harmonious shared society.

The peace-building turn in the 1990s generated a new moral grammar and discourse about conflict, with value-laden discussions about these various processes: "truth recovery", "dealing with the past", "legacy issues", "justice", "trauma", "victims", "perpetrators", "reparations", "restoration", "apology", building "respect" and "trust", "conflict transformation" and the goal of "harmony" and a "shared society" and so forth. The metaphor of a "journey" and the processual quality of reconciliation for re-establishing harmony and cooperation between antagonists are common themes (Fisher 2001, 26). Galtung identified twelve distinct processes and approaches to reconciliation that inform the work of peacebuilders which are primarily rooted around agency, dialogue and inter-personal contact (2001).

Questioning the use of "toleration" as a positive value, Brown has critiqued the "global renaissance in tolerance talk" since the 1980s (2009, 2). She observes how it was used in the past to legitimize intolerance and oppression (as in Jim Crow), and has now been transformed into "a historically protean element of liberal governance", and as a legitimizing "discourse of power and a practice of governmentality", in the Foucaultian sense of organizing the "conduct of conduct" (Brown 2009, 8, 11). In sum, discourses about toleration are often intolerant. Moon has also criticized the vague prelapsarian circularity to much of the reconciliation discourse, which assumes that harmonious group relations preceded the conflict, and a return to such relations was possible irrespective of the nature and dynamics of the conflict (Moon 2004).

Much of the debate on reconciliation pivots on a chicken and egg dilemma: Is reconciliation a precondition for a desired outcome, or the actual end goal itself? A much broader understanding of reconciliation is taken by Schaap (2005), who views the politics of reconciliation as not distinctive but rather inherently ordinary in the contentious politics of liberal democracy, accepting that there are always problems of exclusion and injustice that require reconciliation. Countering Schaap and others, Bashir (2012) challenges the notion that the inclusion of historically excluded and oppressed social groups can be achieved by deliberative democracy, arguing that reconciliation should be conceived "as a necessary requirement that must be fulfilled before deliberation is pursued" (Bashir 2012, 136–137).

Janus-like, reconciliation is backward looking, seeking to rectify the historical grievances of a dystopian past, and forward-looking, aiming to build a new bright future of a shared society. These two aims do not seem to be logically mutually compatible and reinforcing. Doxtader, however, has suggested that the contradictions between reconciliation as a forward-looking enterprise, and the need for recognition of different historical narratives and identities, is a positive Hegelian dynamic (Doxtader 2007). Similarly, Muldoon's critique of the roles of selective memory in reconciliation in South Africa and Australia suggests that the antagonistic narratives of conflict should be embraced as part of a "truth-telling" process of democratic discourse (Muldoon 2003). These positions rightly draw our attention to the fact that political engagement on reconciliation is more about small steps than making quantum leaps.

Reconciliation and contact theory

The roles of agency and contact theory are given prominence in explanations for the major cases that are considered to be successful examples of post-conflict reconciliation (Germany and France after the Second World War), and reducing societal prejudice (the ending of the Jim Crow system in the USA from the 1950s). Social and policy practitioners of inter-personal inter-group contact long preceded the social science theoretical elaboration about the importance of "contact", not only in the USA, but also as in, for example, the work of French Jesuit Jean du Rivau after 1945, who organized extensive grassroots contacts and exchanges between French and German people (Ackermann 1994). Such exchanges were later formalized and funded by governments. In the case of post-War Germany, which was a clear loser in the war, however, there was a meta-level shape-change in thinking about identity among its governing elites. Adenauer eschewed any German narrative of grievance about the war and forged a new consensus on democratic values, partly to facilitate a speedy post-war integration into the new European order and other international institutions (Feldman 2012). The shift from segregation in the USA was much slower, and resisted more intensely in the Deep South, a process which is analysed in Allport (1954), the classic study of prejudice.

The contact theory in social psychology is derived from Allport (1954) and has informed thinking on the importance of agency in the overcoming of prejudice and pathways to reconciliation globally. Allport proposed that inter-group prejudice may be overcome and trust built by promoting positive interaction between groups in non-hierarchical and non-threatening settings. In sum, he proposed equal status contacts towards achieving common goals. His work has been the theoretical foundation for the design of much of the social psychology research in divided societies. Allport shied away from proposing large scale social engineering of structural change to overcome prejudice, and favoured the use of essentially soft coercive change through top-down agential leadership responses by "executive action" and judicial activism (as in US desegregation) to change the "conditions of conformity". When Allport argued that "it is wiser to attack segregation and discrimination than to attack prejudice directly", he means changing values and behaviour, not attacking the structures of discrimination and segregation per se (Allport, 1954, 509).

Contact has also indirectly informed the theory of consociationalism, which since the 1990s has become a mainstay of political peace processes and institutional engineering to end conflicts in deeply divided societies. Lijphart's notion of a "spirit of accommodation" among elites is central to his ideas about how power-sharing institutions work to produce peace by making elites work positively together through routine contact

(1968). Peace agreements, consociational or otherwise, however, can be made without the conflict groups (elite or mass) agreeing on a narrative of the conflict: its root causes, its dynamics (interpreting key events and the development of the conflict over time), and the apportionment of fault ("blame", defining "victim", distinguishing between victim and perpetrator), or accepting that "we are all victims", or recognizing the "little perpetrator in each one of us" (Doxtader, 133 citing the South African Truth and Reconciliation Commission). Moreover, while consociationalism accepts the necessity for profound structural institutional change, and transformed elite mentalities, it is also paradoxically grounded in an acceptance of deep structural segmentation of politics and society, in a sense accepting segregation and providing no mechanisms for transcending it. It is important to recognize that the conditions produced by consociational peace processes are not favourable to a shared identity or societal reconciliation.

Contact theory informs peace processes broadly through the idea of "dialogue". In a conflict setting, this almost always refers to elite talks. Such dialogue is almost always conducted in secret, and while that may or may not insulate elites from other radical "outbidders", or recalcitrant constituencies, it is seen as a vital way to build trust among elites – but it does exclude society. Perhaps the most recognized use of the idea of "dialogue" is in the faith-based approaches to reconciliation. The process of dialogue is less about negotiation as such, and much more derived from the Christian humanist idea that by "bringing people together" in a process of dialogue it is possible to overcome divisions irrespective of their nature, structure, ideological or material basis. Such an approach is most closely associated with Christian religious leaders and practitioners in the field such as Jean Paul Lederach and Desmond Tutu. Lederach's and Tutu's works stress the interaction of the personal and communal and specific social psychological aspects of individual transformation in post-conflict peace-making (Lederach 1995, 1997, 1999, 2003; Tutu 1999). In particular, it is Lederach who is the guru of the concept of "transformation", which is concerned with developing reconciliation in society and among individuals by psychocultural means, and primarily by a focus on the "self". Lederach is dismissive of the institutional engineering of peace-making, criticizing the "narrowness of resolution approaches" that are focused on institutions and politics, because while they may solve problems in the short term they do not create a dynamic of "constructive change". But what kind of "constructive change" does Lederach envisage? Lederach loosely uses ill-defined concepts such as building positive "relationships", "changing lives for the better", and building "capacities which are creative, responsive, constructive, and non-violent" (Lederach 2003, 69, 70), without specifying how any of this will be achieved in practice or addressing the structural context of conflict.

Reducing power asymmetries so that all groups perceive equality of opportunity for material and social advancement is understood to be critical for positive inter-group contact (Malloy 2008). At the maximum groups perceive that mutual dependence and mutual respect will lead to positive outcomes for all. Here, we see a significant divergence in the studies of reconciliation between those that tend to stress the material rewards from cooperation, in terms of the ending of conflict and economic development, and those that are informed by religious belief in the spiritual benefits of recognizing common humanity. However, the basic premise at work here is that contact creates a virtuous cycle of mutual respect, shared narratives leading to a common identity, and thereby the possibilities of cooperation increase, and the potential for conflict decreases. When social scientists have attempted to measure the effects of contact, the results suggest that it has positive effects, seemingly confirming the theory. A meta-analysis of 515 studies over many decades on prejudice suggests that, even allowing for selection bias and "file drawer" problems (not reporting results that negate the theory), even unstructured intergroup contact reduces prejudice and improves attitudes toward outgroups, while the effect is enhanced under Allport's optimal conditions (Pettigrew and Tropp 2006). The question then is not whether contact theory works, but whether it can work effectively in societies that are structurally segregated. After all, segregation is a huge structural limitation to contact in deeply divided societies.

Segregation, trust and reconciliation

Given the centrality of agency for achieving reconciliation in the various iterations of contact theory, the very absence of opportunities for regular contact posed by structural forms of segregation such as residential area, education, cultural rituals, social spaces, etc. constitute a huge challenge. Residential segregation profoundly shapes interethnic relations by reinforcing mutual ignorance of the "other", and instilling negative emotions such as fear, hatred and resentment. Sociologists have long recognized that even if it is the case that identities were not conflictual prior to their mobilization, the dynamics of violent conflict produce a breakdown in social relationships which can itself further structure and deepen antagonisms by hardening group identities and rivalries (Coser 1956). Prior to their mobilization for conflict, identities may also be hardened by structural factors – the spatial and demographic features of a divided society – and the cleansing, targeting, and other forms of discrimination against groups. The canvas of these structural divisions is usually broad, ranging from various forms of institutionalized discrimination between groups, but perhaps one of the most embedded aspects of structural division is group segregation.

Dominant groups in divided societies often seek to harden the segregation by destroying shared communities and spaces, or by public policies which obstruct their emergence. Apartheid is an extreme case but that regime's forced removals policies, and illustrated by its destruction of District Six, a vibrant cosmopolitan multiracial community in Cape Town in 1960, demonstrate the symbolic and practical importance attached to separation by such regimes. We could consider the segregation of Israeli Jewish and Palestinian communities both inside Israel and in the Occupied Territories to be in a similar vein. In cases such as Northern Ireland and Israel, the social segregation is even visibly demonstrated by the construction of massive physical barriers between communities. The "contact" theory, consequently, tends to be decontextualized from its structural environment, in particular, where segregation greatly limits the opportunities for positive routine contact between groups.

As noted earlier, Allport's confidence in "contact" and the use of state agential power in executive actions and law reform as the primary means for changing "conformity" on prejudice did not challenge the structures of segregation directly. Such an approach does not grasp accurately the question of what constitutes social conformity. The problem was encapsulated by Woodward, who observed that:

> laws are not an adequate index of the extent and prevalence of segregation and discriminatory practices in the South. The practices often anticipated and sometimes exceeded the law. It may be confidentially assumed – and it could be verified by present observation – that there is more Jim Crowism practiced in the South than there are Jim Crow laws on the books. (Woodward 1955, 87)

When social scientists analyse the effects of structural segregation they find that it seriously constrains the "contact" theory. Putnam critiques the "allure" of contact theory by citing a wide range of studies showing a negative relationship between ethnic diversity and indicators of social capital and cohesion, concluding that "diversity fosters out-group distrust and in-group solidarity" (2007, 141–142). His solution is a top-down public policy of promoting an overarching "shared citizenship" and building "meaningful opportunities" for bridging capital at local level – not dissimilar to the "contact" theory he criticizes (2007, 164). Putnam also misses the target, for in a gallop to attack diversity, he overlooks the pivotal importance of segregation. Other research that digs down into what constitutes a "diverse" neighbourhood or city, draw conclusions opposite to Putnam. It is not diversity but residential segregation that drives down inter-group trust.

Generalized trust is the belief that "most people can be trusted," even those different from ourselves, or considered to be the "other" (Uslaner 2002, ch. 2). Trust is a form of "bridging" or connecting capital between groups rather than "bonding" capital within groups. Using values data from US and British cities,

Uslaner (2011) has shown that people are somewhat less trusting in diverse cities, but people living in well integrated cities who have diverse social networks are much more likely to be trusting than people who live in segregated cities with homogenous social networks, though this effect is more pronounced for whites than for non-whites. Other research suggests that residential segregation perpetuates discriminatory social structures, inequalities and racist value-systems, transmitting their contexts inter-generationally (Sharkey 2008). The effects occur as much through in-group socialization as by any of the other conventionally highlighted effects (income inequalities, labour markets, housing markets, asymmetries in opportunities, and of course prejudice). A continuity of racial context from youth to young adulthood is consistent with the logic of the place stratification model. Young white, African-American, and Latino adults are residentially segregated from each other because they grew up in segregated neighbourhoods (Goldsmith 2016).

The agency of contact theory seems to break against the structure of perpetuation theory. If segregation persists then it blocks routine contact and perpetuates deep prejudices, while at the same time providing a laager for the socialization of in-group values and a geographical basis for activity segregation and political polarization. Let us now explore critically the dynamics between these two theories in an important case of ethnic conflict and conflict resolution: Northern Ireland. This is a case that is characterized not only by deep segregation, but also where there was no conclusive victory in a conflict, and where antagonistic identities, selective memory and particularistic narratives, and social structures, endure into the post-conflict arena.

Northern Ireland: perpetuated segregation as a barrier to reconciliation

The peace in Northern Ireland has been widely marketed internationally as a positive model for conflict resolution and peace-building by the British, Irish and US governments, and by the EU. It is also part of the canon of cases used to illustrate the debates about consociationalism and conflict resolution mechanisms. It is also, however, under-theorized as a case illustrating the inherent dynamic tension between agency and structure in reconciliation processes. Political elite discourses in the UK, Ireland and internationally, have emphasized the transferable lessons of a peace process of elite "dialogue" that ended one of the most protracted conflicts to afflict an advanced democracy in modern times, while also downplaying the actual complex elite power-sharing consociational institutional engineering that secured the peace (Clinton 2000; Hain 2007; Obama 2013). The recent collapse of the Northern Ireland Executive in January 2017, followed by a deeply polarizing election, requires a critical lens to be focused on the question of what are the lessons to be drawn from the Northern Ireland conflict and the Good Friday

Agreement (GFA) of 1998, and why progress on reconciliation there has been so problematical.

Structural segregation is a defining feature of Northern Irish society and politics. Rooted in settler colonialism and constructed over centuries, it is today perpetuated in many spatial and cultural activity dimensions: residence, education, work, sport and leisure, marital and personal relationships, social spaces, transport, use of public services and so on. Here, I will focus on residential segregation as the primary dimension, though it is important to note that education is the other salient domain (about 93 per cent of primary and secondary school children attend single faith schools) (Rutherford and Fergus, 2013).

The second 2011 census release revealed that of 1.8 million citizens, protestants account for 48 per cent (down from 53 per cent in 2001), catholics almost 46 per cent (up from 44 per cent in 2001), and the rest are either other religious minorities or atheists. The trend is for a growing catholic population and a declining protestant population (Northern Ireland Statistics and Research Agency 2011). Approximately 35–40 per cent of the Northern Irish population live in totally segregated neighbourhoods (Hughes et al. 2007). Residential segregation is predominantly a working class and urban phenomenon and there is covariance between levels of segregation and social class, and deprivation (Shirlow and Murtagh 2006). However, research that uses a time series analysis to model the effect of relative deprivation (using unemployment as a proxy) on political violence in Northern Ireland in 1922–85, shows that there is no association between deprivation and conflict (Thompson 1989). The weak association between segregated space, deprivation *and* conflict over time is further supported by the fact that while the conflict violence in 1969–98 was concentrated in deprived areas (according to official criteria), those same areas were deprived and peaceful for long periods during the Stormont period from 1922, and remain the most deprived after the GFA of 1998, and yet were/are generally peaceful.

Spatial segregation of ethnic communities in Northern Ireland is viewed by some scholars as the deliberate action of "ethnic entrepreneurs" to facilitate political mobilization, as ethno-religious "enclosures" allow for more intense "propaganda conditioning" (Shirlow 2003, 77), to strengthen the "reification of 'cultures'" (Todd and Ruane 2010, 3–4), and to distort collective memories by inculcating particularistic historical "truths" (McGrattan 2013). Studies of Belfast based on available census data have demonstrated that periodic sectarian violence is a key push factor in the intensification of segregation in a "ratchet effect" over time (after episodes of interethnic violence after partition in the early 1920s, in 1935 during the Great Depression, and in the period from 1969 (Boal 1969; Doherty and Poole 1997; Murtagh 2002). The further concentration of residential segregation from 1969 is strongly correlated with the spatial distribution of violence, in particular killings, in the early 1970s as these were concentrated along the interfaces between the segregated working class areas of north and west Belfast or in catholic "ghettos" (about 45 per cent of all conflict related deaths occurred in Belfast) (O'Duffy 1995; Fay, Morrissey, and Smyth 1999; O'Leary and McGarry 2001). It is estimated that violent ethnic cleansing in the Belfast area alone between August 1969 and February 1973 affected about 60,000 people (Darby and Morris 1974, summary page c).

A neglected aspect is the role of the state in hardening segregation as an instrument of security policy. The British Army constructed at least forty-one security barriers, sometimes referred to locally as "peace lines", in Belfast along the interfaces between the catholic and protestant communities in north, west, south-west and east Belfast after the beginning of the conflict in August 1969 (Jarman 2005). The state helped to embed structural segregation through policies in both social housing and education. Cunningham (2014) has revealed from the study of recently declassified British state documents from the 1970s and 1980s that the state security agencies in Northern Ireland played a key role in subordinating the planning and redevelopment of Belfast to military needs, the aim of which was to spatially isolate by new motorways and create a cordon sanitaire around the main areas of conflict, in the nationalist north and west of the city (Cunningham 2014, 456).

From the early 1970s, the segregation of social housing and to some extent other social provision was preserved and reinforced by state agencies, such as the Housing Executive, through a policy of prioritizing security and client "wishes" (Shirlow and Murtagh 2006, 59–60). By 2003 more than 70 per cent of Housing Executive estates were more than 90 per cent protestant or more than 90 per cent catholic (Community Relations Unit 2003). In subsequent years, the figure for segregated social housing rose to 94 per cent in Belfast (Shuttleworth and Lloyd 2009). The Housing Executive has a statutory duty under Section 75 (2) of the Northern Ireland Act 1998 to promote community "good relations" and "community cohesion" but its policy is to develop integrated housing only when it is "practicable, desirable and safe". It has developed a programme of "shared neighbourhoods" (by now there are some 50 such estates), but these social housing estates tend to be located in peripheral areas outside the main conurbations, and the Housing Executive uses a very low threshold of 10 per cent protestant or catholic residents to classify an estate as "integrated" (Housing Executive 2015). The high level of social housing segregation contrasts with survey data which reveals that the majority (about 70 per cent) of people aspire to live in mixed neighbourhoods, and the results are essentially the same for both protestants and catholics (Life and Times Survey 2014).

The contact thesis in Northern Ireland: individuals against structure

Community relations activists and professionals working in Northern Ireland have promoted a narrative which holds that the GFA would have been impossible without decades of work by civil society on justice, equality and dialogue (Fitzduff 2001, 256). The commodification of reconciliation expanded rapidly in the 1990s as a result of the increased allocation of state funds (UK and Irish) and other international funds, but most of all as a result of the EU Peace Programmes for Northern Ireland (1995–2013). The grand total of peace-building funding for the period from the early 1980s to 2006 from the EU, British and Irish governments and international foundations, was approximately £1.35 billion. The bulk of these funds went into building social capital within ethnic communities rather building bonding capital across communities, and while reconciliation was a stated goal, there was no coherence about how programmes and projects should actually deliver on this goal or be measured (Deloitte 2007, 24–27; Hughes 2009). By the time of the GFA in 1998, there were approximately 5,000 voluntary and community organizations in Northern Ireland providing employment to some 33,000 people, with a gross annual income for the sector of around £500 million (Consultation Document on Funding for the Voluntary and Community Sector, Department for Social Development, April 2000, 3).

Research suggests, however, that there is much political division and confusion over the concept of reconciliation and its implementation among officials, professionals and activists (Hamber and Kelly 2005). There is a tendency to gloss over the unpalatable realities about reconciliation work in Northern Ireland during the conflict: that "community relations" was a highly politicized arena, that it was securitized as part of the British government's strategy for managing the conflict, and that British government and Army "community relations" units were rejected by catholics, that civil society organizations were overwhelmingly polarized on sectarian grounds, that much of the effort was grounded in religious organizations, not in secular civil society, and paramilitaries often benefitted from community relations funds (especially after the GFA). Contact and dialogue between government, political parties and paramilitaries was often facilitated most effectively by low-level religious figures, sometimes seen as mavericks (Brewer, Higgins, and Teeney 2013; Hughes 2014).

In the case of Northern Ireland, we can observe two main forms in which the contact thesis has been pursued. Firstly, there was bottom-up civil society efforts to promote inter-communal contact and dialogue, the most prominent of which was the reconciliation work of the ecumenical religious community at Corrymeela. Founded in 1965 (prior to the violence) by a Presbyterian pastor, Ray Davey, it provided a combination of neutral haven and forum for dialogue, where a team of experienced managers would act as "enablers" of dialogue and the outcome would be "networks for peace" and friendship circles (Braniff and Byrne 2014, 51). He was inspired by the reconciliation activities of other European Christian peace movements whose work centred on contact (the Anglo-German movement based at Coventry, and the

Agape centre in Italy). Its funding from public and private sources expanded throughout the period from the early 1970s-present. By 1990, it was hosting about 8,000 people per annum on residential courses, plus many thousands of day visitors annually. Its range extended from school groups, to community groups, religious groups and groups of professionals, politicians, as well as victims and "perpetrators" (usually understood here as referring to ex-prisoners). This "gatekeeper" approach to mediating contact did not produce the sought after result of ending the conflict, nor a peaceful coexistence through to deeper forms of reconciliation.

Secondly, studies by social psychologists whose research designs are informed by contact theory have aimed to measure the effects of out-group friendship in mitigating prejudice, and generating support for more generalized positive attitudes to the out-group in Northern Ireland. While this work is innovative, the inherent methodological problems of selection bias remain – that the prejudiced avoid contact, and perhaps also avoid being surveyed. Most of the research is focused on schoolchildren and university students. Schoolchildren have long been a focus of government efforts at value and behavioural change in Northern Ireland, partly because they are a captive audience who will determine generational change, and partly to reach parents through the children. Pairing (of protestant and catholic schools and classes), and developing a curriculum around mutual understanding of culture and identity have been developing since the 1970s. Research indicates that direct and indirect cross-group friendship between catholics and protestants reduces out-group prejudice via an anxiety-reduction mechanism (Paolini et al. 2004; Hughes et al. 2007), and promotes trust (Hewstone et al. 2008; Tam et al. 2009), which is seen as an essential condition for sustained positive contact. The contact thesis is also being stretched beyond the face-to-face contacts envisaged by Allport. Turner et al. (2013) have shown that in addition to cross-group friendships, "extended" contact by schoolchildren, i.e. indirect forms of contact that involve learning about in-group members who have out-group friends, is also significantly associated with prejudice reduction. Potentially, this is an important finding in Northern Ireland, where structural segregation is such an immense barrier to face-to-face contact.

Reconciliation after the GFA of 1998

The initial euphoria around the GFA has steadily waned and given way to increasingly critical discourses about the lack of transitional justice mechanisms, and the failure to build consensus on addressing so-called "legacy" issues (victims, historical criminal investigations, commemoration and so on) – issues which remain deeply contentious as evidenced by the failure of the "fresh start" process in 2015 (Northern Ireland Executive 2015). The GFA is also criticized for failing to engage seriously with the issue of reconciliation. Reconciliation is cited as an aspiration in the preamble-like "Declaration of Support". There was also a separate section on "Reconciliation and Victims of Violence". Several components were highlighted: addressing the needs of victims; a commitment to fund organizations engaged in reconciliation work; and, an aim of encouraging a "culture of tolerance" and mixing in housing and education. The Agreement did not specify how these components were to be achieved (Belfast Agreement 1998, section 6). Jonathan Powell, a key British negotiator of The Agreement, has suggested that the negotiating parties were too overwhelmed by the complex institutional arrangements and issues such as decommissioning of weapons to pay much attention to the issue of reconciliation (Powell 2015). The GFA's approach to reconciliation is seen as being too much driven "from above" by the British and Irish states, and the peace process culminating in the consociational power-sharing institutions is critiqued for being too top-down elitist (Byrne 2001; Taylor 2009).

The critical discourse on the GFA focuses on the way that consociationalism entrenches ethnic power and provides no mechanism for transcending ethnic and sectarian divisions to create a "shared identity". The alternative perspectives to elite-centred consociationalism have concentrated around ideas about reconciliation originating in Lederach's "conflict transformation" approach (discussed earlier), emphasizing individual change and positive social interactions as key to building shared narratives, common identity, and a new "shared society" (Hamber 2003; Hamber and Kelly 2005). The alternative perspectives, however, shy away from the gargantuan policy challenges their aspirations require: the systematic social engineering of desegregation, creating new shared spaces and new forms of socialization.

Ironically, there was a hardening of sectarian interfaces after the GFA, mainly in Belfast, as the number of barriers has grown to about ninety-nine, running to over twenty miles, and their construction has become more elaborate and higher (Belfast Interface Project 2016). There are also a small number of segregating security barriers in other towns such as Derry and Portadown. When surveyed the overwhelming majority (69 per cent) of those living near security walls favoured their retention due to fear of potential sectarian violence (Gormley-Heenan, Byrne, and Robinson 2013). Peace brought an increase in "chill factors", including new security barriers, and a fortifying of the sectarian boundaries with graffiti, flags, kerb painting and other manifestations of religious and cultural political identity and paramilitary association (Harbison 2002; Hughes 2014).

When the GFA was suspended between 2002 and 2007, the UK government attempted to address the segregation issue by commissioning the so-called Harbison Report (2002) on "A Shared Future" and conducting a "consultation exercize". Harbison presented a stark policy choice for future policy:

"separate development" or "co-existence" versus "a cohesive but pluralist society". The costs of a divided society, he argued, were unsustainable. He advocated "promoting inter-dependence" through two mechanisms: firstly, to incentivize infrastructures "to promote better relations within and between communities" and secondly, to change the policy discourse, abandoning the idiom of "community relations" in favour of the more liberal term "good relations", which had been employed in the Northern Ireland Act 1998 (Harbison 2002, 8, 41–42, 49). The proposals for a "Shared Future" were abandoned by the UK government when the St Andrews Agreement brought the radical Unionist party, the DUP, into the restored power-sharing structures in 2007. From 2007, Northern Ireland was governed by an interethnic coalition, the DUP-Sinn Féin executive, which collapsed in sectarian acrimony and lack of mutual "respect" in January 2017.

The DUP-Sinn Féin executive produced its own policy on social transformation around the *Programme for Cohesion, Sharing and Integration* (Office of the First Minister and Deputy First Minister (hereafter OFMDFM), 2010). The *Programme for Cohesion* document shifted the policy direction away from tackling segregation to one that elevated the notion of "mutual accommodation", on the assumption that "cultures" and identities are not only relatively fixed and enduring, but are to be valued: "pride in who we are and confidence in our different cultural identities" (OFMDFM 2010, 2.3). The document reflected both an absence of political will at the elite level to address the structures of division in Northern Irish society, and a realistic acceptance of the perpetuation of an "intercultural society" – a euphemism for segregation.

Conclusion

The challenge posed by reconciliation is encapsulated in Allport's observation that: "It is easier to smash the atom than a prejudice" (Allport 1954, xvii). Contact theory, developed by Allport as a process for positively transforming race relations in the USA, is the main conceptual frame underpinning the study of reconciliation more generally, irrespective of whether the deep cleavage is race, religion, ethnicity or other. The theory reifies agency over structure. It reflects a psychological concern with individuals as potential change-agents, whether the "self" or the "other". It assumes that values and behaviour can be modified in a progressive way by regimes of contact between individuals from antagonistic groups, conducted in non-hierarchical and non-threatening conditions, and mediated by an appropriately motivated and trained cadre of professionals. Even if we assume that a "shared identity" can be built in this way, contact theory does not take sufficient account of the social structures of segregation which often characterize divided places and societies, nor does it recognize that conflicts may not always end cleanly with a clear victor, which may facilitate the imposition of a dominant shared narrative of the conflict.

Segregation can be understood as a bridging concept which allows us to analyse why agential reconciliation is so problematical. Often deeply rooted in long histories of antagonism, segregation can operate across multiple dimensions to perpetuate prejudice. By hindering, and blocking even, opportunities for sustained routine contact in the positive ways envisaged by contact theory, segregation renders the theory ineffective in terms of societal transformation. The case of Northern Ireland widely extolled as an exportable model for peace-building, demonstrates that a peace agreement between elites is possible, though as recent events show even this is problematical, without any significant steps of reconciliation at the level of society, and with the persistence of deep segregation. This is a good case also to illustrate the under-theorization of the relationship between agency and structure in reconciliation, and the disjuncture between elites and society in a peace process.

Disclosure statement

No potential conflict of interest was reported by the author.

References

Ackermann, Alice. 1994. "Reconciliation as a Peacebuilding Process in Postwar Europe. The Franco-German Case." *Peace and Change* 19 (3): 229–250.

Allport, Gordon W. 1954. *The Nature of Prejudice*. Reading, MA: Addison-Wesley.

Bashir, Bashir. 2012. "Reconciling Historical Injustices: Deliberative Democracy and the Politics of Reconciliation." *Res Publica (liverpool, England)* 18 (2): 127–143.

Belfast Interface Project. 2016. http://www.belfastinterfaceproject.org/interfaces-map-and-database-overview.

Bloomfield, David. 2006. On Good Terms: Clarifying Reconciliation. Berghof Report No. 14. Accessed October. http://www.berghof-center.org.

Boal, Fredrick. 1969. "Territoriality on the Shankill-Falls Divide, Belfast." *Irish Geography* 6 (1): 30–50.

Braniff, Máire, and Jonny Byrne. 2014. "Circle of Friends: Unravelling the Networks of Peacebuilding in Northern Ireland." *Peacebuilding* 2 (1): 45–63.

Brewer, John D., Gareth I. Higgins, and Francis Teeney. 2013. *Religion, Civil Society and Peace in Northern Ireland*. Oxford: Oxford University Press.

Brown, Wendy. 2009. *Regulating Aversion Tolerance in the Age of Identity and Empire*. Princeton, NJ: Princeton University Press. Online resource.

Byrne, Sean. 2001. "Consociational and Civic Society Approaches to Peacebuilding in Northern Ireland." *Journal of Peace Research* 38 (3): 327–352.

Clinton, William J. 2000. *Keynote Address at the Odyssey Arena*. Belfast: Lagan Waterfront. December 13, 2000. Accessed 6 November, 2011. http://cain.ulst.ac.uk/events/peace/docs/bc131200.htm.

Community Relations Unit. 2003. "A Shared Future A Consultation Paper on Improving Relations in Northern Ireland January 2003." Stormont: Office of the First Minister and Deputy First Minister. http://cain.ulst.ac.uk/issues/community/cru03.htm.

Consultation Document on Funding for the Voluntary and Community Sector, Department for Social Development, April. 2000. http://www.dsdni.gov.uk/harbison_report.pdf.

Coser, Lewis. 1956. *The Functions of Social Conflict*. New York: The Free Press.

Cunningham, Tim. 2014. "Changing Direction: Defensive Planning in a Post-conflict City." *City* 18 (4–5): 455–462.

Darby, John, and G. Morris. 1974. *Intimidation in Housing*. Belfast: The Northern Ireland Community Relations Commission.

Deloitte. 2007. "Research into the Financial Cost of the Northern Ireland Divide, April 2007." Accessed August 28, 2013. http://cain.ulst.ac.uk/help/caindex.htm.

Doherty, Paul, and Michael M Poole. 1997. "Ethnic Residential Segregation in Belfast, Northern Ireland, 1971–1991." *Geographical Review* 87 (4): 520–536.

Doxtader, Erik. 2007. "The Faith and Struggle of Beginning (with) Words: On the Turn between Reconciliation and Recognition." *Philosophy and Rhetoric* 40 (1): 119–146.

Fay, Marie-Therese, Mike Morrissey, and Marie Smyth. 1999. *Northern Ireland's Troubles. The Human Costs*. London: Pluto Press.

Feldman, Lily Gardner. 2012. *Germany's Foreign Policy of Reconciliation: From Enmity to Amity*. Lanham, MD: Rowman & Littlefield.

Fisher, Ronald J. 2001. "Social-psychological Processes in Interactive Conflict Analysis and Reconciliation." In *Reconciliation, Justice, and Coexistence, Theory and Practice*, edited by Mohammed Abu-Nimer, 25–46. Lanham, MD: Lexington Books.

Fitzduff, Marie. 2001. "The Challenge to History: Justice, Coexistence, and Reconciliation Work in Northern Ireland." In *Reconciliation, Justice, and Coexistence, Theory and Practice*, edited by Mohammed Abu-Nimer, 255–274. Lanham, MD: Lexington Books.

Galtung, Johan. 2001. "After Violence, Reconstruction, Reconciliation, and Resolution. Coping with the Visible and Invisible Effects of War and Violence." In *Reconciliation, Justice, and Coexistence, Theory and Practice*, edited by Mohammed Abu-Nimer, 3–23. Lanham, MD: Lexington Books.

Goldsmith, Pat Rubio. 2016. "Perpetuation Theory and the Racial Segregation of Young Adults." *Social Science Research* 56: 1–15.

Gormley-Heenan, Cathy, Jonny Byrne, and Gillian Robinson. 2013. "The Berlin Walls of Belfast." *British Politics* 8 (3): 357–382.

Hain, Peter. 2007. "Peacemaking in Northern Ireland: A Model for Conflict Resolution." Secretary of State for Northern Ireland. Chatham House, June 12, 2007. Accessed August 28, 2013. http://cain.ulst.ac.uk/issues/politics/docs/nio/ph120607.pdf.

Hamber, Brandon. 2003. "Transformation and Reconciliation." In *Contemporary Peacemaking: Conflict, Violence and Peace Processes*, edited by John Darby, and Roger Mac Ginty, 224–234. Basingstoke: Palgrave MacMillan.

Hamber, Brandon, and Gráinne Kelly. 2005. *A Place for Reconciliation? Conflict and Locality in Northern Ireland*. Democratic Dialogue Report 18 September.

Harbison, Jeremy. 2002. *Review of Community Relations Policy: Main Report*. Belfast: Community Relations Unit (CRU), OFMDFM.

Hewstone, Miles, Ed Cairns, Jared Kenworthy, Joanne Hughes, Nicole Tausch, Tania Tam, Alberto Voci, von Ulrich Hecker, and Catherine Pinder. 2008. "Stepping Stones to Reconciliation in Northern Ireland: Intergroup Contact, Forgiveness and Trust." In *The Social Psychology of Intergroup Reconciliation*, edited by Arie Nadler, Thomas E. Malloy, and Jeffrey D. Fisher, 199–226. Oxford: Oxford University Press.

Hirsch, Alexander Keller. 2012. *Theorizing Post-conflict Reconciliation: Agonism, Restitution and Repair*. London: Routledge.

Housing Executive (Northern Ireland). 2015. "Community Cohesion Strategy 2015–2020." http://www.nihe.gov.uk/index/corporate/strategies/good_relations_strategy.htm.

Hughes, James. 2009. "Paying for Peace: Comparing the EU's Role in the Conflicts in Northern Ireland and Kosovo." *Ethnopolitics* 8 (3): 287–306.

Hughes, James. 2014. "Reconstruction without Reconciliation: Is Northern Ireland a 'Model?'" In *National Identity and Armed Conflict in Europe 1918–2011*, edited by Bill Kissane, 245–272. Philadelphia: University of Pennsylvania Press.

Hughes, Joanne, Andrea Campbell, Miles Hewstone, and Ed Cairns. 2007. "Segregation in Northern Ireland – Implications for Community Relations Policy." *Policy Studies* 28: 35–53.

Jarman, Neil. 2005. "Mapping Interface Barriers." Belfast Interface Project's Interface Mapping Project. http://www.belfastinterfaceproject.org/publication9.html.

Kymlicka, Will, and Bashir Bashir, eds. 2008. *The Politics of Reconciliation in Multicultural Societies*. Oxford: Oxford University Press.

Lederach, Jean Paul. 1995. *Preparing for Peace: Conflict Transformation across Cultures*. Syracuse: University Press.

Lederach, Jean Paul. 1997. *Building Peace: Sustainable Reconciliation in Divided Societies*. Washington, DC: U.S. Institute of Peace.

Lederach, Jean Paul. 1999. *The Journey toward Reconciliation*. Scottdale, PA: Herald Press.

Lederach, Jean Paul. 2003. *The Little Book of Conflict Transformation*. Intercourse, PA: Good Books.

Life and Times Survey (Northern Ireland). 2014. http://www.ark.ac.uk/nilt/2014/Community_Relations/MXRLGNGH.html.

Lijphart, Arend. 1968. *The Politics of Accommodation. Pluralism and Democracy in the Netherlands*. Berkeley: University of California Press.

Malloy, Thomas E. 2008. "Intergroup Relations and Reconciliation: Theoretical Analysis and Methodological Implications." In *The Social Psychology of Intergroup Reconciliation*, edited by Arie Nadler, Thomas E. Malloy, and Jeffrey D. Fisher, 345–368. Oxford: Oxford University Press.

McGrattan, Cillian. 2013. *Haunted by History: Memory, Identity and Politics*. Basingstoke: Palgrave Macmillan.

Moon, Claire. 2004. "Prelapsarian State: Forgiveness and Reconciliation in Transitional Justice." *International Journal for the Semiotics of Law Revue internationale de Sémiotique juridique* 17 (2): 185–197.

Muldoon, Paul. 2003. "Reconciliation and Political Legitimacy: The Old Australia and the New South Africa." *Australian Journal of Politics and History* 49 (2): 182–196.

Murtagh, Brendan. 2002. *The Politics of Territory. Policy and Segregation in Northern Ireland*. Basingstoke: Palgrave.

Nadler, Arie, Thomas E. Malloy, Jeffrey D. Fisher, eds. 2008. *The Social Psychology of Intergroup Reconciliation*. Oxford: Oxford University Press.

Northern Ireland Executive. 2015. "A Fresh Start." The Stormont Agreement and Implementation Plan. *An Agreement to Consolidate the Peace, Securest* Ability, Enable Progress and Offer Hope. Belfast. Accessed March 22, 2017. https://www.northernireland.gov.uk/publications/fresh-start-stormont-agreement-and-implementation-plan-0.

Northern Ireland Statistics and Research Agency. 2011. "Census 2011, Key Statistics for Northern Ireland. Belfast." Accessed March 28, 2013. http://www.nisra.gov.uk/Census/key_report_2011.pdf.

Obama, Barack. 2013. "Remarks by President Obama and Mrs. Obama with Youth of Northern Ireland." Belfast Waterfront. Belfast. Northern Ireland June 17. Accessed March 28, 2013. http://www.whitehouse.gov/briefing-room.

O'Duffy, Brendan. 1995. "Violence in Northern Ireland 1969–1994: Sectarian or Ethno-national?" *Ethnic and Racial Studies* 18 (4): 740–772.

Office of the First Minister and Deputy First Minister. 2010. "Programme for Cohesion, Sharing And Integration." Consultation Document. 2010. Stormont. Accessed June 16, 2016. http://cain.ulst.ac.uk/issues/politics/ofmdfm/ofmdfm_270710_sharing.pdf.

O'Leary, Brendan, and John McGarry. 2001. *The Politics of Antagonism: Understanding Northern Ireland*. 2nd ed. London: Athlone Press.

Paolini, Stefania, Miles Hewstone, Ed Cairns, and Alberto Voci. 2004. "Effects of Direct and Indirect Cross-group Friendships on Judgments of Catholics and Protestants in Northern Ireland: The Mediating Role of an Anxiety-reduction Mechanism." *Personality and Social Psychology Bulletin* 30 (6): 770–786.

Pettigrew, Thomas F., and Linda R Tropp. 2006. "A Meta-analytic Test of Intergroup Contact Theory." *Journal of Personality and Social Psychology* 90 (5): 751–783.

Powell, Jonathan. 2015. Private Communication to Author.

Putnam, Robert D. 2007. "E Pluribus Unum: Diversity and Community in the Twenty-first Century: The 2006 Johan Skytte Prize Lecture." *Scandinavian Political Studies* 30: 137–174.

Rutherford, Adrian, and Lindsay Fergus. 2013. "Public Mood in Northern Ireland is for an End to Segregation in Schools." *Belfast Telegraph*. June 26.

Schaap, Andrew. 2005. *Political Reconciliation*. Abingdon: Routledge.

Sharkey, Patrick. 2008. "The Intergenerational Transmission of Context." *American Journal of Sociology* 113 (4): 931–969.

Shirlow, Peter. 2003. "Ethnocentrism and the Reproduction of Fear in Belfast." *Capital and Class*. 80: 77–93.

Shirlow, Peter, and Brendan Murtagh. 2006. *Belfast. Segregation, Violence and the City*. London: Pluto Press.

Shuttleworth, Ian, and Chris Lloyd. 2009. "Mapping Segregation in Northern Ireland Northern Ireland Housing Executive Estates Outside Belfast, a Report Commissioned by the Northern Ireland Housing Executive from Queens University, Belfast., NIHE, Belfast 2009." Accessed June 21, 2014. http://www.nihe.gov.uk/mapping_segregation_in_northern_ireland_-_northern_ireland_housing_executive_estates_outside_belfast.pdf.

Tam, Tania, Miles Hewstone, Jared Kenworthy, and Ed Cairns. 2009. "Intergroup Trust in Northern Ireland." *Personality and Social Psychology Bulletin* 35 (1): 45–59.

Taylor, Rupert, ed. 2009. *Consociational Theory. McGarry and O'Leary and the Northern Ireland Conflict*. Abingdon: Routledge.

The Agreement. 1998. "Agreement Reached in the Multi-party Negotiations." 10 April. Accessed November 7, 2011. http://cain.ulst.ac.uk/events/peace/docs/agreement.htm.

Thompson, J. L. P. 1989. "Deprivation and Political Violence in Northern Ireland, 1922–1985 a Time-series Analysis." *Journal of Conflict Resolution* 3 (4): 676–699.

Todd, Jennifer, and Joseph Ruane. 2010. *From "A Shared Future" to "Cohesion, Sharing and Integration". An Analysis of Northern Ireland's Policy Framework Documents*. York: Joseph Rowntree Charitable Trust. Accessed October. www.jrct.org.uk/core/documents/download.asp?id=429.

Turner, Rhiannon N., Tania Tam, Miles Hewstone, Jared Kenworthy, and Ed Cairns. 2013. "Contact between Catholic and Protestant Schoolchildren in Northern Ireland." *Journal of Applied Social Psychology* 43 (Suppl. 2): E216–E228.

Tutu, Desmond. 1999. *No Future Without Forgiveness*. New York: Doubleday.

Uslaner, Eric M. 2002. *The Moral Foundations of Trust*. New York: Cambridge University Press.

Uslaner, Eric M. 2011. "Trust, Diversity, and Segregation in the United States and the United Kingdom." *Comparative Sociology* 10: 221–247.

Woodward, C. Vann. 1955. *The Strange Career of Jim Crow, 1908–1999*. Oxford: Oxford University Press.

Decolonization as reconciliation: rethinking the national conflict paradigm in the Israeli-Palestinian conflict

Nadim N. Rouhana

ABSTRACT

This paper argues that thinking about reconciliation in the Israeli-Palestinian conflict requires a paradigmatic shift in conflict analysis. The international community has approached the Israeli-Palestinian conflict as a national conflict between Zionism, as the national movement of the Jewish people, and the Palestinian National Movement. The partition plans proposed from before 1947 until the recent "two-state solution" formula have all been based on this assumption. I argue that the premise of national conflict is fundamentally flawed, and, therefore, reaching a settlement based on partition – let alone reconciliation – is becoming increasingly unlikely. A new paradigm (in the Kuhnian sense) is needed that applies a settler-colonial framework to the conflict while also taking into consideration the national component. Reconciliation in this conflict is conceived as decolonization within a transitional justice framework. This approach overcomes major pitfalls in the hegemonic discourse on reconciliation in this conflict, including the symmetrical analysis and psychologizing the process.

Introduction

The term "reconciliation" is loosely used within and across disciplines and spheres of discourse, except for in the context of transitional justice (Rouhana 2011). In political discourse and international media, for example, the term includes a wide scope of outcomes: reaching an agreement over a border dispute, approaching a ceasefire, or initiating a political negotiation between parties. In many cases, academic discourses also fail to provide a specific definition that identifies reconciliation as a process intended to reach peaceful relations founded on the transformation of power structures and political relationships. The term gains its clearest meaning within the politics of transitional justice – the transformation of authoritarian regimes and regimes involved in mass human rights violations into democracies that face their histories and seek to overcome past atrocities by introducing social reconciliation and restorative justice (see also Crocker 1999; Dwyer 1999; Van Zyl 1999). When minorities in Western democracies challenged the ability of a majoritarian political system to eliminate explicit forms of discrimination, ethnic hierarchies, and political and cultural inequalities, the concept of a "politics of difference" nourished the debate on reconciliation and provided the term with its most necessary substance. Most notably this debate led to more effective ways to introduce past injustices and historical accountability into the definition of democracy and equality, and generated ideas about how to better guarantee democratic processes (see e.g. Bashir and Kymlicka 2008; Rouhana 2008). The interaction between the two – introducing multicultural and democratic citizenship as integral to post-transition societies and recognizing the historical dimension in the politics of difference – continues to influence how the concept of reconciliation is defined.

In my work, I have distinguished between *reconciliation* and two other qualitatively different processes in the conflict studies literature: *conflict settlement* and *conflict resolution* (Rouhana 2004). First introduced in 2004, other scholars later adopted the distinction among the three processes, (see e.g. Kelman 2006) including those who studied reconciliation in the Israeli-Palestinian conflict (e.g. Hammack 2010; Vollhardt 2009). I argued that the three processes differ in terms of the end goals between parties in conflict, the extent to which publics are involved in the agreements, the nature of the desired societal and political relationship, the importance of mutual acceptance to the parties, the examination of past injustice and collective responsibility, the prerequisites for changes in political institutions and constitutional arrangements, and the psychological dynamics involving the societies Previously, the literature had addressed the distinction between political settlement and conflict resolution, most notably by Burton (1990) and adherents of human needs theory (Richmond 2001).

In brief, *conflict settlement* is a process in which the parties to a conflict, through negotiation mediation, seek an agreement of formal termination of a dispute based on calculations of mutual interests and reflecting the power relations that exist on the ground at the time the settlement is reached. Conflict settlements often do not reflect equitably the parties' broader collective needs and do not address the weaker party's long-term interests. A settlement is not typically intended to effect a deeper transformation of relations between societies or reach genuine mutual recognition between the parties. *Conflict resolution processes* seek to address the underlying causes of conflict and reach an agreement designed to address the basic political needs and concerns of both sides regardless of the power relations between them. Within these processes – usually negotiated by political elites – the aim is to achieve peaceful relations not only between governments, but also between societies. Burton's Basic Human Needs theory (see e.g. Burton 1990; Kelman 2006; Mitchell 1990) heavily influenced the conceptualization of this process, which is most appropriate for addressing social conflicts that involve mutual violence and deep grievances related to identity and recognition.

I argue that these methodologies and approaches are not appropriate for addressing conflicts that involve massive and asymmetric human rights violations such as mass killings, military occupation, systematic human rights violations, colonization, ethnic cleansing, and war crimes, particularly when the parties' futures are interdependent and the societies are not separate. The above approaches, for various reasons, purposely and wilfully avoid core issues such as historical responsibility, justice, truth, and other transitional justice-related issues.

In contrast to the two processes described above, *reconciliation* is a process that seeks a genuine, just, and enduring end to the conflict and a profound transformation of the dynamics of relationships between the societies through a course of action involving intertwined political and social changes. Reconciliation addresses both politically structural issues such as distribution of power and constitutional arrangements as well as intangible issues such as historical truth and historical responsibility (Rouhana 2004, 2011). As such, this process has psychological correlates for the parties involved that emerge concurrently with its unfolding. However, the process is in essence social and political – it demands reaching agreements not only based on restructuring the power distribution, democratic arrangements, and constitutional guarantees for equality and human rights within a framework of restorative justice, but also on reaching inter-subjective agreements on historical truths and reckoning with the historical responsibilities for the mass violations of human rights that have occurred. As a result, this process becomes founded on *mutual legitimacy* that is gained within a new moral and political framework.

In previous papers, in line with the transitional justice literature, I identified four key issues that must be addressed for a reconciliation process to achieve its goals (Rouhana 2004): justice, truth, historical responsibility, and restructuring the social and political relationship between the parties within a framework that guarantees constitutional rights, democracy, and equality of groups and individuals. In this paper I seek to apply the reconciliation process to the Israeli-Palestinian conflict while considering a different analytical paradigm.

Reconciliation in the Israeli-Palestinian conflict

During the last quarter century, since the beginning of direct negotiations between Israel and the PLO (first secretly in 1992 and then openly in 1993), it is hard to point to significant steps toward a political settlement between Israelis and Palestinians, let alone reconciliation as defined above. The main issues that define reconciliation such as justice, truth, and historic responsibility, were, by and large, absent from the formal negotiations. The senior Israeli official who participated in the first meeting that brought together PLO and Israeli officials, reported that after a brief exchange about history

> [we] arrived at our first understanding. Never again would we argue about the past. This was an important step, for it moved us beyond an endless wrangle over right and wrong. Discussing the future would mean reconciling two rights, not readdressing ancient wrongs. (Savir 1998, 15)

In addition, the Israeli prime minister and foreign minister set a major condition before starting what became known as the Oslo process: the parties would not resort to international arbitration, such as security-council resolutions. The Palestinians acquiesced and so history and justice were permanently excluded from the negotiating process.

This absence of any discussion of real reconciliation has characterized the approach to the "peace process" since the negotiation started in 1993. Discourse among Israelis who support a political settlement with the Palestinians – even those who support a two-state solution – has been dominated by the call for full separation from the Palestinians. Israeli politicians and the media frequently recite the phrase "we are here and they are there", overlooking any discussion of the requirements for reconciliation. Among Palestinians, the discourse has centred on a "just and durable peace", which exceeds a political settlement as defined above. Palestinians have consistently sought to include the return of Palestinian refugees in their formula for peace: a Palestinian state on the territories occupied in 1967, East Jerusalem as its capital, and the return of refugees. For many Palestinians, this formula addresses a major element of justice: the return of refugees.

The hegemonic academic discourse on reconciliation in the Israeli-Palestinian conflict suffers from three main pitfalls this paper seeks to overcome. First, the paradigm that has guided the thinking on reconciliation assumes a conflict between two national movements – Zionism and the Palestinian National Movement (PNM) – over a land on which they both have legitimate claims. This paradigm has almost completely ignored the settler-colonial analysis of the conflict. Second, hegemonic discourse imposed a symmetrical analysis that in effect obscured the fundamental elements of the conflict. Third, much of the analysis overemphasized the psychological side of reconciliation at the expense of the political side.

The national conflict paradigm

The Palestinian-Israeli conflict, according to mainstream Western academic approaches, represents a clash between two national movements (see e.g. Tessler 2009). The United Nation's General Assembly's resolution 181, grounded in this interpretation, offers the partition of Palestine into two states as the most desirable solution. Official and unofficial conflict resolution efforts have focused on how to reach this outcome, especially after the Oslo Accords in 1993. By then Israel had recognized the PLO and the latter had recognized Israel's right to exist – a mutual but asymmetrical recognition.

This paradigmatic conception (in the Kuhnian sense, see Kuhn 2012) of the conflict as a clash between two national movements differs from the mainstream Zionist and Palestinian understandings of the conflict. The mainstream Zionist movement does not see the Palestinians as a nation and conceives of the conflict as a fight between a nation returning to their God-promised ancient homeland and the "Arab inhabitants" of that homeland. For Zionism, it is a conflict between the obvious right of the Jewish people to return to their Biblical lands and establish an exclusive state and the Arab groups who have resisted this project. From its inception, mainstream Zionism and later Israeli political thought and practice denied Palestinian nationalism. Israel's recognition of the PLO in 1993 and the establishment of the Palestinian Authority in the West Bank and Gaza led many to a limited acknowledgment of Palestinian nationalism, as many Israelis began to consider a two-state solution.

Palestinians, too, did not originally conceive of the conflict with Zionism as a national fight. Before and immediately following the Zionist project's successful establishment of the state of Israel in part of historic Palestine in 1948, Palestinians framed the conflict within a settler-colonial paradigm. From the early days of the Zionist project – even before the formation of a distinct Palestinian national identity, Palestinians saw the Zionist movement as a settler-colonial project that aimed to take over their homeland (Said 1979; Sayegh 1965). Therefore, Palestinians defined their goals in terms of halting Jewish colonial settlement in Palestine, thwarting the project of constructing a Jewish homeland on their lands, and achieving national independence from the British Mandate. Until 1948, the Palestinians also resisted the Western powers' plans for the partition of Palestine into two states – one Arab and one Jewish – and rejected by consensus the UNGA's partition resolution 181.

When the Palestinians in exile revived the PNM in the 1960s, the PLO and all its factions identified Israel as a settler-colonial state. The PLO understood this settler colonialism in similar terms to French settler colonialism in Algeria, and thus conceptualized resistance within a decolonization framework articulated by many peoples in the Third World. The Palestinians did not seek a return to the borders of the UNGA's partition plan (which gave Israel about fifty-five per cent of Palestine while it in effect conquered a total of about seventy-eight per cent of the country), nor did they call for the retreat of Israel to the borders of the partition plan. They did not demand – nor did the Arab countries – the establishment of a Palestinian state in the West Bank and Gaza or within borders the 1947 UN Partition Plan designated to the Arab state. For the Palestinian leadership at the time, demanding anything less than "return and liberation" (which in Palestinian discourse meant the return of the expelled Palestinians to their homes, and the liberation of all of Palestine from Zionist rule) signified a final collapse of Palestinian existence and Palestinian identity.

The PNM's objective remained clear from the establishment of the PLO in 1964 until 1974, when the Palestinian National Council (PNC), after long deliberations, accepted a document known as the "Ten Points Document". The document, which called for establishing a Palestinian state "on any liberated part of Palestine", laid the foundations of a gradual shift to a new paradigm that implicitly began to articulate the Palestinian conflict with Israel as a "national conflict". Approving this document reflected the Palestinian understanding that within the existing international and regional balance of power after 1973, the demand of "return and liberation" along the lines of the Algerian model became unattainable. Egypt and Syria instigated the 1973 October War to liberate their own occupied territories; liberating Palestine was not one of their objectives. The war also revealed the Arab states' limitations to using armed confrontation with Israel. At the same time, international pressure, specifically from the Soviet Union, pushed the PLO to accept a two-state formula in return for diplomatic support.

This paradigm peaked with the resolutions submitted at the PNC's nineteenth meeting, which openly endorsed a two-state solution in November 1988 (see Khalidi 1990). Since then, mainstream Palestinian political discourse has gradually shifted from a discourse consistent with a paradigm of a national liberation movement in conflict with a settler-colonial project to embracing a discourse consistent with a paradigm that assumes, even if not clearly articulated, that the conflict is between two national movements that claim the same land. In the latter paradigm, it is logical to negotiate the terms of partition, compromises over borders, security conditions, economic relations, and even issues-related to refugees – as long as the envisioned solution is formulated in a way that avoids historical accounts, restorative justice, and the return of the vast majority of refugees.

The Palestinian political demand for a two-state solution that emerged tacitly in the 1970s and explicitly in the late 1980s is incompatible with a settler-colonial paradigm that emphasizes decolonization rather than partition. It is remarkable, then, to observe how early Palestinian academic discourse on Israel and settler colonialism, which was integral to the analysis of the Palestinian case (Abu-Lughod and Abu-Laban 1974; Hilal 1976; Sayegh 1965), gradually gave way to a literature emanating from the two-state framework. With the Oslo agreements, the political thought that demands partition has become consolidated among the majority of the Palestinian political class.

As I argue elsewhere (Rouhana 2014) Zionism, indeed is a national movement, but this dimension of Zionism should be taken into consideration within a more analytically appropriate paradigm – the settler colonial.

The return of history and the settler-colonial paradigm

Whether conflict resolution efforts guided solely by the national conflict paradigm could have achieved the ultimate goal of political settlement or political reconciliation by partitioning Palestine into two states is an important question, but one that falls beyond the scope of this paper. What is becoming increasingly obvious, however, is that many Palestinians are more aware of the failure of the national conflict paradigm in achieving partition. Indeed, the Palestinian public, the elites, and youth, have dramatically lost their trust in the possibility of achieving a Palestinian state (Hatuqa 2013; Jerusalem Post 2015). In addition, many Israelis increasingly believe that the Zionist project is in trouble precisely because Israel is unable to disentangle itself from the occupation (Ravid 2016). Recently, Palestinian and other academic circles have generated alternative paradigms to the two-state solution, which have permeated both global academic and intellectual discourse, and some political discussions on the conflict. That these alternative paradigms, most commonly a bi-national "one-state solution", have so quickly begun to influence international discourse on Palestine illuminates the seriousness of the difficulties of partition.

In parallel to the discourse that challenges partition, many scholars currently accept the premise that the Zionist project that aimed to establish a Jewish state in Palestine is a settler-colonial project (for just a few examples, see Lloyd 2012; Mamdani 2015; Pappé 2012; Robinson 2013; Rouhana 2014; Sabbagh-Khoury 2015; Shalhoub-Kevorkian 2015; Shihade 2011; Veracini 2010; Wolfe 2006). This project continues to unfold across mandatory Palestine, including Israel (see Amara 2014).

The literature on Zionism and settler colonialism points to important features of Zionism that place it squarely within the settler-colonial paradigm. Among the most important features are the following: (a) Demographic riddance of the native population (when their labour is not needed). This riddance took the form of elimination in many settler-colonial cases; in the 1948 war Zionist forces executed an ethnic cleansing. Since then Israel has applied strict demographic limitations on entrance of Palestinians to Israel and later to the West Bank. (b) Control of space, which, inside Israel itself manifested in the massive expropriation of Palestinian citizens' land and its transfer to Jewish ownership in a process that left the Arab citizens who constitute about seventeen per cent of the population in control of less than 3 per cent of the state's lands (Jabareen 2017). Control of space extends also to the Israeli domination of occupied Palestinian lands in the West Bank and the transfer of major segments of this land to Jewish ownership; (c) Cultural erasure, which took place systematically by Israel and was directed at Palestinian identity, history, geographic names, and cultural expressions. This effort has not been as successful as the previous two (Rouhana and Sabbagh-Khoury 2014). (d) Political domination, which extends over Palestinians in all parts of mandatory Palestine, and is almost total, whether they are settler-colonial citizens inside Israel as Rouhana and Sabbagh-Khoury (2014) theorize, under military occupation in the West Bank, or under siege in Gaza.

However, the examination of Zionism (and Israel) only through a settler-colonial lens is not analytically comprehensive and might overshadow other defining features (see Rouhana 2014). Zionism is also a national movement with a strong religious component that fuses with nationalism. As a national movement, Zionism established national organizations, revived an ancient language, and created a vibrant society. Most importantly, Zionism successfully created a national consciousness with a particular land as its object. But Zionism is not a national liberation movement, even if Zionist jargon purposefully presents it as such in more than one sense: liberating Jews from a diasporic existence and maltreatment in Europe; and liberating the Jewish homeland from the British Mandate. (Hence the 1948 war is called "the war of liberation".) Zionism, even as a national movement, could not have achieved the typical goal of national movements – statehood – without being a colonial project and using settler-colonial strategies in order to establish its state. The effect of this combination of settler colonialism and nationalism on the dynamics of conflict (and on reconciliation) should be examined. Zionism embodies an ideology of exclusive nationalism. Because separateness from the natives and exclusivity are defining features of this nationalism, the presence of the natives became, by definition, an obstacle to the goal to establish an exclusive Jewish state. Separateness and exclusivity were pursued through the eliminatory component of the settler-colonial project and have resulted in the expulsion of the natives.

The fact that Zionism was both a settler-colonial project and a national movement has been detrimental to the dynamics of the conflict with the Palestinians. Zionism's combination of being both a colonial project that did not seek to create a racial hierarchy in which the natives could be incorporated to the benefit of the colonial society, and its exclusive nationalist goals, explains why the expulsion of the natives was favoured over their subjugation. Some Zionists, when they do acknowledge the expulsion of the Palestinians, argue that it only occurred because of circumstantial conditions of war. Benny Morris is one of a handful of "new historians" (Morris 2009) who articulate this explanation, although it seems to simply fulfil the elaborate justificatory system of Zionism. And when Zionists admit expulsion was a deliberate act, as in the recent case of Ari Shavit's description of the Lydda expulsion (Shavit 2013), this displacement of Palestinians from their homes and homeland by force is considered as the worthy price of the success of Zionism, and the worthy price of a Jewish state.

Another distinct feature of Zionism is the fusion of religious claims and religion with the national and the settler-colonial. For example, in Israel Jewish religion and Jewish nationalism overlap completely. An individual's nationality is Jewish only if they are Jewish in their religion. If they leave the Jewish faith, they will no longer be Jewish by nationality (see Bishara 2017). Furthermore, religious claims are central to the justificatory system of the colonial claim to Palestine. Even secular Zionism used religious arguments to establish the claim and to transform Jewish cultural ties to biblical history into a modern political claim: the sovereign (and exclusive) right over Palestine.

These historical and ideological features should problematize the simplistic application of a settler-colonial framework to Zionism and its century-long conflict with the Palestinians.

The symmetrical analysis of rights, recognition, and legitimacy

As mentioned above, the national conflict paradigm is most conducive to a symmetrical analysis, which in turn is used to support this paradigm. By taking two examples from leading scholars on the Israeli-Palestinian conflict, I will try to demonstrate that this pervasive analysis, in many of its manifestations, obfuscates the fundamentals of the conflict and does not contribute to reconciliation as defined here.

In one of the most comprehensive volumes on the Israeli-Palestinian conflict, the author states that his volume, "seeks not only to present a balanced and accurate history of the Israeli-Palestinian conflict, it also strives to encourage a sympathetic understanding of the parties involved" (Tessler 2009, viii). The author then explains that his work proceeds on the assumption that "both Jews and Arabs have legitimate political rights in Palestine; that the validity of these rights does not depend on the absence of corresponding rights possessed by the other party to the conflict and that these rights are inalienable". So he clearly takes what he calls a "normative" and symmetrical position on the conflict. He also asserts that most Israelis, Palestinians, and members of the international community support the establishment of a Palestinian state in the West Bank that "would live in peace with the Jewish state next door". (viii) Tessler's normative view of balance is reflected in his support for the establishment of a Palestinian state and a specifically "Jewish" state, which he mistakenly assumes that most Palestinians support. But the evidence overwhelmingly shows that Palestinians refuse to recognize Israel as a Jewish state (see Ghanim 2014).

The author clearly assumes that both Jews and Arabs[1] have legitimate rights to the land. The assertion that Jews have "rights" to Palestine is at the core of Zionist claims, and this assertion of "rights", (not historical connections) is stated as a matter of fact. Tessler's symmetrical approach is further revealed when he writes that

> only if each party to the conflict is persuaded that the other … has valid claims and has been motivated over the years by legitimate national aspirations is there likely to be agreement on any formula for compromise and peace, no matter how reasonable that formula might be. (xix)

Tessler's views echo the extensively and repeatedly explicated views of one of the most influential scholars in the field of conflict resolution, Herbert Kelman. Kelman's work on mutual denial of nationhood and the need for mutual recognition and legitimacy constitute the foundational analysis for why the two sides in the Israeli-Palestinian conflict, as well as the international community, should accept the symmetrical solution of a Palestinian state and a Jewish state, as proposed by Tessler. For example, in his discussion of "mutual denial of national identity" in the Israeli-Palestinian conflict, Kelman claims that what

> is especially pronounced, if not unique, about this conflict, is that it is marked by a principled non-recognition at the very basic level. Neither side fully recognizes the other's national identity and its right to exist. … Thus the core element of the Israeli-Palestinian conflict is mutual denial of the adversary's national identity. (Kelman 1978, 167)

Kelman wrote this statement long before the Oslo Agreements, and it has been repeated in different forms since then. Its importance emanates from the symmetrical reference that Kelman seeks to establish between Zionism and Palestinian nationhood. In effect, he is symmetricizing the Palestinians' denial to recognize Zionism – not simply the reality of Israel's existence – and Israelis' denial to accept the existence of Palestinians as a nation. Thus, he argues that to address this mutual denial the two sides must mutually accept each other's nationhood: Palestinians should accept Israel's legitimacy, which is "a confirmation of the moral basis" of the Jewish state. Thus

> various conceptions of Zionism and Israel that are offered – such as those describing Zionism as a form of racism, Israel as a settler state or outpost of western imperialism – evade the fact that Zionism is a nationalist movement and Israel is the political expression of that movement. (167)

In return, Israelis should accept the Palestinians' existence as a national group and recognize their nationhood. Thus, the parties have to deal with the symmetric denial by offering mutual symmetric acceptance. Both the denial and the acceptance are treated symmetrically.

Using basic human needs theory Kelman argues that, "each side needs recognition (in the psychological sense) from the other to satisfy its need for identity, justice, and security" (Kelman 1987, 357). This can be achieved in a "framework based on mutual recognition of the other's right to self-determination in the land they both claim" (358). Again, Palestinians must recognize Zionism (in the psychological sense) mutually with Israelis' recognition of the right of Palestinian self-determination in the West Bank and Gaza.

The two examples above both presume that reconciliation can be achieved based on mutual recognition of a Jewish state and a Palestinian state, as Tessler argues, or Zionism and Palestinian nationhood, as Kelman has tirelessly argued. Both scholars, like many others, fail to see why Palestinians cannot recognize a Jewish state or Zionism, even though this inevitable Palestinian response has been clearly stated by many Palestinian scholars and political leaders (Bishara 2017; Falah 2015; Jabareen 2014; Khalidi 2011; Rouhana 2006) This failure is rooted in the shortcomings of the symmetrical analysis and the refusal to accept that Zionism is an active, ongoing settler-colonial project, both in the West Bank and inside Israel. It is precisely because Palestinians consider Zionism a (continuing) settler-colonial project that they cannot lend legitimacy to the Jewish state. This blind spot is both a cause for the symmetrical analysis and is strengthened by it. Reconciliation between Israelis and Palestinians will benefit from discarding this type of analysis and advancing new foundations for true reconciliation.

Psychologizing the reconciliation process

The national conflict paradigm, which posits that partition is the most commonsense arrangement for both Israelis and Palestinians, also emphasizes that the parties' resistance to reaching an agreement emanates from psychological barriers. According to this rationale, if only the mutual fear, mistrust, denial, and dehumanization can be addressed, then the parties will be able to achieve a peaceful agreement and perhaps even reconciliation. Thus, Tessler believes

> that one of the greatest obstacles to peace has been each side's distrust of the other and, in particular, the fact that this distrust has been fed by stereotypes, misconceptions, and propaganda that lead each side to see its adversary as uninterested in, and unworthy of, genuine compromise. (Tessler 2009, ix)

This statement conflates two fallacies: (a) psychologizing the political and (b) symmetricizing a greatly asymmetric process. In Tessler's view, the primary obstacles to reconciliation are psychological rather than substantive political issues such as full-fledged settler-colonial policies the stronger party relentlessly implements, or the demand of the disadvantaged party for parity in a system of colonial privileges. Elaborating on these views, Tessler argues that the tendency of Israelis and Palestinians (and their foreign supporters) is to view the other as motivated by "unchangeable impulses and even hatreds" (ix). He reaches the climax of this argument when he states that he

> remains convinced that one of the biggest obstacles to peace, and arguably the biggest obstacle of all, is psychological in character. Peace will be possible if, and almost certainly only if, each side and its supporters reject the view that the Israeli-Palestinian conflict is a struggle between good and evil, accept the legitimacy of the other side's aspirations, and conclude from the history reported in this book that neither party has a monopoly on behaviour that is deserving either of respect or of condemnation.

The danger in such an approach is to over-psychologize the conflict and thus obscure its true nature: the power structures, the hierarchies of dominance, the politics of ethnic privileging, and the guiding political and ideological outlooks of each group.

This psychologizing approach is popular among many scholars who study reconciliation in the Israeli-Palestinian case. In a review I conducted earlier (Rouhana 2011), I found that the dominant approach sees reconciliation as essentially a psychologically driven process detached from power relations and illegitimate political practices, such as state-sanctioned discrimination and military occupation. For example, Maoz (2004) refers to reconciliation as "a cluster of cognitive and emotional processes" (225). Noor, Brown, and Prentice (2008) suggest that "at the heart of reconciliation lies the psychological process effecting shifts of one's 'mind and heart' concerning the conflict and the opponent group" (99), which has to address lack of trust and empathy. Kelman (2006) defines reconciliation in terms of a necessary identity change in each party that requires "the removal of the negation of the other as a central component of one's own identity" (119). Bar-Tal and Bennink (2004) claim that "the essence of reconciliation involves socio-psychological processes consisting of changes of motivations, goals, beliefs, attitudes and emotions by the majority of society members" and that "the first condition for reconciliation is legitimization and humanization of the rival" (366).

This approach is characterized by the assumption that the essence of the reconciliation process is psychological, removing psychological manifestations from the context of a broader social and political dynamics. It ignores that the psychological, which indeed contributes to perpetuating the conflict, is largely shaped by these dynamics. This is why the psychological emphasis is often made at the expense of the political requirements of reconciliation, central to which is the transformation of an unjust political order into a new order that addresses past injustice. There are many scholars who do see the reconciliation process as linked to social and political prerequisites and not in purely psychological terms (see e.g. Spears 2008; Stephan 2008). Spears (2008), for example, writing from within the tradition of social identity theory, defines reconciliation as "the stage after group conflict in which real group differences have been made clear, and resolved through struggle, and where groups come to term with the shift in power and status" (338). Groups in a post-conflict situation grant mutual legitimacy; but this becomes possible because of their new equal status and power relations, and because the groups recognize, acknowledge, and work to rectify the illegitimacy of the past system, and fully embrace and engage in the current effort to achieve social justice. This analysis is entirely different than the prevailing discourse in the Israeli-Palestinian conflict, which requires the two groups to mutually recognize each other, despite one group's defining political view of ethnic exclusivity and ethnic privileges that has been generating settler-colonial policies for decades.

The future of reconciliation in the Israeli-Palestinian case

Guided by the settler-colonial paradigm I propose that reconciliation, although difficult to achieve in the near future, should be pursued as decolonization within a framework of transitional justice. I also argue that this paradigm can help explain why the pursuit of a political settlement based on partition has failed. I will first focus on how the colonized and the colonizer conceive of the dominant political settlement, and how these asymmetric conceptions makes the settlement unlikely to be reached. Then I will explore the requirements for reconciliation in a settler-colonial context.

Settlement based on partition in a settler-colonial conflict

The experiences of conflict between settler regimes and native populations have varied depending on the historical era in which each project has emerged, the nature of the colonial project, and the nature and potency of the resistance. Despite the variations, those who resist colonialism have always faced severe human rights violations, ethnic cleansing, crimes against humanity, or extreme forms of structural, political, and military violence. Nevertheless, historically, native populations have not demanded partition, and few settler-colonial projects have ended with a partition of the land between the colonizers and the colonized. Settler-colonial projects have generally evolved in other forms such as extermination of most of the native population (North America), or the defeat and expulsion of the settlers (Algiers). Most relevant to our case is the emergence, after periods of domination and a long, persistent, and visionary struggle by the native population, of a new political order that includes both settlers and natives, such as in South Africa, Zimbabwe, and one can possibly argue, Northern Ireland.

In the Israeli-Palestinian conflict, one major problem with achieving a political agreement based on partition – even if the terms of the agreement have been reached based on parameters of balance of power (for example, the Clinton Parameters of 2000) – are the views that each side holds about the *nature* of such an agreement. Which of the three types of peacemaking described above should be considered? Is it a political settlement or is it reconciliation? The answer to this question immediately introduces questions of historical responsibility and historical justice to the public domain.

Let us assume the Palestinian leadership will, by choice or through international pressure accept a political settlement of two states. For their constituency to support this acceptance, the leadership would have to present it as such: a political settlement in which Palestinians live in coexistence with Israel, without reaching a resolution to the historical dimensions of the conflict, and without achieving justice. Within the parameters of a political settlement based on partition (such as the Clinton Parameters), Israel would not take responsibility for the refugee problem, face the truth of the ethnic cleansing that occurred in 1948, or accept a just solution to the refugee problem at the centre of which is fulfilling the right of return. This will remain, from the point of view of the Palestinian public a *political settlement*. For the native population, a settlement based on partition is only temporary.

Let us assume, too, that the international community, various US guarantees to Israel, and economic incentives can persuade an Israeli government to accept such an agreement. From an Israeli perspective, the extent of concessions that Israel will have to offer – including major territorial withdrawals, removing settlements, concessions on its policies on Jerusalem and recognizing a Palestinian state in reality – cannot be justified by the Israeli public if this arrangement is not seen as a final *reconciliation*. That is, Israel will seek to achieve from the Palestinians – and for that matter, from the Arabs – an agreement that guarantees an end to the conflict and to all historical claims, and recognition of its legitimacy as a Jewish state. This would close the door on the possibility of the return of refugees, and would signify Palestinian consent that Palestinian citizens of Israel will continue to be constitutionally unequal. These Israeli demands are rooted in the profound historical insecurity that Israelis hold about their collective existence in the region – precisely because a settler-colonial project inherently inhabits a site of insecurity when the state lacks legitimacy in the eyes of the natives.

Security, legitimacy, and the nature of the potential political arrangement become intertwined. For Israel to release its total control of the Palestinians, it has to feel secure. But in order to feel secure, Israel, as a Jewish state, needs to achieve legitimacy from its Palestinian victims as well as from the surrounding Arab states; for this security to be achieved Palestinians and the Arabs must explicitly accept it as a legitimate state. They must accept that the history of the encounter that led to Israel's establishment and the creation of the

Palestinian refugee problem was inevitable, understandable, and morally justifiable. Israel will thus seek the empathy of its victims, or at least the understanding or validation of its narrative about the reason Zionists settled in Palestine, claimed the land, and established a Jewish state. This can only happen if Palestinians (and the Arabs) recognize Zionism and recognize Israel as a Jewish state – the same arguments proposed in the context of mutual recognition by many scholars, the limitations and unfeasibility of which I described above.

In this scenario Israel demands in return for a "settlement" it offers the Palestinians a historical reconciliation with Zionism and the erasure of history prior to the 1967 Israeli occupation of the West Bank and Gaza. Historical memory in such an agreement begins not with Israel's creation but with Israel's 1967 occupation of the West Bank and Gaza in order to conveniently bury the heavy history related to the pre- and post-1948 conflict.

Reconciliation as decolonization

My proposed conceptualization of reconciliation between Israelis and Palestinians is based on the understanding that the Zionist project originated and continues to unfold as a settler-colonial project, with features of a national movement and other unique characteristics. Reconciliation between the parties in a settler-colonial conflict should be approached with the intention of decolonization. Such an approach, of course, cannot adopt frameworks of symmetrical analysis as most of the current work on conflict resolution and reconciliation in the Israeli-Palestinian conflict does. Instead, reconciliation as decolonization begins with acknowledging the power structures and asymmetry between colonized and colonizer as the point of departure, with the explicit goal of transforming them into structures of equality and reciprocity in a new democratic political order.

I therefore suggest that reconciliation in this conflict should be conceived as decolonization within a transitional justice framework. This is a dramatic shift from the current "conflict resolution efforts", official and unofficial, and I have no illusions that such a shift can take place swiftly or in the near future, or that the obstacles – such as realities of segregation on the ground, strong animosities, local resistance, non-existent international support, and regional coalitions – are easily surmountable. But a main point of this paper is to argue that for such a shift to have a chance to start compete with the failed existing paradigms, its parameters and principles must be broadly defined, hence the need for a new intellectual project. After these principles are outlined or in parallel to such a process, defining the political structure will have to follow. For example, what do scholars mean by calling for a bi-national state? Who are the two nations and what principles shape their relationship? What democratic structures are necessary?

I do not claim in this paper to have conceptualized a comprehensive framework for decolonization within a transitional justice context. But broadly speaking, such a framework should provide the mechanisms for examining the history of settler colonization, the moral and political framework that propelled it, the injustice it caused to the native population, how responsibility for this project should be assigned, and what mechanisms will be available for restorative justice. The framework should define the privileges that the colonizers enjoy by virtue of their ethnic affiliation, and the characteristics of the new political order in which both national groups will enjoy equal status, mutual acceptance, and security. Such framework should include four interrelated processes:

- *The moral imperative:* This will be based on decolonization within a transitional justice context seeking to transform the power structures that characterize colonizers and the colonized and address the asymmetrical injustice and massive human rights violations. The new moral foundation is defined by social justice, truth, historical accountability, and the establishment of institutions that reflect this framework. Such a framework makes use of tools of transitional justice appropriate to this particular conflict, including truth commissions, measures for restorative justice and reparations, historic reckoning and the use of apology or acknowledgement. These tools cannot be applied mechanically, without negotiations within the new moral framework. The challenges of transitional justice usually take centre place: How do we advance transitional justice without threatening a new democratic arrangement established on these foundations?
- *The political:* Reconciliation as decolonization is a process in which new democratic institutions are created and constitutional transformations are introduced in order to guarantee a future based on equality and democracy and protect against violations of human rights. The constitutional form that guarantees such a future – whether it is integration, federation, bi-nationalism, autonomy, or something else – will be founded on restorative and distributive justice, fair distribution of resources, and power sharing.
- *The social-psychological:* The reconciliation process entails cognitive, emotional, and behavioural changes that support the transformation. These changes become possible within the broader process. These are mainly consequences of the reconciliation framework, although once instigated, they promote its continuation. Similarly, psychological healing can be facilitated and easier to achieve within such moral and political frameworks.
- *The involvement of publics and elites:* These processes are public and involve new political behaviour on the part of the publics and elites of both

societies. Within such frameworks, state institutions can be legitimately employed to generate public and open support that translates into mutual legitimacy for these frameworks and the transformation they guided.

Finally, this type of reconciliation will enable the legitimacy of the Jewish Israeli presence in Palestine. This will require an explicit, open, and public acceptance of the Israeli Jewish national group on fully equal terms and a completely legitimate basis within the new order. The mutual recognition that some scholars so tirelessly but hopelessly argued for will become more likely after decolonization in a joint and mutually accepted political framework. Admittedly though, there are currently no significant political forces on the ground pushing in this direction.

Note

1. Note specifically that the author refers not to Israelis or Israeli Jews, but to Jews in general.

Disclosure statement

No potential conflict of interest was reported by the author.

References

Abu-Lughod, Ibrahim, and Baha Abu-Laban. 1974. *Settler Regimes in Africa and the Arab World: The Illusion of Endurance*. Wilmette: The Medina University Press.

Amara, Ahmad. 2014. "Plans for Bedouin Resettlement in the Naqab." *The Mada Files* 1: 1–12.

Bar-Tal, Daniel, and Gemma H. Bennink. 2004. "The Nature of Reconciliation as an Outcome and as a Process." In *From Conflict Resolution to Reconciliation*, edited by Yaacov Bar-Siman-Tov, 11–38. Oxford, NY: Oxford University Press.

Bashir, Bashir, and Will Kymlicka. 2008. "Introduction: Struggles for Inclusion and Reconciliation in Modern Democracies." In *The Politics of Reconciliation in Multicultural Societies*, edited by Bashir Bashir and Will Kymlicka, 1–24. Oxford: Oxford University Press.

Bishara, Azmi. 2017. "Zionism and Equal Citizenship: Essential and Incidental Citizenship in the Jewish State." In *Israel and the Palestinian Citizens: Ethnic Privileges in the Jewish State*, edited by Nadim N. Rouhana, 137–155. Cambridge: Cambridge University Press.

Burton, John. 1990. *Conflict: Resolution and Prevention*. New York: St. Martin's Press.

Crocker, David. 1999. "Reckoning with Past Wrongs: A Normative Framework." *Ethics & International Affairs* 13 (1): 43–64.

Dwyer, Susan. 1999. "Reconciliation for Realists." *Ethics & International Affairs* 13 (1): 81–98.

Falah, Ghazi-Walid. 2015. "The Implications of Israel's Demand to Be Recognized by the Palestinians as a 'Jewish State'." *The Arab World Geographer* 18 (3): 192–220.

Ghanim, Honaida. 2014. *On Recognition of the "Jewish State."* Ramallah: The Palestinian Forum for Israeli Studies.

Hammack, Phillip. 2010. *Narrative and the Politics of Identity: The Cultural Psychology of Israeli and Palestinian Youth*. Oxford: Oxford University Press.

Hatuqa, Dalia. 2013. "Analysis: Palestinians See Peace Process as 'Doomed Experiment.'" *Al Jazeera English*, September 8. Accessed June 18 2016. http://america.aljazeera.com/articles/2013/9/8/analysis-palestiniansseelatesttalksashopeless.html.

Hilal, Jamil. 1976. "Imperialism and Settler-Colonialism in West Africa: Israel and the Arab Palestinian Struggle." *UTAFITI* 1 (1): 51–70.

Jabareen, Hassan. 2014. "The Legal Meaning of the 'Jewish State' and the Nakba." In *On Recognition of the "Jewish State,"* edited by Honaida Ghanim, 39–48. Ramallah: The Palestinian Forum for Israeli Studies.

Jabareen, Yosef. 2017. "Controlling Land and Demography in Israel: The Obsession with Territorial and Geographic Dominance." In *Israel and the Palestinian Citizens: Ethnic Privileges in the Jewish State*, edited by Nadim N. Rouhana, 238–255. Cambridge: Cambridge University Press.

Jerusalem Post. 2015. "Poll Finds Fading Support for Two-State Solution Between Israelis, Palestinians." *Jerusalem Post*, June 26, Accessed June 18. http://www.jpost.com/Arab-Israeli-Conflict/Poll-finds-fading-support-for-two-state-solution-between-Israelis-Palestinians-407222.

Kelman, Herbert. 1978. "Israelis and Palestinians: Psychological Prerequisites for Mutual Acceptance." *International Security* 3 (1): 162–186.

Kelman, Herbert. 1987. "The Political Psychology of the Israeli-Palestinian Conflict: How Can We Overcome the Barriers to a Negotiated Solution?" *Political Psychology* 8 (3): 347–363.

Kelman, Herbert. 2006. "Interests, Relationships, Identities: Three Central Issues for Individuals and Groups in Negotiating Their Social Environment." *Annual Review of Psychology* 57 (1): 1–26.

Khalidi, Rashid. 1990. *Palestinian Identity: The Construction of Modern National Consciousness*. New York: Columbia University Press.

Khalidi, Ahmad. 2011. "Why Can't the Palestinians Recognize the Jewish State?" *Journal of Palestine Studies* 40 (4): 78–81.

Kuhn, Thomas S. 2012. *The Structure of Scientific Revolutions*. Chicago: University of Chicago Press.

Lloyd, David. 2012. "Settler Colonialism and the State of Exception: The Example of Palestine/Israel." *Settler Colonial Studies* 2 (1): 59–80.

Mamdani, Mahmood. 2015. "Settler Colonialism: Then and Now." *Critical Inquiry* 41 (3): 596–614.

Maoz, Ifat. 2004. "Social-Cognitive Mechanisms in Reconciliation." In *From Conflict Resolution to Reconciliation*, edited by Yaacov Bar-Siman-Tov, 197–224. Oxford, NY: Oxford University Press.

Mitchell, Christopher. 1990. "Necessitous Man and Conflict Resolution: More Basic Questions about Basic Human Needs Theory." In *Conflict: Human Needs Theory*, edited by John Burton, 149–176. New York: St. Martin's Press.

Morris, Benny. 2009. *1948: A History of the First Arab-Israeli War*. New Haven: Yale University Press.

Noor, Masi, Rupert Brown, and Garry Prentice. 2008. "Prospects for Intergroup Reconciliation: Social-psychological Predictors of Intergroup Forgiveness and

Reparation in Northern Ireland and Chile." In *The Social Psychology of Intergroup Reconciliation*, edited by Arie Nadler, Thomas E. Malloy, and Jeffrey D. Fisher, 97–116. Oxford, NY: Oxford University Press.

Pappé, Ilan. 2012. "Shtetl Colonialism: First and Last Impressions of Indigeneity by Colonized Colonizers." *Settler Colonial Studies* 2: 39–58.

Ravid, Barak. 2016. "Ehud Barak Hints at Return to Politics: If Government Won't Get Back on Track, We Must Topple It." Ha'aretz English. June 16. Accessed June 18 2016. http://www.haaretz.com/israel-news/.premium-1.725482.

Richmond, Oliver. 2001. "A Genealogy of Peacemaking: The Creation and Re-creation of Order." *Alternatives: Global, Local, Political* 26 (3): 317–348.

Robinson, Shira. 2013. *Citizen Strangers: Palestinians and the Birth of Israeli Liberal Settler State*. Redwood: Stanford University Press.

Rouhana, Nadim. 2004. "Group Identity and Power Asymmetry in Reconciliation Processes: The Israeli-Palestinian Case." *Peace & Conflict* 10 (1): 33–52.

Rouhana, Nadim. 2006. "'Jewish and Democratic'? The Price of a National Self-deception." *Journal of Palestine Studies* 35 (2): 64–74.

Rouhana, Nadim. 2008. "Reconciling History and Equal Citizenship in Israel: Democracy and the politics of historical denial." In *The Politics of Reconciliation in Multicultural Societies*, edited by Will Kymlicka and Bashir Bashir, 70–93. Oxford, NY: Oxford University Press.

Rouhana, Nadim. 2011. "Key Issues in Reconciliation: Challenging Traditional Assumptions on Conflict Resolution and Power Dynamics." In *Intergroup Conflicts and Their Resolution: A Social Psychological Perspective*, edited by Bar-Tal, 291–311. New York: Psychology Press.

Rouhana, Nadim. 2014. "'The Palestinian National Project: Towards Restoring the Settler Colonial Paradigm." *Majjalat al-Dirasat al-Filistiniyah (Journal of Palestine Studies)* 19: 18–36.

Rouhana, Nadim, and Areej Sabbagh-Khoury. 2014. "Settler-Colonial Citizenship: Conceptualizing the Relationship Between Israel and Its Palestinian Citizens." *Settler Colonial Studies* 5 (3): 205–225.

Sabbagh-Khoury, Areej. 2015. "Colonization Practices and Interactions at the Frontier: Ha- Shomer Ha-Tzair Kibbutzes and the Surrounding Arab Villages at the Margins of the Valley of Jezreel/Marj Ibn 'Amer, 1936–1956." Ph.D diss., Tel Aviv University.

Said, Edward. 1979. "Zionism from the Standpoint of its Jewish Victims." *Social Text* 1: 7–58.

Savir, Uri. 1998. *The Process*. New York: Vintage Books.

Sayegh, Fayez. 1965. *Zionist Colonialism in Palestine*. Beirut: Palestine Liberation Organization Research Center.

Shalhoub-Kevorkian, Nadera. 2015. *Security Theology, Surveillance and the Politics of Fear*. Cambridge: Cambridge University Press.

Shavit, Ari. 2013. "Lydda, 1948." *The New Yorker*, October 21.

Shihade, Magid. 2011. *Not Just a Soccer Game: Colonialism & Conflict among Palestinians in Israel*. Syracuse: Syracuse University Press.

Spears, Russell M. 2008. "Social Identity, Legitimacy, and Intergroup Conflict: The Rocky Road to Reconciliation." In *The Social Psychology of Intergroup Reconciliation*, edited by Arie Nadler, Thomas Malloy, and Jeffrey D. Fisher, 319–344. Oxford, NY: Oxford University Press.

Stephan, Walter G. 2008. "The Road to Reconciliation." In *The Social Psychology of Intergroup Reconciliation*, edited by Arie Nadler, Thomas Malloy, and Jeffrey D. Fisher, 369–394. Oxford, NY: Oxford University Press.

Tessler, Mark. 2009. *A History of the Israeli-Palestinian Conflict*. 2nd ed. Bloomington: Indiana University Press.

Van Zyl, Paul. 1999. "Dilemmas of Transitional Justice: The Case of South Africa's Truth and Reconciliation Commission." *Journal of International Affairs* 52 (2): 647–667.

Veracini, Lorenzo. 2010. "The Settler-Colonial Situation." *Native Studies Review* 19 (1): 101–118.

Vollhardt, Johanna. 2009. "The Role of Victim Beliefs in the Israeli–Palestinian Conflict: Risk or Potential for Peace?" *Peace and Conflict: Journal of Peace Psychology* 15 (2): 135–159.

Wolfe, Patrick. 2006. "Settler Colonialism and the Elimination of the Native." *Journal of Genocide Research* 8 (4): 387–409.

Transitional justice and political order in Rwanda

Cyanne E. Loyle

ABSTRACT

The gacaca transitional justice process in Rwanda has strong proponents and sharp critics. At the core of these critiques is the argument that gacaca has been used by the government in Rwanda to consolidate political power around a single narrative of the conflict and the dominant political party. This article advances this critique by arguing that it was not simply the implementation of gacaca which was used for a specific political purpose, but rather the process itself which was structured in a way to consolidate political order for the Rwandan Patriotic Front government. Through the Rwanda case, this article advances an understanding of transitional justice adoption which focuses on the ways in which governments use transitional justice as a tool of political order. Within this framework, transitional justice is adopted to address security, resource, and legitimacy challenges for a post-conflict or post-transition government.

In 2001, the Rwandan government adopted the gacaca courts to much international acclaim. These courts were designed as a wide-reaching, domestic institution to address crimes of genocide in Rwanda based on a historical indigenous practice of dispute resolution. The courts were heralded by many as a traditional justice mechanism worthy of emulation which incorporated Rwandan values with a regard for accountability in line with international norms (UNDP 2006). Despite this acclaim, gacaca has sparked heated debate in Rwanda and abroad. Some argue that gacaca is uniquely designed for dealing with the specific justice and legacy issues emerging from the genocide (Clark 2007; Kirkby 2006), whereas others question the legality of the process (Chakravarty 2006) and its ability to achieve societal reconciliation (Thomson and Nagy 2011). Gacaca has been criticized by the legal community for failing to follow international legal conventions of due process, not providing legal counsel for defendants, a lack of an unbiased jury, and the use of lay judges (Clark 2009). Reduced sentences potentially undermine accountability and threaten Rwandan security by failing to hold perpetrators fully accountable for their actions (Corey and Joireman 2004; Human Rights Watch 2011). Furthermore, by prosecuting only those accused of committing genocide while ignoring crimes against Hutu committed by Tutsi including the alleged crimes of the Rwandan Patriotic Front (RPF), gacaca fails to overcome the very inequities and political marginalization which contributed to the genocide in the first place (Loyle 2011; Thomson and Nagy 2011).[1]

Those critical of gacaca have made the argument that the process has been used as a policy tool by the Rwandan government to strengthen political order in the country and consolidate the control of a de facto single party state, yet this work has not clearly established why the government chose the specific justice path that it did. In the decade that followed gacaca's adoption, scholars and policy-makers alike have argued that given the conditions that persisted in Rwanda – overcrowded prisons, a decimated judiciary, and the sheer scope of participation in the genocide – gacaca was the *only* possible solution for bringing accountability and reconciliation to the country. This path-dependent argument fails to engage with the many ways in which the narrative around justice and accountability in Rwanda was structured towards a particular political end. In this article, I trace the adoption of gacaca and argue that it was a series of strategic guiding principles concerning issues of justice and accountability in Rwanda which led the government to select and advocate this process. Had these post-conflict challenges been framed differently by the government, the justice solution would have changed. Rather than solely advancing unity and reconciliation – the often-ascribed goals of transitional justice – the Rwandan government selected and supported gacaca as a tool for projecting political power following the conflict (Des Forges and Longman 2004). This aim was visible at the outset in the way that issues of justice were defined and a justice solution was constructed.

The last decade has seen a precipitous rise in the use of domestic transitional justice following political transitions and the termination of armed conflict.[2] Sikkink (2011) has attributed the growth in use of transitional justice polices to a justice cascade in which a global coalescence around international and domestic demands for accountability has increased the pressure for domestic justice. Furthermore, transitional justice has become a staple in the liberal peacebuilding agenda (Paris 2004) as the international community incentivizes the use of transitional justice (Subotić 2012). Yet, our focus on the growing norm of accountability, and the now seeming inevitability of "justice", moves us away from earlier thinking about the structural incentives for transitional justice adoption causing us to overlook the inherently political nature of institutional choices (Meierhenrich 2005; Moe 2005).

Given the many international and domestic incentives for using transitional justice, there is growing evidence that states are using the institutional form of transitional justice without maintaining a commitment to the normative goals presumed by domestic and transnational advocacy actors (Loyle and Davenport 2016). While on the surface post-conflict countries appear to be readily adopting transitional justice as a means of addressing past violations of human rights, in many cases, these institutions are being used to mask the domestic political agendas of their governments (Cronin-Furman 2015). In this way, the expanding use of transitional justice in the current period can be attributed only in part to the justice cascade; we must also consider the functionality of transitional justice for achieving alternative political aims.

Though arguably a unique case in many respects, Rwanda offers broader lessons about the political use of transitional justice following armed conflict and political transitions. While much work has been done to expose the ways in which transitional justice has been used for political purposes (e.g. Lake 2017; Nalepa 2010; Simmons 2017; Subotić 2009), we have yet to link this understanding to broader theories of post-conflict institutional change. In this article, I argue that it is the ability of transitional justice to address specific concerns of political order which has contributed to the increased use of these processes. This argument problematizes recent discussions about the proliferation of transitional justice emerging from a growing norm of accountability (Sikkink 2011) attributing the growth, instead, to the functionality of transitional justice and its ability to achieve certain domestic political aims.

I begin this article by tracing the adoption of the gacaca courts in Rwanda. I use this case to illustrate the ways in which transitional justice in Rwanda was selected based on three guiding principles which were conceptualized from the outset to strengthen the political power of the ruling party. Building from this case, I theorize the instrumentalization of transitional justice as a tool for achieving political order. In particular, transitional justice processes can be used to achieve important post-conflict aims such as the provision of security, resources, and legitimacy. I close with a discussion of the broader applications of this theory and its applicability to other cases.

Transitional justice and political order in post-conflict Rwanda

Gacaca is an important case for understanding the use of transitional justice because of the global attention the process has received and the claim that this process could be a model for other nations pursuing locally adapted accountability processes.[3] These claims press us to better understand how gacaca was chosen and ultimately to what ends it was pursued. To develop this case, I conducted over 10 months of fieldwork in Rwanda across four trips between 2009 and 2013. This fieldwork included interviews with 20 government leaders, academics, and civil society actors. Interviews were semi-structured and in many cases took place over multiple meetings. In some cases, information received from these interviews is not attributed in order to protect the individuals who participated in the research. Interviews were supplemented by archival work in the Gacaca Archives in Kigali, Rwanda which houses documentation of all gacaca trials.

I begin with an overview of the conflict and post-conflict period in Rwanda detailing the three justice policies that were pursued by the Rwandan government and the international community: national court trials, an international criminal tribunal, and gacaca courts. I then trace how the gacaca policy was selected. In particular, I describe the three principles adopted by the Rwanda government which made gacaca appear as an "inevitable" policy option. And finally, I turn to how gacaca, once selected, was able to aid in the political consolidation of the RPF regime.

The evolution of conflict and post-conflict in Rwanda

The contemporary conflict in Rwanda began in October 1990 with the onset of a civil war. The rebel forces, calling themselves the RPF, had the military goal of winning political participation and legitimacy for Tutsi refugees who had fled Rwanda during pogroms against Tutsi in the 1960s and 1980s. In 1992, the United Nations brokered a peace agreement which ended the conflict and resulted in the deployment of a UN peacekeeping mission, UNAMIR, to monitor the ceasefire. Tensions mounted through 1993 as Hutu hardliners in the transition government proved unwilling to accept the negotiated peace and the RPF resumed military attacks with the intention of forcing the government to abide by its agreement (Kuperman 2004).

On 6 April 1994, President Habyarimana, the president of the transitional government and Rwanda's president for the past 20 years, was killed in a plane crash over Kigali International Airport.[4] Habyarimana's death became the inciting event for the genocide (Adler et al. 2008). From the early weeks of April, violence was rampant and included one-on-one killing using machetes, farm instruments, and blunt objects. In addition to personalized killings, there were more systematic attempts at extermination such as the deliberate military targeting of civilian areas including churches and schools (African Rights 1995; Human Rights Watch 1999; Straus 2006). Over the course of 100 days, approximately 800,000 people were killed.[5] The civil war and genocide ended in July when the RPF, led by General Paul Kagame, took control of the capital city and Interahamwe militia, soldiers, and a large number of civilians fled to neighbouring countries.

Once the war ended, the RPF formed a transitional government, the Government of National Unity, similar in structure to the one proposed by the UN in 1992. This government was to represent all major political parties; however, it did not include members from the more radical Hutu power parties, nor those individuals who had been politically or socially aligned with the previous regime. While on the surface it appeared that the new government was a broad-based political coalition, in reality it was criticized for shutting out opposition and concentrating power around supporters of the RPF (Prunier 1997; Reyntjens 2004).

Post-conflict justice in Rwanda

The RPF and the transition government faced a number of pressing challenges in the post-conflict period, including issues of governance, security, and the economy; but justice (i.e. the punishment of those responsible for crimes during the conflict) and an end to impunity for ethnic violence were seen as important prerequisites to these other goals.[6] The post-conflict justice strategy in Rwanda took a three-tiered approach encompassing national court proceedings, an international criminal tribunal, and the gacaca courts.

In the beginning, the Rwandan government advanced its justice strategy through the national courts with genocide crimes prosecuted through a special chamber. Yet, the Rwandan judiciary lacked the legal and physical capacity for the task. Under Habyarimana, there was no functioning Bar Association and of the 708 magistrates operating in Rwanda at that time, only 45 held university law degrees.[7] The legal system had a strong history of being merely an extension of executive power which continued to undermine confidence in the national courts even after power had shifted. Furthermore, the massive levels of participation in the violence quickly led to an untenable situation in the prisons. By early 1995, more than 6,500 suspected genocide perpetrators were being held. By 2005, that number was close to 72,000 (USIP 1995).[8] Trials in the special chambers began in the final week of December 1996. This effort was extensive. By early 2000, UN Special Representative Michel Moussalli reported that 2,406 people had been tried (Schabas 2009). This pace, however, could not keep up with the growing prison population and international pressures to address worsening conditions in the prisons.

At the same time that Rwanda was structuring its judicial response through the national courts, the Rwandan government petitioned the United Nations to address violations of international law around the planning and implementation of the genocide. Created by the UN Security Council in 1994, the International Criminal Tribunal for Rwanda (ICTR) was intended to handle the "prosecution of persons responsible for genocide and other serious violations of international humanitarian law committed in the territory of Rwanda between 1 January 1994 and 31 December 1994" (United Nations 1994). Despite the Rwandan government's initial request for assistance, the creation of the ICTR was controversial. While the international community and permanent members of the Security Council were in seeming alignment, Rwanda held the rotating position on the Council and represented the one dissenting vote. The Rwandan government's objections included to the prohibition on the use of capital punishment, the limitation of the temporal jurisdiction of the process to 1994, the lack of an independent prosecutor and appeals chamber (these were shared with the International Criminal Tribunal for the Former Yugoslavia), and the decision to locate the tribunal outside of Rwanda (Schabas 2009). Despite objections, the ICTR issued its first indictments on 12 December 1995.

The third component of the Rwanda justice strategy was inkiko gacaca, the gacaca courts. On 16 January 2001, the Transitional National Assembly of Rwanda adopted Organic Law No. 40/2000 which called for the establishment of "gacaca jurisdictions", loosely based on the traditional, pre-colonial justice structure in Rwanda (Schabas 2005).[9] Gacaca courts function like a community meeting using locally elected judges trained by the Rwandan government on specific law and relevant court proceedings. Gacaca proceedings were public and took place in individual communities encouraging public confession of crimes, truth telling, and community service in exchange for reduced punishments. Crimes tried in gacaca courts include property crimes, assault, and joining with and assisting killers in finding the location of targeted individuals. The accused in gacaca managed their own defence, while members of the community volunteered information and their own experiences about a particular crime (Clark 2010). All members of the community were asked by the government to attend.[10] Before closing in 2014, gacaca processed over 1.5 million cases (Kanyesigye 2011); approximately one out of every five adults in Rwanda.

Given the limitations of the national special courts, overcrowded prisons, and domestic challenges to the ICTR, gacaca is often presented as an inevitable process. In other words, given these conditions, there was simply no other solution; however, the decision to use gacaca was a product of three strategic decisions concerning the centrality of punishment and how to define crimes of genocide.

Guiding principles of the RPF's post-conflict justice strategy

The first formal reference to the potential of using traditional gacaca courts came in December 1995 as part of an international response conference. The government of Rwanda, with financial support from USAID and the Government of Ireland, held a conference in Kigali tasked with receiving international input into the pressing problems of the time. This conference discussed issues including the management of political, economic, and social consequences of the violence. The working group responsible for debating ways to bring perpetrators to justice raised the possibility of using the historical dispute resolution mechanism, gacaca. This proposal was reportedly made by a group of academics, including Rwandan historians and anthropologists who had studied gacaca.[11] The use of gacaca was further debated at the Urugwiro Reflection Meetings held at President Bizimungu's residence from May 1998 to March 1999 (Karekezi, Nshimiyimana, and Mutamba 2004). These weekly meetings were large, private assemblies of eminent persons in Rwandan politics and civil society where participants were tasked with discussing the major challenges of rebuilding the state. It was as part of these meetings that momentum coalesced behind the idea of gacaca. Of note, while much of the justification for the implementation of gacaca focuses on the backlog in the national courts, the original idea for gacaca was presented before national trials were underway.

While alternative judicial configurations were proposed and debated at this time, including the strict reliance on domestic prosecutions and the use of amnesty, there were three guiding principles which led to the adoption of gacaca. First, the RPF made accountability and punishment a priority for *all* individuals involved in the genocide (Gahima 2007), what Jennie Burnet has termed "maximal prosecution" (Burnet 2010). As Jean de Dieu Mucyo, former Minister of Justice, argued:

> Justice was the priority. You can't sit there and look at someone who killed your husband or your children and keep moving forward while still seeing him before you.[12]

Discussions of justice in early 1995 were linked very closely to the RPF's conceptualization of Rwandan history. In numerous interviews, top RPF officials cited the impunity for previous episodes of anti-Tutsi violence as a precipitating factor of the genocide. In speaking about his work on the 1994 RPF Human Rights Commission, Tito Rutaremara said:

> We were finding people who committed genocide in '62, '64, then '72, '91. Finding people who committed genocide four, five times and each and every time, the former regimes would give amnesty.[13]

Under the Habyarimana regime, impunity for ethnic crimes, particularly those against Tutsi, was the norm (Uvin 1999). As Paul Rutayisire, director of the Center for Conflict Management, argued, "One of the key causes of the tragedy was impunity. So now to reconstruct, we [the RPF] had to put an emphasis on justice."[14] Punishment for crimes against Tutsi became a prevailing component of the RPF's post-conflict strategy; in order to prevent the violence and instability that Rwanda had experienced from happening again, these crimes needed to be addressed. Based on the priority of accountability, once the conflict ended the transitional government initiated a massive plan of arrests for suspected perpetrators (USIP 1995) as it was determined that "every single participant in the genocide, from the central planners down to coerced peasant farmers and opportunist looters, would be prosecuted and punished for their crimes" (Burnet 2010, 97).[15]

The RPF's goal of complete accountability and punishment eliminated alternative transitional justice options, such as amnesty. Amnesty, even for rank and file participants in the violence, was viewed as directly contradictory to the idea of overcoming impunity in the country.[16] While other countries, such as South Africa, have chosen to pardon members of the previous regime in order to enhance stability in the transition to democracy, the RPF chose a different path. Despite the overwhelming nature of the task, the RPF never deviated from its core principle that *all* those responsible for the genocide should be punished.[17]

Second, the RPF focused on accountability solely for crimes of genocide, but defined these crimes broadly.[18] The large number of genocide perpetrators in Rwanda is due in part to the way the government has chosen to define crimes of genocide. Crimes of genocide under Rwandan law range on a scale from organization of the violence at one extreme to low-level participation on the other where participation can include property crimes, "pillaging" and "showing" or divulging the location of someone in hiding (Longman 2009). In some cases, these low-level crimes were motivated by "genocidal ideology" (Ingelaere 2009), but it is also possible that people participated in looting and more superficial acts of violence against Tutsi because of the social and political breakdown at the time (Adler et al. 2008; Davenport and Stam 2009; Kalyvas 2003). Longman and Rutagengwa (2004) find that while the RPF narrative of the violence focuses on a genocidal ideology, Rwandans were more likely to see the genocide as caused by fear and ignorance. While these violations have been classified as crimes of genocide, it is extremely difficult to prove genocidal intent through the gacaca courts (Karbo and Mutisi 2008; Morrill 2004).

Third, the RPF insisted on a "Rwandan", domestically controlled, justice process. While this dialogue has shifted over time, in the late 1990s, there was a strong emphasis on the root causes of the genocide as driven by ethnic divisionism in Rwandan society which was created and enforced during Colonial times.[19] The argument is that in Rwandan society, Hutu, Tutsi, and Twa coexisted relatively peacefully before German and Belgian colonial rule. The logic therefore follows that any attempt to "fix" this divisionism would be best served with a Rwandan solution independent of international influence (Des Forges and Longman 2004). The idea of the negative influence of the international was reinforced by the perceived lack of support by the international community towards Rwandan reconstruction and RPF rule (Prunier 1997, 336–345). This resistance to the international was further strengthened and by the challenges faced by the ICTR. For example, there were accusations of genocide collaborators being hired by the ICTR and subsequent abuse or lack of protection for witnesses (Peskin 2005). As President Kagame stated in a 2007 genocide Commemoration speech, "It is inconceivable that foreigners should judge Rwandans" (quoted in Ingelaere

2009). The creed which emerged at this time was one of strong, national, self-reliance; a local justice process was an important component of that agenda.

The focus on accountability for all individuals involved in genocide, broadly defined, necessitated the creation and use of a broad-based justice process capable of holding tens of thousands of individuals to account. Coupled with the desire to initiate a local process, free from international influence, the gacaca courts were adopted. Furthermore, these strategic principles provided a concrete justification for the construction of a transitional justice programme which contributed to the consolidation of the RPF political regime.

Transitional justice as a tool of political order

The RPF chose to pursue accountability in this way, but to what effect? Below, I argue that gacaca was an effective tool in the development and maintenance of political order in Rwanda – a key goal of the RPF government. Transitional justice polices are particularly well suited for advancing domestic political order and consolidating power behind a given regime. While transitional justice and political order has mostly been theorized in regard to democratic consolidation (Loyle and Davenport 2016), the Rwanda case demonstrates the way in which transitional justice processes can be effective in consolidating an emerging authoritarian regime. The "justice cascade" has theorized a move towards domestic justice driven by a normative commitment to individual accountability (Sikkink 2011); however, it may be that we are seeing the increased use of transitional justice because of the ability of these processes to advance alternative or additional aims. The flexibility around the characteristics of transitional justice institutions (e.g. their mandate and how they are structured) and the focus on the use of domestically adopted mechanisms allows for these processes to be more easily manipulated by domestic actors, than say international or hybrid tribunals. While there are numerous incentives for addressing issues of accountability following armed conflict, governments are able to use calls for justice and accountability for achieving essential post-conflict aims, namely the provision of political order through regime consolidation.

Political order refers to the ability of a leader to "secure compliance with particular directives or to mold attitudes so as to assure political stability through the voluntary acceptance of a given authority structure, its norms or social conduct, and its directives" (Dallin and Breslauer 1970, 2). In other words, political order is a leader's ability to securely govern in the way he chooses. Political order is an important issue for post-conflict governments given the uncertainty that exists in post-conflict situations (Collier et al. 2003). To overcome this uncertainty, a leader will select policies most likely to address the post-conflict challenges undermining his rule, focusing on broader concerns about security, resources, and the legitimacy of the government itself (Dallin and Breslauer 1970). As leaders set about trying to restore and maintain political order following armed conflict, all three of these challenges must be successfully addressed. Transitional justice can be a useful institution for addressing these challenges of peacebuilding, state building, and/or nation-building.

First, transitional justice processes can address security challenges by identifying, marginalizing, or eliminating political challenges to the leader. Through trials, exiles, and purges, challengers can be identified and removed from the political arena. For example, human rights trials could be held for former rebel leaders who committed crimes during the conflict. If these leaders are found guilty of those crimes, they will be imprisoned, marginalizing them from political life. Lustration laws or purging processes can be used to prevent entire political parties from running for office or taking part in governing (Nalepa 2010; Stan and Nedelsky 2015). Transitional justice can also be used to indirectly decrease the influence of individuals or opposition groups. For example, when a truth commission publicly identifies previous human rights violators, those individuals may have a harder time running for political office or gaining broad-based popular support.

Second, transitional justice can provide the material incentives necessary to address resource challenges and shore up the support of a needed constituency. In line with Grodsky (2010), transitional justice can be used as a political good for appealing to important constituencies, thus bolstering a leader's winning coalition and strengthening his position in power. For example, Smith (2012) found that war crimes trials often "serve to consolidate power to the extent that the trials expand the political influence or control of the mechanisms of government of those conducting the trials or appease some constituent group upon which those conducting trials rely" (19). Material incentives to constituents can include direct reparation payments or victim funds, but they can also include public good provisions such as an economic incentive package for a region hard hit by the conflict.

Finally, transitional justice can be used to construct and reinforce a politically beneficial narrative legitimizing the government through framing events of the conflict and post-conflict period in a particular light. Framing, in this context, "refers to the process of selecting and highlighting some aspects of a perceived reality, and enhancing the salience of an interpretation and evaluation of that reality" (Entman 2004, 26). Transitional justice consolidates the emerging narrative around the conflict by focusing national and international attention on certain events, actions, and perpetrators (Brass 1997). Criminal guilt following armed conflict, for example, is determined by which groups and individuals are charged and ultimately prosecuted for certain crimes. In his review of war crimes tribunals, Smith (2012) found that "the winner [of the previous conflict] defined justice and constructed the framework of a trial for his political purposes" (50). Truth commissions can serve similar functions by "narrowing the range of permissible lies" (Ignatieff, cited in Hayner 2011, 25). Through public testimony, statement gathering, and the publication of a final report, truth commissions write a narrative of conflict events (Taylor and Dukalskis 2012). However, this range of "permissible lies" is unlikely to refer solely to the "truth" but rather the *permissible* truth as identified and accommodated by those in power (Loyle 2011).

Political order and gacaca

Based on three principles of accountability and punishment in Rwanda, the RPF was able to select and subsequently construct a unique institutional response to the challenges of justice in post-genocide Rwanda. Gacaca has gone on to be an effective tool in the consolidation of the political regime in Rwanda, as theorized above, through marginalizing political opponents, provide material benefits to the RPF's constituency, and constructing a political narrative which helped to legitimate the party in advance of democratic elections.

Gacaca has been effective at *marginalizing political challengers* within the country as individuals associated with the crimes of the past regime are imprisoned and physically removed from the political space. Further to this point, because gacaca only recognizes violence perpetrated by the former Rwandan Army, Interahamwe militia groups, and vigilante individuals, it has been an effective means of specifically targeting those individuals in potential opposition to RPF rule. The 2007 Freedom House country report on Rwanda describes gacaca as "one-sided" and argues that its failure to prosecute RPF war crimes from 1990 through 1995 or violence in the Congo from 1996 through 2000 opens the critique that gacaca is simply victor's justice. "Survivors and relatives of the victims of RP[F] violence frequently express frustration over the failure of both the formal justice system and the gacaca courts to investigate and prosecute these offences" (Gahima 2007, 174). In this way, transitional justice in Rwanda only acknowledges violence in which the RPF government cannot be implicated (Des Forges and Longman 2004; Longman 2009).[20] As Gahima writes (2007, 173), "Gacaca proceedings are selective, partisan and discriminatory judicial processes."

Gacaca has also provided *material incentives* for the RPF's constituency, specifically Tutsi genocide survivors, shoring up the RPF's major base of support (Longman 2009). Genocide survivors receive special compensation for school fees, property, and other allotments through national genocide survivor funds such as FARG (Fonds National pour l"Assistance aux Rescapés du Génocide/National Fund for the Assistance of Survivors of Genocide). Gacaca included compensation and community service (T.I.G.) as potential punishment for accused perpetrators. While these dispensations can in no way compensate for their experiences during the genocide and those loved ones who were lost, a strong effort is made to assist survivors in their current living conditions. In addition, genocide survivors received the less tangible benefits of post-conflict justice through the gacaca courts; where survivors are provided with additional information about the violations they experienced. Genocide survivors were also given an opportunity to participate in the potentially cathartic experience of testifying against their aggressor(s).[21] These benefits were subsequently not given to those individuals who experienced other types of violence committed during the civil war or by the RPF.[22]

Finally, gacaca was an essential piece in constructing the pervasive and *legitimating narrative* regarding the RPF's role in governing post-genocide Rwanda. The political narrative in Rwanda elevates the genocide against the Tutsi as the penultimate violence that the country experienced. This period of conflict is called "the Genocide Against the Tutsi" by the Rwanda government to further highlight the targeting of the Tutsi ethnic group over Hutu political moderates who were killed at the same time.[23] The current government uses the violence from the Genocide to create what Reyntjens (2004) calls a "genocide credit" which serves to remind people of the horrible and disruptive violence that took place in 1994 and the "bad leadership" that brought the country to that place. Strategically, gacaca's focus on the genocide justifies a demand for strong RPF leadership in order to prevent a return to violence and disorder. The RPF was able to use this narrative to legitimate its own rule and consolidate political power both at home and internationally. As Reyntjens describes it:

> of course the genocide is a massive reality with a lasting impact, but it has also become a source of legitimacy astutely exploited to escape condemnation. [T]he 1994 genocide has become an ideological weapon allowing the RPF to acquire and maintain victim status and, as a perceived form of compensation, to enjoy complete immunity. (Reyntjens 2004, 199)

Gacaca's reach has marginalized dissent by creating a tightly constructed narrative about good and evil in Rwandan society. The public and widespread nature of gacaca allowed the Rwandan government to use the process to transmit this narrative throughout the country and to enforce the message through targeted punishments and mandatory weekly meetings strengthening RPF legitimacy through this normative policy.

Conclusions

New work in the field of transitional justice draws attention to the way in which rule of law processes, such as human rights trials and amnesties, are being used as "weapons of war" during and following armed conflicts (Lake 2017; Loyle and Binningsbø 2017; Loyle, Gates, and Binningsbø 2017; Simmons 2017). The gacaca courts in Rwanda are an important part of this story. While the legacy of gacaca has yet to be determined, there is evidence to suggest that the use of this process, in part, to consolidate the RPF party has contributed and will contribute to a politicization of the genocide and a weakening of rule of law in the country more broadly (e.g. Longman 2009; Loyle 2011; Thomson and Nagy 2011). In some ways, gacaca can be classified as a success. Prisons were emptied. Perpetrators living within the country (and some tried in abstentia) have been held to account. There is a prevalent message that crimes of genocide will not be tolerated and that the era of impunity in Rwanda has ended.

Yet, despite these achievements, Gacaca has been effective in furthering the government's aims of regime consolidation. Political opposition in Rwanda has been largely silenced and the continued focus on the message of preventing genocide and ethnic divisions have served to legitimate the oppressive tendencies of the government. As Uvin (1999) writes "The main strength of ... [the regime] lay not in its oppression, but in its capacity to legitimize itself." Gacaca was an essential component of that legitimization. Some suggest that a failure to provide justice to all Rwandans has entrenched rather than eradicated ethnic divisions within the country (Sebarenzi 2011). Furthermore, the search for the truth has been sacrificed to the government's goal of universal prosecution. Penal Reform International cites the lack of open discussion and debate during a number of the proceedings as reinforcing "the impression among some that the gathering of information was done 'under the influence' of the local authorities" (PRI Gacaca 8 Years).

The story of transitional justice in Rwanda is really a story about domestic politics played out in the guise of a peace-promoting, rule-of-law institution. With much international support and acquiescence, gacaca has been effective in addressing the post-conflict challenges of the Rwandan government despite claims of loftier aims, such as societal reconciliation. There are other cases where we see similar patterns. Subotić (2009) highlights the ability of the Bosnian and Serbian governments to fake compliance with the International Criminal Tribunal of the Former Yugoslavia in order to appease domestic constituents while still courting international favour from EU member states. The Liberian government eagerly adopted a truth commission following the civil war, but has failed to adopt many of the recommendations from the process due to domestic constrains. While not all transitional justice processes are merely a guise for domestic agendas, the potential for governments to strategically adopt these institutions should cause scholars and policy-makers to systematically reflect on the role of post-conflict justice and its potential for misuse. In particular, the flexible institutional construction and local control of transitional justice processes have led them to become useful institutions for the consolidation of authoritarian regimes.

Disclosure statement

No potential conflict of interest was reported by the author.

Notes

1. For a review of the legal and human rights critique against gacaca, see Clark (2009).
2. I focus my argument exclusively on the government use of transitional justice following armed conflict.
3. UNDP's "Governance for the Future" report highlighted Rwanda for its "innovative methods in search of justice" and argued that gacaca was a potential transitional justice model for other nations (UNDP 2006, 130).
4. While culpability has never been determined, evidence suggests that the plane was deliberately targeted by heavily armed individuals (or troops).
5. The total number of people killed and the ethnic composition of that number are highly debated (Straus 2004). Early estimates emerged from Human Rights Watch and African Rights of around 500,000 people killed; however, later it was admitted that this was a conservative number. At one point, IBUKA, the Rwandan survivor organization placed the number around 1.2 million. The quoted figure of 800,000 people represents a median consensus in the literature. Original sources believe this number to be made up almost entirely of Tutsi victims; however, recent work has suggested that a large part of this figure, over 50 per cent, could have been Hutu deaths (see Davenport and Stam 2009). Due to the nature of the data, this work is inconclusive.
6. Interview, Bernadette Kanzayire, November 8, 2013.
7. Final report from Urigwiro Reflection Meeting 1998.
8. See also: http://news.bbc.co.uk/2/hi/africa/4726969.stm. Accessed December 30, 2010.
9. For an overview of the international community's role in the construction of gacaca, see Oomen (2005).
10. http://www.inkiko-gacaca.gov.rw/En/Generaties.htm.
11. Author interview, Philbert Kagabo, November 8, 2013.
12. Author interview, Jean de Dieu Mucyo, November 8, 2013.
13. Author interview, Tito Rutaremara, November 7, 2013.
14. Author interview, Paul Rutayisiri, November 11, 2013.
15. Rwandan Organic Law 40/2000.
16. Author interview, Paul Rutayisiri, November 11, 2013.
17. Of note, this principle was later contradicted by gacaca's plea-bargaining scheme (Clark 2010).
18. While the Rwandan government tried a limited number of RPF soldiers accused of crimes during the civil war, the focus of their justice policy was on crimes of genocide.
19. Author interview, Abdul Karim Harelimana, November 9, 2013.
20. The 'double genocide' hypothesis emerged in recent literature on Rwanda, suggesting that there were two genocides, one committed by the Hutu against the Tutsi and another committed by Tutsi (specifically the advancing RPF) against the Hutu. For a detailed explanation, see Verwimp (2003).
21. The psychology and transitional justice literature actively debates the benefits of public testimony (Stover and Weinstein 2004).

22. This is not to say that all genocide survivors agree with RPF policies towards justice and reparations nor that all survivors feel that all their post-conflict needs are addressed by the government.
23. In 2009, there was a shift in the name of the conflict from "The 1994 Genocide" to the "Genocide Against the Tutsi". There is speculation that this change was made to exclude Hutu political moderates from the national narrative (Author's Interviews, 2009).

References

Adler, Reva, Cyanne E. Loyle, Judith Globerman, and E. Larson. 2008. "Transforming Men into Killers: Attitudes Leading to Hands-on Violence During the 1994 Rwandan Genocide." *Global Public Health: An International Journal for Research, Policy and Practice* 3: 291–307.

African Rights. 1995. *Rwanda: Death, Despair and Defiance*. London: African Rights.

Brass, P. R. 1997. *Theft of an Idol: Text and Context in the Representation of Collective Violence in India*. Princeton, NJ: Princeton Univ. Press.

Burnet, Jennie E. 2010. "Truth, Reconciliation, and Revenge in Rwanda's *Gacaca*." In *Transitional Justice: Global Mechanisms and Local Realities After Genocide and Mass Violence*, edited by Alexander Hinton, 95–118. New Brunswick, NJ: Rutgers University Press.

Chakravarty, Anuradha. 2006. "Gacaca Courts in Rwanda: Explaining Divisions Within the Human Rights Community." *Yale Journal of International Affairs* 1: 132–145.

Clark, Phil. 2007. "Hybridity, Holism and Traditional Justice: The Case of the Gacaca Courts in Post-Genocide Rwanda." *George Washington International Law Review* 39: 765–837.

Clark, Phil. 2009. "The Rules (and Politics) of Engagement: The Gacaca Courts and Post-Genocide Justice, Healing and Reconciliation in Rwanda." In *After Genocide: Transitional Justice, Post-Conflict Reconstruction and Reconciliation in Rwanda and Beyond*, edited by Phil Clark and Zachary D. Kaufman, 297–320. New York: Columbia University Press.

Clark, Phil. 2010. *The Gacaca Courts, Post-Genocide Justice and Reconciliation in Rwanda*. Cambridge, UK: Cambridge University Press.

Collier, Paul, V. L. Elliott, Håvard Hegre, Anke Hoeffler, Marta Reynal-Querol, and Nicholas Sambanis. 2003. Breaking the Conflict Trap: Civil War and Development Policy. Washington, DC: World Bank and Oxford University Press.

Corey, Allison, and Sandra Joireman. 2004. "Retributive Justice: the Gacaca Courts in Rwanda." *African Affairs* 103: 73–89.

Cronin-Furman, Kate. 2015. "Just Enough: The Politics of Accountability for Mass Atrocities." Diss., Columbia University.

Dallin, Alexander, and George Breslauer. 1970. *Political Terror in Communist Systems*. Stanford, CA: Stanford University Press.

Davenport, Christian, and Alan Stam. 2009. "Rwandan Political Violence in Space and Time." Working Paper and Dataset.

Des Forges, Alison, and Timothy Longman. 2004. "Legal Responses to Genocide in Rwanda." In *My Neighbor, My Enemy: Justice and Community in the Aftermath of Mass Atrocity*, edited by Eric Stover and Harvey M. Weinstein, 49–68. Cambridge: Cambridge University Press.

Entman, R. M. 2004. *Projections of Power: Framing News, Public Opinion, and US Foreign Policy*. Chicago, IL: University of Chicago Press.

Gahima, Gerald. 2007. "Alternatives to Prosecution: The Case of Rwanda." In *Atrocities and International Accountability: Beyond Transitional Justice*, edited by Edel Hughes, William Schabas, and Ramesh Thakur, 159–181. New York, NY: United Nations University Press.

Grodsky, Brian. 2010. *The Costs of Justice: How New Leaders Respond to Previous Rights Abuses*. Notre Dame, IN: University of Notre Dame Press.

Hayner, Priscilla B. 2011. *Unspeakable Truths: Facing the Challenge of Truth Commissions*. New York: Routledge.

Human Rights Watch. 1999. *Leave None to Tell the Story: Genocide in Rwanda*. New York: Human Rights Watch.

Human Rights Watch. 2011. *Justice Compromised: The Legacy of Rwanda's Community-Based Gacaca Courts*. New York: Human Rights Watch.

Ingelaere, Bert. 2009. "'Does the Truth Pass Across the Fire Without Burning?' Locating the Short Circuit in Rwanda's Gacaca Courts." *The Journal of Modern African Studies* 47 (4): 507–528.

Kalyvas, Stathis N. 2003. "The Ontology of 'Political Violence': Action and Identity in Civil Wars." *Perspective on Politics* 1 (3): 475–494.

Kanyesigye, Frank. 2011. "Only 97 Cases Pending in Gacaca." *The New Times*, June 10, 1.

Karbo, Tony, and Martha Mutisi. 2008. "Psychological Aspects of Post-Conflict Reconstruction: Transforming Mindsets, The Case of Gacaca in Rwanda." Paper prepared for the Ad Hoc Expert Group Meeting on Lessons Learned in Post-Conflict State Capacity: Reconstructing Governance and Public Administration Capacities in Post-Conflict Societies, Accra, Ghana, October 2–4.

Karekezi, Urusaro Alice, Alphonse Nshimiyimana, and Beth Mutamba. 2004. "Localizing Justice: Gacaca Courts in Post-Genocide Rwanda." In *My Neighbor, My Enemy: Justice and Community in the Aftermath of Mass Atrocity*, edited by Eric Stover and Harvey M. Weinstein, 69–84. Cambridge: Cambridge University Press.

Kirkby, Coel. 2006. "Rwanda's Gacaca Courts: A Preliminary Critique." *Journal of African Law* 50: 94–117.

Kuperman, Alan J. 2004. "Provoking Genocide: a Revised History of the Rwandan Patriotic Front." *Journal of Genocide Research* 6 (1): 61–84.

Lake, Milli. 2017. "Building the Rule of War: Postconflict Institutions and the Micro-Dynamics of Conflict in Eastern DR Congo." *International Organization* 71 (2): 281–315.

Longman, Timothy. 2009. "An Assessment of Rwanda's Gacaca Courts." *Peace Review* 21 (3): 304–312.

Longman, Timothy, and Théonèste Rutagengwa. 2004. "Memory, Identity, and Community in Rwanda." In *My Neighbor, My Enemy: Justice and Community in the Aftermath of Mass Atrocity*, edited by Eric Stover and Harvey M. Weinstein, 162–182. Cambridge: Cambridge University Press.

Loyle, Cyanne E. 2011. "Regimes of Truth: The Microfoundations of Post-Conflict Justice." Ph.D. diss., University of Maryland.

Loyle, Cyanne E., and Helga Malmin Binningsbø. Forthcoming. "Justice During Armed Conflict: A New Dataset on Government and Rebel Strategies." *Journal of Conflict Resolution*.

Loyle, Cyanne E., and Christian Davenport. 2016. "Transitional InJustice: Subverting Justice in Transition and Post-Conflict Societies." *Journal of Human Rights* 15 (1): 126–149.

Loyle, Cyanne E., Scott Gates, and Helga Malmin Binningsbø. 2017. "Amnesty as a Weapon of War: Government Strength and Justice Processes During Conflict." Presented at the International Studies Association Annual Conference, February 23.

Meierhenrich, Jens. 2005. "The Invention of *Gacaca*: A Logic of Institutional Choice." Working Paper. http://fsi.stanford.edu/sites/default/files/evnts/media// Meierhenrich%2C_The_Invention_of_Gacaca.pdf.

Moe, Terry. 2005. "Power and Political Institutions." *Perspectives on Politics* 3 (2): 215–233.

Morrill, Constance F. 2004. "Reconciliation and the Gacaca: The Perceptions and Peace-Building Potential of Rwandan Youth Detainees." *Online Journal of Peace and Conflict Resolution* 6 (1): 1–66.

Nalepa, Monika. 2010. *Skeletons in the Closet: Transitional Justice in Post-Communist Europe*. New York, NY: Cambridge University Press.

Oomen, Barbara. 2005. "Donor-Driven Justice and Its Discontents: The Case of Rwanda." *Development and Change* 36: 887–910.

Paris, Roland. 2004. *At War's End: Building Peace After Civil Conflict*. Cambridge, UK: Cambridge University Press.

Peskin, Victor. 2005. "Beyond Victor's Justice? The Challenge of Prosecuting the Winners at the International Criminal Tribunals for the Former Yugoslavia and Rwanda." *Journal of Human Rights* 4 (2): 213–231.

Prunier, Gérard. 1997. *The Rwanda Crisis: History of a Genocide*. New York: Columbia University Press.

Reyntjens, Filip. 2004. "Rwanda, Ten Years On: From Genocide to Dictatorship." *African Affairs* 103 (411): 177–210.

Schabas, W. A. 2005. "Genocide Trials and Gacaca Courts." *Journal of International Criminal Justice* 3: 879–895.

Schabas, William A. 2009. "Post-Genocide Justice in Rwanda." In *After Genocide: Transitional Justice, Post-Conflict Reconstruction and Reconciliation in Rwanda and Beyond*, edited by Phil Clark and Zachary D. Kaufman, 207–228. New York: Columbia University Press.

Sebarenzi, Joseph. 2011. "Justice and Human Rights for All Rwandans." In *Remaking Rwanda: State Building and Human Rights After Mass Violence*, edited by Scott Straus and Lars Waldorf, 343–353. Madison, WI: University of Wisconsin Press.

Sikkink, Kathryn. 2011. *The Justice Cascade: How Human Rights Prosecutions Are Changing World Politics*. New York: W. W. Norton.

Simmons, Alan. 2017. "Domestic Attitudes Towards International Jurisdiction over Human Rights Violations." *Human Rights Review*. doi:10.1007/s12142-017-0459-1.

Smith, Charles Anthony. 2012. *The Rise and Fall of War Crimes Trials: From Charles I to Bush II*. New York, NY: Cambridge University Press.

Stan, Lavinia, and Nadya Nedelsky, eds. 2015. *Post-Communist Transitional Justice: Lessons from Twenty-Five Years of Experience*. New York, NY: Cambridge University Press.

Stover, Eric, and Harvey M. Weinstein, eds. 2004. *My Neighbor, My Enemy: Justice and Community in the Aftermath of Mass Atrocity*. Cambridge: Cambridge University Press.

Straus, Scott. 2004. "How Many Perpetrators Were There in the Rwandan Genocide? An Estimate." *Journal of Genocide Research* 6: 85–98.

Straus, Scott. 2006. *The Order of Genocide: Race, Power, and War in Rwanda*. Ithaca, NY: Cornell University Press.

Subotić, Jelena. 2009. *Hijacking Justice: Dealing with the Past in the Balkans*. Ithaca, NY: Cornell University Press.

Subotić, Jelena. 2012. "The Transformation of International Transitional Justice Advocacy." *International Journal of Transitional Justice* 6 (1): 106–125.

Taylor, L. K., and A. Dukalskis. 2012. "Old Truths and New Politics: Does Truth Commission 'Publicness' Impact Democratization?" *Journal of Peace Research* 49 (5): 671–684.

Thomson, Susan, and R. Nagy. 2011. "Law, Power and Justice: What Legalism Fails to Address in the Functioning of Rwanda's Gacaca Courts." *International Journal of Transitional Justice* 5: 11–30.

UNDP (United Nations Development Programme). 2006. *Governance for the Future: Democracy and Development in the Least Developed Countries*. New York, NY: United Nations.

United Nations. 1994. *Statute of the International Criminal Tribunal for the Prosecution of Persons Responsible for Genocide and Other Serious Violations of International Humanitarian Law Committed in the Territory of Rwanda and Rwandan Citizens Responsible for Genocide and Other Such Violations Committed in the Territory of Neighbouring States, between 1 January 1994 and 31 December 1994*. New York, NY: United Nations.

USIP (United States Institute of Peace). 1995. "Rwanda: Accountability for War Crimes and Genocide." Special Report No. 13.

Uvin, Peter. 1999. "Ethnicity and Power in Burundi and Rwanda: Different Paths to Mass Violence." *Comparative Politics* 31: 253–271.

Verwimp, Philip. 2003. "Testing the Double-Genocide Thesis for Central and Southern Rwanda." *Journal of Conflict Resolution* 47: 423–442.

Norm contestation and reconciliation: evidence from a regional transitional justice process in the Balkans

Denisa Kostovicova and Aude Bicquelet

ABSTRACT

We have limited understanding of how ethnic groups can achieve an agreement on tackling the legacy of war crimes, because transitional justice scholars have been focused primarily on challenges to post-conflict reconciliation. Addressing this gap, we investigate whether contestation over the norm of transitional justice prevents inter-ethnic reconciliation, operationalized by us as reconciliatory discourse. Empirical evidence is drawn from the study of debates conducted by a transnational advocacy network (RECOM), which proposes a regional fact-finding commission in the Balkans. Applying text analysis to identify key themes in these debates, we find reconciliatory discourse in those debates where there is norm contestation. Also, the spatial scale of a transitional justice process matters. We identify different patterns of discourse at different levels of debates. Debates containing norm contestation are associated with ethnically centred arguments at the national level, but with sustained scrutiny of proposed solutions at the regional level despite ethnic divisions.

Introduction

Transitional justice is the study and practice of how states and societies engage with past wrongs (Teitel 2000). Post-conflict justice practices are deemed to be crucial for promoting discussion about the violent past and for providing a pathway to reconciliation (Cohen 2001, 96). While transitional justice has become an accepted norm of international peace-making (Sharp 2013, 152), its implementation in post-conflict contexts has turned out to be a deeply contested process. Sites and sources of contestation are many. In post-conflict contexts, transitional justice as a global norm is at times resisted due to a perceived tension with local norms (Sokolić 2016). The

Supplemental data for this article can be accessed at https://doi.org/10.1080/01419870.2018.1380211

norm of transitional justice is also contested between ethnic groups (Kostić 2008), as well as within ethnic groups (Gordy 2013).

Contestation of the norm of transitional justice is invariably equated with elusive reconciliation. This article queries the relationship between norm contestation, understood as "a mode of critique through critical engagement in a discourse about [the norms]" (Wiener 2017, 109), and reconciliation. It asks: does norm contestation necessarily prevent reconciliation? We explore how ethnic groups achieve an agreement on addressing the war crimes legacy despite deep divisions. In doing so, we further our understanding of the dynamics of inter-ethnic reconciliation in the aftermath of mass atrocity. This article complements the dominant agenda in transitional justice research that focuses on negative, unintended effects of transitional justice norms that stymie its emancipatory goals (Subotić 2009). We argue that the field also needs to investigate whether a divisive impact of contestation of transitional justice can be overcome, and how.

Reconciliation is broadly understood as societal transformation in the aftermath of conflict (Chapman 2009), yet there remains a lack of scholarly consensus on the concept's precise meaning, on the different levels of reconciliation, or how to achieve it (Pankhurst 1999). As Kriesberg (2001, 60) notes, "[r]econciliation is never total, never including all members of antagonistic parties, not including every dimension of reconciliation completely, nor being fully reciprocal between parties". While recognizing the ambiguity of the concept in theory and practice, we approach reconciliation as a discursive process, rather than an outcome. More precisely, we define reconciliation as a steady process of overcoming "obstacles presented by – among other things – culture, race, religion and politics" through communication (Komesaroff 2008, 5). Cohen (2001, 238) specifies that "[w]hen rhetoric of reconciliation is genuine, it looks for tolerance, forgiveness, social reconstruction and solution of social conflicts in ways other than punishment". Although reconciliation may not ever be total, it still represents "a radical way of confronting the past" (Cohen 2001, 239). In this article, we investigate whether contestation of the norm of transitional justice is at odds with reconciliation understood as reconciliatory discourse.

We explore the effects of norm contestation by examining the process of norm adoption in transnational activist networks (TANs). Empirical evidence is drawn from a regional civil society network in the Balkans, known by its acronym RECOM, which advocates the establishment of a regional fact-finding commission. Norm adoption is an understudied aspect of network activity (Carpenter 2011), in contrast to later stages in a norm "life cycle" (Finnemore and Sikkink 1998), such as diffusion of norms (Carpenter 2007, 101). We are guided by the "local turn" in the scholarship on transitional justice, to which we also contribute. Like the theories of critical peace-building, this scholarship brings into focus the local agency (Baker and Obradovic-

Wochnik 2016, 288–289). We investigate the local dimension of norm contestation and justice-seeking by going beyond the currently prevalent approaches, which evaluate the "local" almost exclusively in the context of the "justice cascade" (Sikkink 2011), framed by the diffusion of norms from the global to the local level. In contrast, we study how a range of disparate local actors, with different identities, interests and values, contest various aspects of the norm of transitional justice, during its operationalization into an elaborate policy proposal.

The paper proceeds as follows. A theoretical approach focusing on norm adoption is outlined, proposing a study of contestation of aspects of norms, rather than of norms themselves, within a transnational advocacy network. The case study of the RECOM network is then introduced. It is followed by sections that detail the data and method, and present our findings. The conclusion reflects on the broader theoretical implications of this work, which finds that norm contestation does not necessarily prevent reconciliatory discourse.

Norm adoption and contestation in transnational advocacy networks

Transitional justice is a contested subject and area of practice involving a multitude of post-conflict actors. These actors may have conflicting positions about the violent past and face political constraints (Zalaquett 1991–1992; Orentlicher 2007), which shape their views on transitional justice, and may include their opposition to it. When addressing the issue of norm contestation, transitional justice scholars have queried: whose norm is it? And, how well does it represent various stakeholders' interests or resonate with their values? Yet, they have stopped short of unpacking the norm itself. We address this gap in the scholarship by introducing a sociological definition of norms into theorizing of TANs. Approaching a TAN as a space of contestation, we foreground contestation about aspects of the norm of transitional justice. TANs are also sites of discursive interaction (cf. Watts 2004, 254). Thematic patterns of these interactions provide a novel perspective on the effects of norm contestation.

Networks, including the TANs, are voluntary arrangements. Membership in a network is not binding, and members enjoy the option to exit. Neither members nor their commitments can be "locked in". This means that networks need to produce benefits for their members, which ensure their continued existence (Sikkink 2009, 230). In line with this conceptualization, we investigate the construction of norm consensus about transitional justice around which network members coalesce. While networks constrain actors, they are also simultaneously constituted by "subjective meaning and motivation, including the *normative commitment* of their actors" (Emirbayer and Goodwin 1994, 1413). Norm consensus reinforces a stake in the existence of the network form. It also reinforces the message that a network sends out to its targets, such as states or international organizations (van Raaij 2006, 267).

Furthermore, emphasis in the network theory scholarship has generally been on reciprocity and trust in a network form, as opposed to other organizational forms premised on a more adversarial posture (Podolny and Page 1998, 61). TANs are "a space for the negotiation of meanings", while the political learning within the network also involves "normative shifts in understanding of shared identities and responsibilities" (Keck and Sikkink 1998, 215–216). Learning and subsequent adjustments within a network are outward-oriented (Bob 2007), because the goal is to enhance the efficiency of the network in order to bring about normative change in its targets. However, the possibility that a norm, its meaning and prescription *within* the network may be contested, or even manipulated, has been all but dismissed until recently.

O'Toole and Meier (2006, 271) have criticized the prevalent understanding of networks as neutral producers of collective goods, which derives from "an implicitly benign perspective regarding the importance and necessity of using multiple interdependent social actors, often multiple organizational actors, to achieve collective purposes". Their argument resonates with the political approach to TANs, which is premised on recognition of differential interests and capabilities of network nodes (Kahler 2009, 11–16; cf. Lake and Wong 2009, 130), while powerful network members get to determine the adoption of specific norms. The political approach conceives of the process of norm adoption as contentious: a norm is either adopted in a given form, or it is not. It thus stops short of allowing for the possibility of contestation of aspects of the norm. The definition of norms in sociological studies enables analysis of the contestation over the aspects of a norm *rather* than the norm itself.

The understanding of norms in the international relations literature, preoccupied with TANs, are informed by a diffusionist perspective that stresses their prescriptive, rule-like character, which is consistent with a theoretical preoccupation with explaining norm-induced change. Finnemore and Sikkink (1998, 891–892) argue that appropriateness of a given behaviour is established in reference to the judgements of a community or a society, i.e. a shared assessment. Sociologists studying norms have queried their shared quality, which is "an essential ingredient of a norm", and shifted attention to variance centred on aspects of a given norm, for example, intensity or strength in individuals' attachment to the norm (Jasso and Opp 1997, 948). Normative disagreements appear to be more frequently centred around degrees of adherence to an agreed-upon normative system, as opposed to the outright rejection of the norm (Rossi and Berk 1985, 343). Consequently, it is not necessarily contestation between different norms, but contestation among different aspects or segments (Wiener 2014, 19–20) of a norm, that can provide analytical traction. This is particularly relevant for the RECOM process in the Balkans, where participants agreed on the norm of transitional justice through establishment of facts of war crimes. But, they, simultaneously, disagreed about specific aspects and applications of that norm, that Deitelhoff and Zimmermann (2013, 5) call "applicatory contestation". It is reflected in the debates about the articles of the draft Statute of the proposed regional fact-finding commission, which we study.

Norm adoption, as Carpenter (2007, 115) puts it, is premised on "the possibility of contestation". As we demonstrate above, contestation may also concern aspects of a norm, rather than a norm itself. Contestation creates a challenge for the researcher: "understanding how multiple insider sympathists negotiate disagreements about framing new ideas will require methodologies that can trace and capture this process" (Carpenter 2007, 115). In addition, norms prompt justification for action and leave an extensive trail of communication among actors that we can study (Finnemore and Sikkink 1998, 892). In this article, we apply a bespoke text analysis technique to investigate one such trail contained in the transcripts of the RECOM's consultations.

The RECOM network in the Balkans: the background

The Coalition for RECOM, which is the abbreviation for the Regional Commission for Establishing the Facts about War Crimes and other Serious Human Rights Violations in former Yugoslavia from 1 January 1991 to 31 December 2001, is "a network of non-governmental organizations, associations, and individuals who support and affirm the Initiative for RECOM" (Jakovčić 2009). The RECOM initiative is a type of a transnational advocacy network, which is defined by "the centrality of principled ideas or values" (Keck and Sikkink 1998, 1). This locally driven civil society network advocates the establishment of a regional fact-finding commission. It emerged as a response to the complex legacy of conflict in the successor states of the former Yugoslavia, and to the limits of the international criminal justice strategy focused on the perpetrator and punishment (Nettelfield 2012). In contrast to the International Criminal Tribunal for former Yugoslavia at The Hague, the RECOM is concerned with victims and seeks to acknowledge their suffering as a means for promoting reconciliation (*Istorijat inicijative o osnivanju REKOM-a* 2009).

Three non-governmental organizations (NGOs): Documenta from Croatia, the Research and Documentation Centre from Bosnia and Herzegovina, and the Centre for the Humanitarian Law from Serbia, launched a debate on how best to address the legacy of mass atrocity in May 2006. It resulted in the establishment of the Coalition for RECOM in October 2008, marking the beginning of a regional transitional justice process in the Balkans (Kandić

2007). The coalition membership includes nearly 2,000 NGOs, victims, veterans, lawyers, artists, journalists, academics and youth – from all ethnic groups in the former Yugoslavia. The leading NGOs envisaged the consultations as a public platform for debating transitional justice. The network reached out more broadly to local communities and involved some 6,000 people in a consultative process. The consultations about a regional approach to transitional justice were held at the regional, national and local levels, with sessions lasting from half a day to two days. The network also consulted on the commission's Statute, which was adopted in 2011, and encompassed all aspects of the commission's work: the aims of the commission, the country location of its seat, the make-up of the commission, its relationship with criminal justice, etc. Support from the Balkan states for a regional transitional justice instrument has not been forthcoming. Nevertheless, the RECOM process provides valuable insight into how a norm of post-conflict justice is contested inside a TAN, and to what effect.

This unique transnational advocacy network has been studied through the lens of norm diffusion, qualifying the RECOM's approach to justice-seeking as an imposed agenda (Rowen 2012, 699) and dismissing its advocacy as alienating discourse (Obradovic-Wochnik 2013). A power politics approach attributed norm adoption to the assertion of power by the RECOM's leading NGOs (Rowen 2012, 705–708). Exploring the substance of debates, scholars drew attention to divisive inter-ethnic and intra-ethnic positions in this multi-ethnic network (Irvine and McMahon 2013; Kostovicova 2010), the rejection of concepts, such as truth and reconciliation (Touquet and Vermeersch 2016, 65–68), and the discussions over definitions, such as that of a victim (Kurze and Vukusic 2013). Lastly, scholars revealed domestic opposition to inter-ethnic cross-border collaboration in justice-seeking (Kostovicova 2013; Di Lellio and McCurn 2013).

The empirical evidence and analytic traction produced by this scholarship are limited by the methods of qualitative inquiry applied in the study of the RECOM process. Scholars have scrutinized at best a handful of transcripts of consultations, or only just one. They have provided some insight into normative disagreements, but have been unable to reveal comprehensively patterns either of discourse or contention throughout this multi-year, multi-ethnic process. Similarly, mechanisms or conditions explaining the findings have remained outside the purview of these studies (for example, all studies are conducted at the national level, overlooking the regional dimension of the RECOM's available data). Furthermore, these studies have conflated RECOM's Statute and non-Statute consultations (Rowen 2012). Their distinction is essential because it embodies different types of contention. Our consideration of relevant variables and application of a quantitative text analysis method allows us to overcome these conceptual and methodological limitations.

Data and method

We analyse the transcripts of twenty-one consultation sessions held by the RECOM initiative. The RECOM's data base, which is publicly available on the RECOM's website, includes transcripts of 134 consultations and 10 regional and international fora about transitional justice.[1] We are interested in the stage of the consultative process that included consultations on the draft Statute of the regional commission as well as general consultations about a regional approach to transitional justice from 29 May 2010 to 23 January 2011. The transcripts were selected by a purposive sampling strategy (Oliver 2006, 245), capturing variation in relation to country locations of consultations, the types of participants (victims, general civil society or professionals), and the level of consultations (local, national or regional). RECOM's transcripts are available in Serbian, Bosnian, Croatian, Montenegrin, Slovenian, Macedonian and Albanian languages,[2] and were prepared for computer-assisted text analysis by translating the entire corpus into a single variant of the Serbian language.[3] The textual data amounts to 488,737 words, and consists of 2 corpora: a contentious corpus (14 consultations about the draft Statute, whose articles were contested) and a non-contentious corpus (7 general consultations).[4] These corpora contain 2,893 speeches by moderators and discussants. Each speech was tagged with variables indicating characteristics of speakers and consultations.[5] The total of 868 speakers (100 moderators and 768 discussants) took part in the analysed consultations.[6] The high number of discussants, who brought their diverse viewpoints into the norm adoption process, reflects the broad nature of the RECOM's consultations.

We build on the analytical traction gained by applying quantitative text analysis to study transitional justice and the RECOM data (Kostovicova 2017). Here, we apply a computer-assisted method, implemented with the Alceste software,[7] drawing on its applications by other scholars, and their analyses of political speeches (Schonhardt-Bailey 2005; Schonhardt-Bailey 2013), parliamentary debates (Schonhardt-Bailey 2008; Bicquelet, Weale, and Bara 2012; Weale, Bicquelet, and Bara 2012) and opinion polls (Brugidou 2003). The Alceste method is suited for identifying themes in political debates and their association with specific variables of interest for the analysis (Weale, Bicquelet, and Bara 2012, 647; Schonhardt-Bailey 2008). In this study variables of interest are the level at which the consultations were held: regional, national and local; and the type of speaker: moderator or discussant.

The Alceste software is designed to quantify the text in order to extract its most significant structures (Brugidou 2003), by relying upon co-occurrence analysis, which is the statistical analysis of frequent word pairs in a text corpus.[8] It conducts a particular reading of the text that does not take into account the meaning of words (Vallès 2014, 128). In its initial phase, the software breaks down the corpus into Context Units (*CUs*) of two different kinds: Initial Context Units (ICUs) and Elemental Context Units (ECUs). ICUs are sampling units corresponding to the divisions of the text specified by the user, to which one or several variables can be assigned. In the analysis below, each speech by a discussant or a moderator constitutes an ICU. The corpus is then fragmented into ECUs, which are "gauged sentences that the program automatically constructs based on word length and punctuation in the text" (Schonhardt-Bailey 2005, 705). ECUs are classified according to the distribution of their vocabulary, producing a number of classes of words that should be representative of the main themes of the analysed text.

Identifying which class a sentence from a RECOM consultation will fall into is a statistical function entirely dependent upon the structural properties of that corpus. Most important among these properties is the frequency of association or co-occurrence of used key terms, in this case, by participants in consultations. Consequently, *post hoc* qualitative interpretation by an analyst is required to give overall meaning to the classes (Bara, Weale, and Bicquelet 2007). This is done by examining the key terms and sentences within each class (Vallès 2014, 128). In sum, this method

> [...] guards against researchers and coders infusing their own biases into the coding. Second, it can provide an impression of a voluminous data corpus within a very short space of time. Third, and following on from that, the issue of reliability which arises with human coding is no longer relevant. (Schonhardt-Bailey 2005, 703)

Next, we present and analyse the results of the application of the Alceste method to the RECOM's textual data.

Results and analysis

We seek to find out whether contestation, stemming from diversity of perspectives among participants about different aspects of the regional commission, prevents reconciliation, understood as reconciliatory discourse. These perspectives are underpinned by ethnicity but also intersect with participants' identities as victims, human rights activists, lawyers, journalists, teachers, etc. We compare two corpora. One is the corpus that contains non-contentious consultations. These debates aimed to solicit participants' views and opinions on the regional commission. In our study, their transcripts make up the corpus without norm contestation. By contrast, the other corpus contains contentious consultations. They are characterized by intense contestation over different articles of the regional commission's Statute. Therefore, their transcripts comprise the corpus with norm contestation, and, more precisely, the contestation over different aspects of the norm of transitional justice. We present the findings first by comparing the themes in the non-contentious and contentious consultations, and then explore these findings by focusing on the level of debates. We draw on different tools provided by the Alceste analysis, of which "two are particularly useful – characteristic words and characteristic ECUs" (Schonhardt-Bailey 2008, 395). Tables 1 and 2 below summarize, respectively: the classes and their size, measured by the percentage of all ECUs classified within each class (Schonhardt-Bailey 2008, 395); their labels with a short descriptive summary, which is based on the interpretative analysis of the most representative ECUs (Schonhardt-Bailey 2008, 396); the most characteristic meaningful words and their Phi coefficients,[9] which indicate the theme or frame of argument that unifies a class (Schonhardt-Bailey 2008, 385), and the variables, including the strength of association with a given class or theme. The analysis below illustrates a class with representative ECUs selected from the first ten Phi values for each class with the most meaningful words in bold.[10]

Thematic analysis: comparing non-contentious and contentious consultations

Non-contentious consultations

There are four classes in non-contentious consultations that are presented below (see Table 1).

Class 1 is an *explanatory* class. It explains why a regional commission should be established, the origins of the idea of the regional commission since 2008, and the commission's aims as well as the working methods of the commission. This class, which is associated with the role of moderators, also outlines the commission's contribution to the goals of transitional justice, along with its intended effect on institutional reform and recognition of victims, as in:

> also, the fourth **goal** of the **commission** is to **contribute** so that the **political** elites and **societies** in signatory **states**, those who endorse the **establishment** of the RECOM, should accept the **facts** about the **war crimes** and other **grave violations** of **human rights**

Class 2 is a *procedural* class, weakly associated with moderators, that offers insight into the running of the consultations. From this class we learn about the spirit of the debate. The stress is on openness of the debate, solicitation of a variety of different views and welcoming of all critical comments and suggestions, as in:

> you will absolutely **get** the **floor**, but since there are many who would like to speak, i will not be able to give the **floor** to everyone, and **please** if you can stick to two, three minutes, be as concise and with as many concrete suggestions

Class 3 is a *reflective* class. Participants reflect on the challenges and hopes for the regional commission. This class is associated with discussants and is particularly focused on the engagement with broader society and political elites in pursuit of

Table 1. Non-contentious corpus: classes, keywords and key variables.

Classes and their distribution (%)	Class name and description	Keywords and φ	Key variables and φ
Class 1 43%	*Explanatory* (justification of the regional commission and its aims)	rights (0, 23) commission (0, 21) victims (0, 21) human (0, 21) facts (0, 17) former (0, 16) crimes (0, 15) societies (0, 14) yugoslavia (0, 14) conflicts (0, 14) regional (0, 13) war (0, 13)	moderator (0, 21) national level (0, 06) local level (0, 04)
Class 2 20%	*Procedural* (protocol and formalities of running a consultative session)	thank (0, 22) please (0, 17) monte (0, 16) negro (0, 16) questions (0, 15) hope (0, 14) president (0, 14) draft (0, 13) greet (0, 13) municipalities (0, 13) colleagues (0, 12)	moderator (0, 08) local (0, 05)
Class 3 26%	*Reflective* (consideration of challenges and expectations from the regional commission)	issue (0, 17) people (0, 15) think (0, 15) want (0, 11) good (0, 10) see (0, 10) campaign (0, 09) aware (0, 09) works (0, 08) signatures (0, 08)	discussant (0, 13) national level (0, 05)
Class 4 11%	*Interpretative* (ways of understanding conflict and obstacles to post-conflict justice)	serbs (0, 19) roma (0, 16) never (0, 16) committed (0, 15) done (0, 14) live (0, 13) minorities (0, 13) croats (0, 13) slovenia (0, 13) bosnia (0, 13) nationality (0, 13) culpable (0, 13)	discussant (0,26) regional level (0,18)

justice. Such preoccupation reflects participants' awareness of a need to ensure the legitimacy of their initiative by winning popular support, as in:

> my starting position is that this commission should not be influenced **politically**. i share that fear too. that would not be good, the commission will not **succeed** in that **case**, do you understand

Class 4 is an *interpretative* class. This class, associated with discussants, sheds light on the role of an ethnic dimension in a transitional justice process. Prominent in this class is the use by the participants of the concept of ethnicity to interpret what happened during the conflict, and as an obstacle to post-conflict justice, as in:

> Example 1: that's what he[11] **said**, too, that the situation that is not ripe for reconciliation in the **context** of the investigation of war crimes. many say, as do **serb** representatives in the **croatian** parliament, many immediately ask questions, who **started**, why did they **start** it, and how? which is why the other **speaker** responded that we should avoid politics

> Example 2: that is discrimination in the constitution of the **republic** of **serbia**, but also of **croatia**, **bosnia**, **national minorities** are only mentioned. **definitely**, a distinction should be made between **national minorities** and the indigenous **national minorities**

Contentious consultations

Unlike the non-contentious consultations, the contentious consultations have an *argumentative* and *reconciliatory* class, while sharing an *explanatory*, *interpretative* and *procedural* class with the non-contentious consultations (see Table 2).

Class 1 in this corpus is *explanatory*, focusing on the prospective regional commission's tasks, and is associated with moderators. Because it is about the Statute and its specific provisions, the debate is more detailed. As in the non-contentious consultations, participants are focused on the commission's broader contribution to transitional justice, but also strive to debate merits of different versions of the draft articles of the Statute, as in:

> under **point** (a) is to **collect** data on **gross violations** of **human rights** and **war crimes**, provide their **detailed account** and present patterns of **violations** and their **consequences**. that means that the **fundamental task** of the **commission** is to **collect** data on the cases of **violations** of **human rights**, that is **war crimes**

Class 2 is an *argumentative* class that is unique to the contentious consultations. It is more specific than the *explanatory* class in this corpus. It provides insight into how participants scrutinize specific propositions in the draft Statute, how they challenge and query them, and how they demand improvements. It demonstrates participants' sustained and serious engagement with minute details of the proposed Statute, and, by extension, their commitment to the transitional justice process and to finding appropriate solutions, as in:

> Example 1: but the reliability of that statement will have to be verified. therefore i do not support repression when it comes to taking **statements**. the **principle** of **voluntarism** is the principle that should prevail. exceptionally, and in an

Table 2. Contentious corpus: classes, keywords and key variables.

Classes and their distribution (%)	Class name and description	Keywords and φ	Key variables and φ
Class 1 10%	*Explanatory* (justification of proposed articles of the regional commission's draft Statute)	human (0, 65) rights (0, 56) violations (0, 45) war (0, 43) crimes (0, 42) grave (0, 39) armed (0, 37) losses (0, 26) civilians (0, 25)	moderator (0, 10)
Class 2 32%	*Argumentative* (critical scrutiny of proposed articles of the regional commission's draft Statute)	court (0, 20) proceedings (0, 17) commission (0, 16) witnesses (0, 16) punishment (0, 14) statements (0, 14) criminal (0, 14) person (0, 13) act (0, 13) doubt (0, 13)	regional level (0, 28)
Class 3 22%	*Procedural* (protocol and formalities of running a consultative session)	statute (0, 20) draft (0, 20) thank (0, 20) working (0, 17) group (0, 16) consultations (0, 12) suggestions (0, 11) discussion (0, 10) hear (0, 10) comments (0, 10)	moderator (0, 14) national level (0, 07)
Class 4 20%	*Interpretative* (ways of understanding conflict and obstacles to post-conflict justice)	years (0, 24) croatia (0, 18) war (0, 18) bosnia (0, 17) kosovo (0, 17) croatia (0, 15) herzegovina (0, 15) slovenia (0, 12) serb (0, 12) people (0, 12) republic (0, 10)	national level (0, 19) discussant (0, 18)
Class 5 16%	*Reconciliatory* (emphasis on confronting the violent past for the sake of victims, peace and justice)	past (0, 19) society (0, 16) process (0, 14) people (0, 13) future (0, 13) youth (0, 12) responsibility (0, 12) stories (0, 12) journalists (0, 12) initiative (0, 12) victims (0, 12)	national level (0, 04)

> agreement with **signatory states** that could mediate obtaining the **statements** from persons of interest, who do not respond to the summons from the **RECOM** to **give** a **statement**

> Example 2: **point** 2 of **article** 46 envisages that three cumulative and not alternative conditions must be fulfilled for the **commission** to publish a **person's** name in the final **report**. the third conditions is that this person must be given an **opportunity** to respond to the findings within a reasonable **period**

Class 3 is a *procedural class* that reveals how the consultations are unfolding in terms of procedure, such as soliciting comments and suggestions from the participants. Like this class in the non-contentious corpus, it is associated with moderators. However, unlike it, this class in the contentious corpus is much more focused on the actual production of the Statute document, as in:

> this is not the **document** that is being created by a fictitious **working group** of experts, without **considering** the voice of the citizens, on the contrary, you are shaping this **document** and therefore please feel very motivated to join in the **discussion** and tell us what you think would be useful **suggestions**, and ask **questions** about the sections that you do not think are clear

Class 4 in the contentious consultations is an *interpretative* class. In this class, as in the corresponding one in the non-contentious corpus, an ethnic dimension comes to the fore and is associated with the discussants. Ethnicity proves to be central for explaining and understanding how and why the conflict broke out. However, ethnicity is also understood as an obstacle to efforts to come to terms with the past, as in:

> Example 1: i **know** that representatives of the **serbian government**, at every summit where they participate, they get up and leave when the **name** of **kosovo** is mentioned. as long as **kosovo** is mentioned i have an impression that they will be leaving, and this project will come to nothing

> Example 2: i will now speak about my childhood and schooling that were not easy at all and i remember those brutal demonstrations. our schooling was interrupted, that is the **reason** why i want the year 1980 to be included because the ethnically-motivated conflict began then, when the demand for the **republic** of **kosovo** was made

Class 5 is a *reconciliatory* class and is unique to the contentious corpus. It is explicit about a need for post-conflict justice through a regional justice-seeking process. This class demonstrates that injustice is understood primarily as a lack of recognition of the victims both by their own communities and by the opposing side. In this class, therefore, the emphasis is on a need to confront the violent past in the name of the victims, regardless of their ethnicity, as well as on a need to achieve truth and understanding in order to overcome the legacy of the violent past, as in:

> Example 1: to narrow down the **space** for manipulation and create the foundation so that our **societies** in the **region** can achieve mutual understanding of what **took place** in the **past**. RECOM should offer an example and together with its relations with the public contribute to a new model for public debates on these topics.

> Example 2: as a **result** of that i must admit it is wonderful to **hear** that we have **support** even from religious **communities**, which is very **difficult** to get, **support** from **individuals** and **associations**, and it seems to me that the **coalition** for RECOM is **really** enjoying ever **greater** trust despite all challenges along the way.

> Example 3: many former inmates, **victims** of sexual violence, those suffering from the post-traumatic stress syndrome, civilian and military victims of war have been trying for fifteen years to have their status as **victims** resolved at an **official** level. what really hurts the **victims** is the fact that everyone has knowledge about what **happened**, but what the **victims** need is the acknowledgment of their **suffering** and pain, as well as **official** satisfaction.

> Example 4: we have to collect this million signatures, and have to be unified, and put the full stop to all this, and **reach** the **truth**, **achieve justice** and reconciliation since we have to carry on living here **regardless** of how many of us are here.

In sum, at the thematic level, the two sets of consultations have three overlapping themes: *procedural*, *explanatory* and *interpretative*. Minor differences concern the level of specificity in *procedural* and *explanatory* classes in line with the contentious consultations' focus on the specific provisions of the draft Statute. The *interpretative class* in both corpora brings out the importance of the ethnic dimension, as participants articulate their experience of violence and identify obstacles to justice. The distinguishing theme in the non-contentious corpus is the *reflective* theme, which is about consideration of the most appropriate ways to address the legacy of mass atrocity in keeping with the opinion-gathering nature of these consultations. Counterintuitively, we find that the contentious consultations have both an *argumentative* and a *reconciliatory* theme. The *argumentative* class demonstrates participants' focus on finding best possible solutions for the Statute, concentrating on weighing their strengths and weaknesses, despite ethnic divisions. The *reconciliatory* class is unexpected, in view of participants' different identities, values and perspectives, and, especially, in view of scholarly arguments that the contestation of the norm of transitional justice undermines reconciliation. In the next section, we examine the relevance of assigned variables to explain these themes.

Explaining the themes: the relevance of the level of consultations

In order to establish how norm contestation unfolds, we turn our attention to the comparative analysis of the *interpretative* class, which points to the prominence of ethnic identity as a filter for comprehending both the violent past and challenges of addressing it. This class exists both in the non-contentious and in the contentious corpus, and is associated with discussants who come from different ethnic groups and hold diverse views. We observe a change in the association of the level of consultations variable for this theme. In the non-contentious corpus, the *interpretative* class is associated with the regional level, where, as opposed to the national and local level, they resort to ethnically centred arguments. Although we might expect that this pattern of discourse will also remain at the regional level in the contentious consultations because of the diversity of ethnic perspectives, this is not the case: the *interpretative* class is associated with the national level. At the same time, the *argumentative* class, which is unique to contentious consultations, and which reflects participants' sustained focus on finding viable solutions for addressing the legacy of mass atrocity acceptable to all, is associated with the regional level. The size of the *argumentative* class (the biggest of all classes), and the comparative strength of its association with the regional level, indicates the pattern of discourse conducive to inter-ethnic accommodation at the regional level despite norm contestation. With its focus on victims, the *reconciliatory* class in the contentious corpus is only weakly associated with the national level. Nonetheless, its emergence in this corpus demonstrates how potentially divisive dynamics of ethnic framing at this level can be countered. It provides additional evidence that norm contestation, which is underpinned by ethnic divisions, is not incompatible with reconciliation, understood as reconciliatory discourse.

Conclusion

By turning to the early stage in the life cycle of norms, this paper has found that contestation over the norm of post-conflict justice within a transnational advocacy network does not prevent reconciliatory communication that can mitigate a divisive impact of ethnically centred perspectives. In line with sociological theorizing of norms, we focused on contestation of various aspects of a norm. Empirically, the contestation focused on specific provisions of the draft Statute of a regional fact-finding commission in the Balkans. Comparing contentious and non-contentious consultations, we found that reconciliatory discourse that acknowledges victims without reference to their ethnicity is possible despite norm contestation, and emerges in contentious consultations.

The notion of "shared intention" can help us understand this counterintuitive finding: it is "an attitude of mind directed at some particular goal or purpose" and is key to overcoming conflict in divided societies (O'Flynn's 2017, 191). "Shared intention" is conditional on the "commitment on the part of each of the individuals involved to 'mesh' their different sub-plans into a single coherent plan of action" (Bratman 1993, 105–107 in O'Flynn 2017). Our findings, based on the analysis of different themes in a transitional justice discourse, suggest that the commitment of participants in the debates to the operationalization of the norm of post-conflict justice plays a role in countering potentially negative dynamics of contestation.

Our research has sought to understand how inter-ethnic accommodation can be attained through debating how to address the violent past. Specifically, it has sought to reveal how potentially divisive consequences of different ethnic identities, values and political constraints can be overcome inside a transnational advocacy network. This work did not address the issue of norm diffusion beyond the network. In the RECOM's case, much work remains to be done to understand why the targets of its advocacy – the states of former Yugoslavia – have remained impervious to its aspirations.

Our findings provide pointers for future work in the field of transitional justice, which concerns the relevance of the spatial scale of justice-seeking and the evaluation of the impact of transitional justice. Firstly, we identify different patterns of transitional justice discourse at different spatial scales (regional, national or local), which require further theoretical and empirical investigation (Kostovicova 2017). Secondly, our findings also call for rethinking of how we assess the impact of transitional justice. This is an important but little-studied area in the field (Bonacker and Buckley-Zistel 2013, 6). We demonstrate that it ought to capture process-related forms of impact, as well as "sideways" effects of transitional justice-seeking (sentence segments provide evidence of interaction among participants on the side-lines of RECOM's formal consultations, with a likely impact on norm socialization). Such assessment would better align with a non-linear nature of transitional justice as a process. But above all, it would refine our understanding of its impact beyond what may turn out to be a reductionist focus on pre-defined goals and expectations of justice-seeking.

Notes

1. See http://www.recom.link/sr/115677-2/page/5/.
2. Transcripts in Albanian, Macedonian and Slovenian are available in Bosnian–Croatian–Serbian.
3. By Denisa Kostovicova with some research assistance.
4. For descriptive statistics of the analysed consultations, see Table 1 and Table 3, and of the RECOM corpus, see Table 4 in the Supplementary Material.
5. See Table 2 in the Supplementary Material.
6. See Table 3 in the Supplementary Material.
7. Alceste stands for *Analyse des Lexèmes Co-occurents dans les Énnoncés Simples d'un texte* [Analysis of the co-occurring lexemes within the simple statements of a text].

8. Schonhardt-Bailey (2008, Appendix 1) provides a detailed account of the "Alceste methodology."
9. The Phi coefficient allows the comparison of variables of interest in the two analysed corpora as it factors out sample size, and hence sample specificity (Vallès 2014, 129–132).
10. One ECU illustrates each class, but additional illustrations are included for key findings (the *interpretative*, *argumentative* and *reconciliatory* classes). See Table 5 and Table 6 in the Supplementary Material, for first ten ECUs for each class.
11. The name is anonymized for ethical reasons.

Acknowledgements

Both authors thank Cheryl Schonhardt-Bailey, Bill Kissane and the three reviewers for their helpful comments, as well as Ivona Ladjevac for research assistance and Aaron Glasserman for editing assistance. The article benefited from feedback and comments by participants in the Annual Convention of the International Studies Association (ISA), Atlanta, the Annual Conference of the British International Studies Association (BISA), Edinburgh, the workshop "Reimagining Conflict-Transformation" organized by the Centre for Conflict, Rule of Law and Society, Bournemouth University, and the authors' workshop "Rethinking Reconciliation and Transitional Justice after Conflict" held at London School of Economics and Political Science.

Disclosure statement

No potential conflict of interest was reported by the authors.

Funding

Dr Kostovicova acknowledges gratefully the Leverhulme Trust (Research Fellowship RF-2015-262), which supported her research for this paper.

ORCID

Denisa Kostovicova http://orcid.org/0000-0002-6243-4379

References

Baker, C., and J. Obradovic-Wochnik. 2016. "Mapping the Nexus of Transitional Justice and Peacebuilding." *Journal of Intervention and Statebuilding* 10 (3): 281–301.

Bara, J., A. Weale, and A. Bicquelet. 2007. "Analysing Parliamentary Debate with Computer Assistance." *Swiss Political Science Review* 13 (4): 577–605.

Bicquelet, A., A. Weale, and J. Bara. 2012. "In a Different Parliamentary Voice?" *Politics & Gender* 8 (1): 83–121.

Bob, C. 2007. "'Dalit Rights Are Human Rights': Caste Discrimination, International Activism, and the Construction of a New Human Rights Issue." *Human Rights Quarterly* 29 (1): 167–193.

Bonacker, T., and S. Buckley-Zistel. 2013. "Introduction: Transitions from Violence – Analyzing the Effects of Transitional Justice." *International Journal of Conflict and Violence* 7 (1): 4–9.

Bratman, M. 1993. "Shared Intention." *Ethics* 104: 97–113.

Brugidou, M. 2003. "Argumentation and Values: An Analysis of Ordinary Political Competence via an Open-ended Question." *International Journal of Public Opinion Research* 15 (4): 413–430.

Carpenter, R. C. 2007. "Setting the Advocacy Agenda: Theorizing Issue Emergence and Nonemergence in Transnational Advocacy Networks." *International Studies Quarterly* 51 (1): 99–120.

Carpenter, R. C. 2011. "Vetting the Advocacy Agenda: Network Centrality and the Paradox of Weapons Norms." *International Organization* 65 (1): 69–102.

Chapman, A. R. 2009. "Approaches to Studying Reconciliation." In *Assessing the Impact of Transitional Justice: Challenges for Empirical Research*, edited by Hugo van der Merwe, Victoria Baxter, and Audrey R. Chapman, 143–172. Washington, DC: United States Institute of Peace Press.

Cohen, S. 2001. *States of Denial: Knowing About Atrocities and Suffering*. Cambridge: Polity.

Deitelhoff, N., and L. Zimmermann. 2013. Things We Lost in the Fire: How Different Types of Contestation Affect the Validity of International Norms. Peace Research Institute and Hessische Stiftung Friedens- und Konfliktforschung. PRIF Working Papers 18.

Di Lellio, A., and C. McCurn. 2013. "Engineering Grassroots Transitional Justice in the Balkans: The Case of Kosovo." *East European Politics and Societies* 27 (1): 129–148.

Emirbayer, M., and J. Goodwin. 1994. "Network Analysis, Culture, and the Problem of Agency." *American Journal of Sociology* 99 (6): 1411–1454.

Finnemore, M., and K. Sikkink. 1998. "International Norm Dynamics and Political Change." *International Organization* 52: 887–917.

Gordy, E. 2013. *Guilt, Responsibility and Denial: The Past at Stake in Post-Milošević Serbia*. Philadelphia: Pennsylvania University Press.

Irvine, J. A., and P. C. McMahon. 2013. "From International Courts to Grassroots Organizing: Obstacles to Transitional Justice in the Balkans." In *Transitional Justice and Civil Society in the Balkans*, edited by O. Simić and Z. Volčič, 217–237. New York: Springer.

Istorijat inicijative o osnivanju REKOM-a. 2009. Koalicija za REKOM. Public release, March 2009.

Jakovčić, E. 2009. Konsultacije sa lokalnom zajednicom o inicijativi REKOM Brčko, Bosna i Herzegovina. December 5.

Jasso, G., and K.-D. Opp. 1997. "Probing the Character of Norms: A Factorial Survey Analysis of the Norms of Political Action." *American Sociological Review* 62 (6): 947–964.

Kahler, M. 2009. "Networked Politics: Agency, Power, and Governance." In *Networked Politics: Agency, Power, and Governance*, edited by M. Kahler, 1–20. Ithaca, NY: Cornell University Press.

Kandić, N. 2007. "Transitional Justice in the Post-conflict Societies in Former Yugoslavia." *Sudosteruopa Mitteilungen* 4 (1): 73–77.

Keck, M. E., and K. Sikkink. 1998. *Activists Beyond Borders: Advocacy Networks in International Politics*. Ithaca, NY: Cornell University Press.

Komesaroff, P. A. 2008. "Pathways to Reconciliation: Bringing Diverse Voices into Conversation." In *Pathways to Reconciliation: Between Theory and Practise*, edited by P. Rothfield, 1–12. Aldershot: Ashgate.

Kostić, R. 2008. "Nationbuilding as an Instrument of Peace? Exploring Local Attitudes Towards International Nationbuilding and Reconciliation in Bosnia and Herzegovina." *Civil Wars* 10 (4): 384–412.

Kostovicova, D. 2010. "Civil Society in the Western Balkans: Vehicle for or Obstacle to Transitional Justice." In *Conflict and Memory: Bridging Past and Future in SouthEast Europe*, edited by W. Petritsch and V. Džihić, 287–293. Baden-Baden: Nomos Verlagsgesellschaft.

Kostovicova, D. 2013. "Airing Crimes, Marginalizing Victims: Political Expectations and Transitional Justice in Kosovo." In *The Milošević Trial: An Autopsy*, edited by T. W. Waters, 249–259. Oxford: Oxford University Press.

Kostovicova, D. 2017. "Seeking Justice in a Divided Region: Text Analysis of Regional Civil Society Deliberations in the Balkans." *International Journal of Transitional Justice* 11 (1): 154–175.

Kriesberg, L. 2001. "Changing Forms of Coexistence." In *Reconciliation, Justice and Coexistence: Theory and Practice*, edited by M. Abu-Nimer, 47–64. Lanham: Lexington Books.

Kurze, A., and I. Vukusic. 2013. "Afraid to Cry Wolf: Human Rights Activists' Struggle of Transnational Accountability Efforts in the Balkans." In *Transitional Justice and Civil Society in the Balkans*, edited by O. Simić and Z. Volčič, 201–217. New York: Springer.

Lake, D. A., and W. H. Wong. 2009. "The Politics of Networks: Interests, Power, and Human Rights Norms." In *Networked Politics: Agency, Power, and Governance*, edited by M. Kahler, 127–150. Ithaca, NY: Cornell University Press.

Nettelfield, L. 2012. *Courting Democracy in Bosnia and Herzegovina: The Hague Tribunal's Impact in a Postwar State*. Cambridge: Cambridge University Press.

Obradovic-Wochnik, J. 2013. "Serbian Civil Society as an Exclusionary Space: NGOs, the Public and 'Coming to Terms with the Past'." In *Civil Society and Transitions in the Western Balkans*, edited by V. Bojicic-Dzelilovic, J. Ker-Lindsay, and D. Kostovicova, 210–229. Basingstoke: Palgrave Macmillan.

O'Flynn, I. 2017. "Pulling Together: Shared Intentions, Deliberative Democracy and Deeply Divided Societies." *British Journal of Political Science* 47 (1): 187–202.

Oliver, P. 2006. "Purposive Sampling." In *The SAGE Dictionary of Social Research Methods*, edited by V. Jupp, 244–245. London: SAGE.

Orentlicher, D. F. 2007. "'Settling Accounts' Revisited: Reconciling Global Norms with Local Agency." *International Journal of Transitional Justice* 1: 10–22.

O'Toole, Jr., L. J., and K. J. Meier. 2006. "Networking in the Penumbra: Public Management, Cooptative Links, and Distributional Consequences." *International Public Management Journal* 9(3): 271–294.

Pankhurst, D. 1999. "Issues of Justice and Reconciliation in Complex Political Emergencies: Conceptualising Reconciliation, Justice and Peace." *Third World Quarterly* 20 (1): 239–255.

Podolny, J. M., and K. L. Page. 1998. "Network Forms of Organization." *Annual Review of Sociology* 24: 57–76.

Rossi, P. H., and R. A. Berk. 1985. "Varieties of Normative Consensus." *American Sociological Review* 50 (5): 333–347.

Rowen, J. 2012. "Mobilizing Truth: Agenda Setting in a Transnational Social Movement." *Law & Social Inquiry* 37 (3): 686–718.

Schonhardt-Bailey, C. 2005. "Measuring Ideas More Effectively: An Analysis of Bush and Kerry's National Security Speeches." *PS: Political Science and Politics* 38 (3): 701–711.

Schonhardt-Bailey, C. 2008. "The Congressional Debate on Partial-birth Abortion: Constitutional Gravitas and Moral Passion." *British Journal of Political Science* 38 (3): 383–410.

Schonhardt-Bailey, C. 2013. *Deliberating American Monetary Policy: A Textual Analysis*. Cambridge: The MIT Press.

Sharp, D. N. 2013. "Interrogating the Peripheries: The Preoccupations of Fourth Generation Transitional Justice." *Harvard Human Rights Journal* 26: 149–178.

Sikkink, K. 2009. "The Power of Networks in International Politics." In *Networked Politics: Agency, Power and Governance*, edited by M. Kahler, 228–247. Ithaca, NY: Cornell University Press.

Sikkink, K. 2011. *The Justice Cascade: How Human Rights Prosecutions Are Changing World Politics*. New York: W.W. Norton.

Sokolić, I. 2016. "Researching Norms, Narratives and Transitional Justice: Focus Group Methodology in Post-Conflict Croatia." *Nationalities Papers* 44 (6): 932–949.

Subotić, J. 2009. *Hijacked Justice: Dealing with the Past in the Balkans*. Ithaca, NY: Cornell University Press.

Teitel, R. G. 2000. *Transitional Justice*. Oxford: Oxford University Press.

Touquet, H., and P. Vermeersch. 2016. "Changing Frames of Reconciliation: The Politics of Peace-building in the Former Yugoslavia." *East European Politics and Societies* 30 (1): 55–73.

Vallès, D. W. 2014. "The Contours of Political Discourse: Deliberating the Patient Protection & Affordable Care Act." *PhD diss*. London School of Economics and Political Science.

van Raaij, D. P. A. M. 2006. "Norms Network Members Use: An Alternative Perspective for Indicating Network Success or Failure." *International Public Management Journal* 9 (3): 249–270.

Watts, D. J. 2004. "The 'New' Science of Networks." *Annual Review of Sociology* 30: 243–270.

Weale, A., A. Bicquelet, and J. Bara. 2012. "Debating Abortion, Deliberative Reciprocity and Parliamentary Advocacy." *Political Studies* 60: 643–667.

Wiener, A. 2014. *A Theory of Contestation*. New York: Springer.

Wiener, A. 2017. "*A Theory of Contestation* – A Concise Summary of Its Argument and Concepts." *Polity* 49 (1): 109–125.

Zalaquett, J. 1991–1992. "Balancing Ethical Imperatives and Political Constraints: The Dilemma of New Democracies Confronting Past Human Rights Violations." *Hastings Law Journal* 43: 1425–1438.

Implementing transformative justice: survivors and ex-combatants at the Comisión de la Verdad y Reconciliación in Peru

Rebekka Friedman

ABSTRACT
Interest has recently increased in transformative justice. While transformative justice research offers an important contribution to transitional justice, I discuss challenges in its implementation. Drawing on research on affected communities and practitioners at the Comisión de la Verdad y Reconciliación in Peru, I question whether there are tensions between addressing micro and macro causes of conflict and in representing and integrating survivors and ex-combatants. While scholars and practitioners have importantly linked transformative justice to the reconfiguration of macro socio-economic structural injustices, more attention is needed to micro drivers of conflict. I outline a tension for a desire for more established punitive justice (prosecution of perpetrators and reparations for survivors) and the need to engage and reintegrate ex-combatants. These challenges are acute in conflict transitions, where transitional justice has taken on more expansive goals of peace-building. More recognition is also important of lingering legacies of violence and practical impediments.

Introduction

In 2001, Peru's Truth and Reconciliation Commission, the Comisión de la Verdad y Reconciliación (CVR), was set up in a deeply polarized climate, following the Peruvian military's victory over the Shining Path. The CVR adopted the South African Truth and Reconciliation Commission's participatory testimonial model, becoming the only Latin American country to use public hearings. Unlike other participatory truth commissions, however, the Peruvian CVR had limited interactions with the majority of combatants. While the CVR's mandate included an inclusive agenda, in which it sought to provide a space to all sides of the conflict to testify, it eventually put most of its emphasis on empowering and dignifying survivors and furthering state accountability and social solidarity.[1]

In this article, I examine the CVR's understanding of and contribution to conflict transformation.[2] In recent years, "transformative justice" has emerged as an important critique and agenda against transitional justice (Lambourne 2008; Gready and Robins 2014; Lambourne and Rodriguez Carreon 2015).[3] Merging transitional justice, development, and peace-building, transformative justice seeks to address the contextually identified root causes of violence, including socio-economic injustices; facilitate civic participation; and promote a "victim-centered agenda", which emphasizes resistance and resilience.[4] While transformative justice, as I will detail in this article, is a welcome response to challenges and shortcomings in globalized transitional justice, more needs to be done to examine its viability in practice. At present, the transformative justice agenda remains largely normative, and it has insufficiently focused on the attempts of formal and informal processes to implement transformative justice.

The CVR is an important case study, as it is an institution that self-consciously took on a strong transformative justice mandate. Gready and Robins (2014, 355) note, "socio-political interventions such as truth commissions, memorials and education reforms have the greatest potential to take on a transformative agenda". They highlight the Peruvian CVR as a recent transitional justice institution that provided a "platform" for victims' empowerment and participation (Gready and Robins 2014, 359). The CVR consciously decided to remain a domestically staffed process, and while drawing on external influences, is noteworthy in its attempts to advance contextually defined objectives of conflict transformation. At the same time, the Peruvian case also significantly illustrates important challenges facing the implementation of transformative justice. Specifically, I argue that transformative justice needs to further acknowledge tensions between micro and macro processes of conflict transformation, and between various constituencies, particularly, survivors and ex-combatants. It also needs to think about the impact of contextual factors on its objectives and the lingering effects and new vulnerabilities and stigmas produced by long-term experiences of violence.

I divide the article into several sections. I begin by defining transformative justice and putting it into historical context. I then turn to the Peruvian case, and argue that tensions within its mandate and politicization led the CVR to scale down its inclusive platform and engagement with ex-combatants and to favour its survivor- and accountability-centred agenda. I conclude by discussing the importance of both micro and macro drivers of conflict. I also maintain that transformative justice needs to reflect on feasibility and practical and political constraints, which serve as barriers to conflict transformation.

Transformative justice

In recent years, a growing transformative justice agenda has emerged from various directions. Prominent policy institutions and global actors have called for more long-term and participatory orientations to transitional justice, which link transitional justice to peace-building (the United Nations 2008). A small but significant academic literature at the intersection of peace-building and transitional justice has taken up a more critical and multi-faceted approach. This scholarship has defined transformative justice as long-term, sustainable processes embedded in society and the integration of psychosocial, political, economic, and legal views on justice (Lambourne 2008). Transformative justice has criticized the view of justice as a backwards-looking short-term process and seeks long-term fundamental changes in society, particularly in the economic realm. It is both past- and forward-looking in that it incorporates "financial or other material compensation, restitution or reparation for past violations or crimes (historical justice)" and "distributive or socioeconomic justice in the future (prospective justice)" (Lambourne and Rodriguez Carreon 2015, 86). It also strongly espouses a participatory and personally and collectively meaningful *experience* of justice through the use of ritual and culturally embedded practices (Lambourne 2014, 32–34). As Lambourne and Rodriguez Carreon (2016, 86) argue, "the idea is both to create an experience of justice about what occurred in the past and to ensure that structural violence in the future is minimised in order to promote a sustainable peace". Transformative justice emphasizes local ownership and the participation of those most affected by the violence (McEvoy and McGregor 2008; Shaw and Waldorf 2010). Gready and Robins (2014, 355–360) usefully outline strategies for transformative justice, focusing both on ends and process goals. First, transformative justice needs to reframe socio-economic rights and continuities of conflict that persist into the present (Gready and Robins 2014, 355). Second, transformative justice would challenge the idea that ordinary people did not know and could not act, and illuminate opportunities for solidarity and collective action (Gready and Robins 2014, 356). It would thus acknowledge and honour resistance to formal processes of addressing the past in the present and open opportunities for debate and disagreement and critical reflection (Moon 2004; Gready and Robins 2014, 356–357). Third, transformative justice would provide opportunities for participation in transitional justice, particularly for survivors. This participation would empower marginalized groups and provide a platform that "transforms victimhood" (Gready and Robins 2014, 358).

In the post-Cold War period, transformative justice offers an important reorientation to more established formal transitional justice. First, it recognizes the increasingly complex settings of transitional justice, particularly its establishment in post-war contexts. As has been noted (Shaw and Waldorf

2010; Friedman 2017), where early transitional justice processes were often established following transitions from authoritarian rule to democracy, transitional justice institutions have increasingly been established during war to peace transitions. These post-war contexts are marked by high numbers of civilian deaths and high recurrence rates of violence. They present a complex array of peace-building challenges, often beyond the traditional accountability remit of formal justice institutions (Friedman 2017). The transformative justice agenda also plugs into dissatisfaction with legalistic and top-down formal globalized justice processes (Kelsall 2005; Shaw 2005; Laplante and Theidon 2007; Shaw and Waldorf 2010; Robins 2012; Millar, van der Lijn, and Verkoren 2013; Friedman 2017). It acknowledges commonly held community preferences for rectificatory and structural justice (Laplante and Theidon 2007; Millar 2011), and the importance of everyday locally supported recovery efforts (Theidon 2013; Millar, van der Lijn, and Verkoren 2013). Finally, transformative justice links to feminist concerns, relating to the continuation of gendered post-war structures and harms after the termination of violence (Ní Aoláin 2012; Lambourne and Rodriguez Carreon 2015, 89). This scholarship emphasizes the socio-political nature of structural violence and the limited contributions of formal and especially international institutions to addressing gendered inequalities (Boesten and Wilding 2015, 1–2). Transformative justice thus challenges patriarchal norms that hinder the political, social, and economic participation of women (Lambourne and Rodriguez Carreon 2015, 87) and seeks to imagine "new ways of responding to persistent social and political violence" (Boesten and Wilding 2015, 8).

While transformative justice presents a welcome and critical agenda, in this piece, I argue that transformative justice policy and research would benefit from addressing several key areas. First, transformative justice must further reflect on which causes of conflict it seeks to transform. One difficulty is that scholarship on transitional and transformative justice has often insufficiently engaged with and spoken to research on the causes of conflict (Friedman 2017). Importantly, as I will further discuss with the Peruvian case, there is little consensus as to the causes of conflict in particular cases. Academic explanations of the drivers of conflict have varied tremendously, not least as a consequence of diverging disciplinary and methodological starting points, unequal access to field research possibilities, and varying linguistic abilities.[5] The transformative justice scholarship has also tended to remain normative, engaging less systematically with how and whether existing transitional justice processes have sought to contribute to transformative justice.[6]

Second, and going further, as criticisms in the Peruvian case make clear, where transitional justice processes have sought to address root causes of conflict, it is my concern that they often insufficiently examine how long-term experiences of violence have generated new conflicts and inequities. This concern has also been prevalent in the normative transformative justice literature although it emerges to some degree in feminist work on gender justice, which looks at links between wartime and post-war gendered violence (Ní Aoláin 2012). Going further and more generally, post-war contexts often feature high degrees of alcoholism and drug abuses, and fractured families and community structures (Quinn 2009; Friedman 2017). They also often are sites of new patterns and dynamics of marginalization and stigmatization and politics of visibility and invisibility. This particularly applies to affected groups who were on the front lines of violence, including survivors of violence, widows and families of missing persons, and ex-combatants. From a gendered dimension, post-war contexts are also often times of normative realignment, particularly for female combatants, who, in many cases have found that they become highly stigmatized and marginalized during transitions to peace, despite holding an elevated status and more prominent public role during conflict (Giles 2004).

Third, more work is needed on the target constituencies and stakeholders of transformative justice and whether their needs are in tension. In its emphasis on process goals, the transformative justice literature has tended to take a strongly "victim-centred" orientation. Gready and Robins (2014, 357–358) do not discuss perpetrators or combatants in their call for participation in transformative justice, aside from a brief discussion of bystanders and passive responsibility (2014, 356). The limited attention to perpetrators and combatants is significant, particularly given the establishment of transitional justice mechanisms in post-war contexts. These settings are often marked by a high number of non-state "complex" perpetrators, including forced recruits, children, and vigilante civilians, who do not easily fit into a criminal justice regime.[7] They are also often contexts where some form of reconciliation or at least coexistence with perpetrators, is often a pragmatic necessity, particularly where high numbers of people were complicit in violence. In sum, the transformative justice agenda should further think about whether it should offer opportunities to facilitate ex-combatants' participation in transitional justice processes and to facilitate their social, political, and/or economic reintegration. Where repeated outbreaks of violence often occur within the same protracted social conflicts, addressing the micro drivers of violence seems critical for conflict prevention. Less directly and straightforwardly, as I will argue in the Peruvian case, failure to integrate perpetrators and combatants from transitional justice processes may also negatively impact processes that facilitate survivors' empowerment and integration.

Methodology

In this article, I draw on seven months of field research carried out between 2010 and 2011 in rural and urban areas in Peru. My research was divided in

Lima and villages and towns in Ayacucho, Huamanga as the site of the first Shining Path attack and home to a majority of survivors as well as former Shining Path members. My research consisted mainly of interviews, focus groups, and surveys with officials and civil society involved in transitional justice processes, and direct stakeholders, including *afectados* (those affected by violence), ex-insurgents, military officials, students, teachers, academics, and community leaders. It asked questions on the causes of conflict, individuals' conception of the meaning of reconciliation and justice and its drivers, the main legacies of violence, the challenges facing affected communities in the present, and the impact of transitional justice. I encouraged practitioners and stakeholders to assess justice and reconciliation and detail their experiences in their own words. To this end, I held open-ended and semi-structured focus groups and interviews to evaluate popular perceptions of transitional justice and reconciliation. I also spent significant time with practitioners involved in the CVR to understand how the Commission conducted its work, the priorities and dilemmas facing its staff, and why they made particular choices at various points in time. I carried out interviews myself in Spanish, and on several occasions in Quechua through an interpreter. I also drew on truth commission archives, minutes, and videos.

Institutionalizing transformative justice: the Peruvian armed conflict and the CVR

The Peruvian armed conflict began in Ayacucho, Huamanga, in 1980, and lasted for at least two decades. The main actors in the Peruvian armed conflict were Peru's two insurgency movements – the Shining Path and the Movimiento Revolutionario Túpac Amaru (MRTA) – and the Peruvian military. The Shining Path emerged in Ayacucho, Huamanga, in the south central Andes as a Maoist communist party aiming to overthrow the Peruvian state. It eventually recruited and inflicted violence across Peru. The MRTA had several hundred members and sought to establish a communist state. The conflict killed an estimated 69,280 individuals, displacing over 600,000 people and destroying over 400 peasant communities (CVR Report 2004, Volume 1, Chapter 3). A combination of Shining Path brutality and a change in state tactics to less militarized methods, led to the Shining Path's defeat.

In significant regards, the CVR consciously aspired to and implemented a transformative justice agenda. For a year prior to its establishment, CVR President, Dr Salomón Lerner Febres, and commissioners held workshops to discuss how the CVR could advance a contextually sensitive and transformative approach.[8] It took a strong stance that the CVR should address the root causes of conflict in the Peruvian context and that it should utilize methodologies and a participatory process that would strengthen democratic citizenship and individually and collectively empower survivors and affected communities. Conscious of the challenge of addressing a multisided conflict with a strong ethnic and class dimension, the CVR also linked its work to the demands of peace-building, and looked for inspiration from what it saw as more participatory and ambitious truth commissions, including in Sierra Leone and South Africa.[9]

The CVR is also noteworthy for its efforts to address multiple drivers of conflict. On the micro level, the CVR sought to offer an inclusive participatory process that would engage participants on various sides of the conflict. To date, the CVR is the only Latin American commission to use public hearings and to reach out to ex-combatants to solicit public testimony. While, as I will discuss in more detail shortly, the conflict's main protagonists – the military and the Shining Path – generally did not take part in the CVR's public work, the CVR held hearings with numerically less involved actors in the conflict, including members of the police forces and *rondas campesinos* (civil militias). While the CVR offered militants the opportunity to testify, as it did not offer amnesty or other incentives, few came forward. While 1,000 members of the Shining Path and MRTA testified, only four leaders agreed to be video recorded (Root 2012, 82). Tensions went both ways. Shining Path members refused to give statements particularly once the CVR's attribution of responsibility for violence came out and the CVR insisted on recordings rather than hearings to prevent insurgents from promoting the movements within public hearings. High ranking political officials, including former President, Alan Garcia, participated, though former President, Fujimori refused. Not a single military member gave a testimony, though as several within the Commission noted, many participated in private.[10]

In many ways, however, as I will argue in the following analysis, the CVR focused most of its efforts on the macro level and prioritized survivors as its primary constituency. This emerges even in its planning stages where those working at the Commission question the relevance of conceptions of restorative justice between survivors and perpetrators at the South African Truth and Reconciliation Commission and identify their focus to be a broad conception of national reconciliation between society and state (Friedman 2017).[11] The CVR's predominant focus was on transforming macro structural causes of conflict, promoting "victims' justice and empowerment", and contributing to state responsibility and social solidarity. It sought to do this by facilitating survivors' participation, outlining an extensive reparations plan and recommendations for reforms, promoting societal learning and making the case for indirect responsibility, and contributing to transparency and accountability, including criminal justice.[12] Reflecting transformative justice's emphasis on resilience (Gready and Robins 2014), the CVR sought to document resistance as a way to generate solidarity and empower civil society and to advance a participatory "victim-centred" approach. Gathering 17,000 testimonies, mainly from victims, the CVR invited activist, Mama Angelica to testify at the first hearing in Ayacucho, paying respect to her campaigns on behalf of her missing son, and acknowledging her prior experiences of state censorship and stigmatization. Additionally, recognizing the gendered nature of disappearances, the CVR put emphasis on the efforts and activism of women in searching for their missing sons and husbands.

Partial transformation: evaluating the CVR

A wide scholarship within and outside of Peru has examined the effects of Peru's official truth-seeking mechanisms on survivors' empowerment (Laplante 2007; Degregori 2010; Friedman 2017). A foremost success of Peru's truth-seeking process is its generation of a platform and "reference point" for afectados and civil society and its attention to military violence and state responsibility (Laplante 2007; Friedman 2017) and tied itself to public performance places for pre-existing and ongoing community and civil society initiatives in affected regions (Milton 2014, 37–38). This is significant, particularly where survivors came from a marginalized and previously invisible demographic and given long-term patterns of state impunity. At the same time, the CVR has also exposed and reinforced the limits of transformative justice in Peru. Here, scholars have critically engaged with the CVR's impact and approach on gendered (Boesten 2010; Boesten and Fisher 2012) and class and race-based inequalities (Laplante 2007; Laplante and Theidon 2007; Theidon 2013). According to its own mandate, the CVR encountered challenges both in terms of how it carried out its work and in the follow up to its recommendations.

Lack of political and social will: tensions between accountability- and victim-centred justice versus an inclusive- and restorative approach

A first issue that emerges strongly in the Peruvian experience is that contextually defined boundaries and constraints will affect the reach and reception of transformative justice. In Peru, a polarized social climate and strong government and still powerful political and military actors associated with the former regime have limited the possibilities as well as impact of justice and memory initiatives (Friedman 2017). This was clearly the case for the CVR, which was under heavy media and political scrutiny throughout its operation (Theidon 2006, 454–456). In affected areas, where communities had suffered significant military violence and had been marginalized from the state, trust in authority structures was low. Tensions and mistrust were also acute at the communal level, where coexistence required living with individuals who had participated in violence.[13]

This political and social climate has had important procedural consequences. In areas heavily affected by military violence, such as Ayacucho, only a fraction of survivors testified at the CVR. The CVR's formal proceedings and concentration in the capital further alienated it from affected communities. Affected communities and those working with them reported that some did not feel ready to testify so soon after the cessation of violence for fear of reprisals and insufficient confidence building.[14]

These early barriers have left lingering legacies. Many survivors' organizations and affected communities in Ayacucho have taken the stance that the number of victims should be higher than the official citations in the CVR's report. This is particularly important in areas heavily hit by military violence and given the military's practice of hiding and burning bodies or using mass graves.[15] Additional problems emerged when the CVR completed its work, where the Commission's mandate and institutional jurisdiction generated confusion. Affected communities often were not aware that the CVR was only able to make recommendations and did not itself have legal ability to implement reparatory justice. Here, as in other contexts, the Commission's short time frame and its high-profile proceedings also stood in contrast to the lack of changes to individuals' lives.[16] Interviewees emphasized political corruption, in particular, and slow implementation of criminal and structural justice.[17] The persistence of deep-rooted structural inequalities continuously came up as one of the biggest failings of transformative justice.

It is also important to note that transitional justice processes, while seeking to shape normative agendas, can also expose political and social divisions and lack of will to address root causes of conflict and victims' rights. Affected populations in Ayacucho frequently pointed out their dismay over the conservative reactions towards the CVR's truth-seeking process among powerful groups and middle classes in the capital. They also raised criticisms voiced by military members of the CVR's findings as painful and offensive.

Where, as I will detail shortly, the CVR had tense relations with military actors and decided to prioritize survivors and state accountability, it is worrying that tensions with actors in the conflict may negatively affect even survivors' empowerment and justice. This emerges strongly in relation to military violence. Survivors and the organizations representing them, for instance, frequently pointed out that military members knew the location of mass graves and the whereabouts of missing family members but chose not to reveal them. They argued that without the participation of protagonists, particularly in a conflict characterized by long-term impunity, they could not make progress with disappearances and reparations. Interviewees also often raised that the military had not apologized for its part in the violence and had not acknowledged responsibility.[18] As ANFASEP (the National Association for

Relatives of Kidnapped, Detained and Disappeared of Peru) official, Yuber Alcon, put it: "People need to feel dignified, that they are a citizen in this country. How can they feel like citizens, like humans, when they still haven't been told the truth?"[19] Where the CVR offered a significant space for survivors' testimony and provided institutional acknowledgment as an official body established by the state, it did not generally offer answers and acknowledgment from those who had carried out abuses.

Second, and relatedly, what has been less discussed in Peru, and in the literature on transformative justice, are tensions between macro and micro processes or logics of conflict transformations. In the CVR's case, this emerged as a tension between a broadly "victim- and accountability-centred" orientation versus an inclusive approach focused on social learning and reconciliation. The CVR struggled to work out its policy towards ex-combatants during its operation (Cueva 2006). Unlike other participatory commissions, as in South Africa or Sierra Leone, contextual factors again limited the CVR's dealings with ex-combatants. Particularly important are that the CVR was established following a military victory, leaving little room for negotiation with non-state actors, and in a context in which the Shining Path was highly stigmatized, particularly among middle classes and in Peru's coastal cities. Additionally, Peru faced strong pressure to prosecute crimes externally and domestically and many commissioners at the CVR had professional training and personal dispositions favouring human rights and criminal justice (Friedman 2017). Given political and social stigmatization of the Shining Path and the CVR's concern about maintaining social and political support for survivors' justice, the CVR faced significant concerns as to how its dealings with ex-combatants would affect its ability to generate political and social support for state accountability and victims' justice.[20]

Nevertheless, compared to other participatory commissions, the CVR took a cautious approach towards ex-combatants, especially to non-state actors, which grew stronger over time. It provided more conditions to ex-combatants' participation, particularly non-state actors, and strongly condemned the legitimacy of insurgent groups.[21] Additionally, it took a strong stance in favour of criminal justice and furthering war crimes trials of military members. Despite an originally expansive inclusive mandate, the CVR prioritized victims' justice and integration and social and political accountability. This orientation was self-reinforcing given an increasingly difficult and conflictual relationship between the CVR and ex-combatants and the fact that the military and Shining Path abstained from testifying at the CVR.

The legacies of political violence: fractured communities and stigmatization

A third crucial issue for the transformative justice agenda is recognition of the ways in which prolonged violence breeds new conflict and processes of marginalization and stigmatization. In the Peruvian case, while the CVR's report emphasized pre-Shining Path structural root causes of the conflict, affected communities and civil society in Ayacucho were very concerned about the new and additional legacies brought on by years of political violence, including widespread alcoholism and drug abuse, domestic abuse, fragmented families, crime, and fractured social and political capital and at the micro and macro levels.[22] Fractured social capital and stained social fabric was particularly acute in rural communities, where lower level insurgents, state collaborators, and survivors coexisted, and fear of self-incrimination and betrayal continued to strain communal relations.[23] These "everyday" concerns were less prevalent in the CVR's agenda, which like formal institutions in other contexts, was foremost concerned with what it identified as political crimes. Yet, for affected communities, they often were a highly relevant priority in structuring their everyday lives.[24]

Taking a longer-term perspective, staff at the CVR often took the position that its transformative agenda would provide a space for ongoing conflict transformation. Those working at the CVR frequently argued that conflict transformation was a long-term process and that the purpose of the CVR was to inspire and mobilize a process that would continue after its cessation.[25] Officials at truth commissions elsewhere and members of international courts have often made similar arguments, maintaining that transitional justice institutions have normative, mobilization, and learning effects, which "trickle down" after they formally finish operation. In Ayacucho, individuals who worked for or had been affiliated with the CVR were active in setting up new programs and organizations, and often linked their agenda to the CVR's work. This was particularly the case for organizations working in human rights and reparations, but also in broader spheres, such as mental health.[26]

At the same time, it is also important to recognize and take into account how transitional justice processes play into and are limited by politics of visibility and invisibility that result from long-term violence. Although, as stated already, the CVR provided a detailed account of the conflict's structural causes, addressing and understanding the micro drivers of insurgent participation has been mainly absent from Peru's transitional justice and conflict reconstruction process.[27] The limited attention to ex-combatant voices and the marginalization of protagonists from Peru's transitional justice process presents a number of challenges. First, and most straightforwardly, the lack of engagement with combatants limits opportunities to examine the micro drivers of violence. Relevant to the CVR's transformative aims, a complex array of macro- and micro-level factors drove Peru's political violence. As in other contexts, academic literature on Peru has employed different lenses of analysis to assess the causes of conflict. While, as discussed, the CVR provided a thorough overview of the political, economic and social structural root causes of the conflict, at the micro level, a significant ethnographic scholarship has focused on the appeal of ideology in an unequal society and the importance of social mobility and recognition in the demographics of insurgent participation (Del Pino 1998; De la Cadena 2008; Degregori 2010; Heilman 2010; La Serna 2012; Portocarrero 2012). This scholarship has paid attention to the Shining Path's instrumentalization of generational grievances and economic, class, gender, and racial inequalities.

Interestingly, in my wider research on Peru, while affected populations (including survivors and ex-combatants) and civil society in Ayacucho and Lima disagreed on how to frame the conflict, there was wide agreement on the structural root causes of the conflict.[28] Interviews and surveys consistently included systematic regional and ethnic marginalization, government corruption, and extreme poverty and underdevelopment as the most important root causes of conflict. At the micro level, explanations of individual motivations for joining armed groups were more complex and varied.[29] Interviewees often recognized ideology as a catalyst to mobilize individual recruits. Others noted the marginalization of youth and personal grievances as motivating factors. My interviews with former MRTA and Shining Path women, for instance, revealed a wide array of insurgent motivations, often intertwining the personal and political realm.[30] One former MRTA woman, who had joined the MRTA, while studying at the Pontificia Católica del Perú in Lima, described feeling inspired by an older socially activist close relative and being already sympathetic to the movement, when members reached the campus. A former Shining Path woman described her devotion to a romantic partner, whom she followed, and her desire to belong given what she described as her low self-esteem and growing up in a "broken home". Another former Shining Path woman cited her enlistment as a response to dishonour, and detailed the military's humiliation of an elderly family member and the state's marginalization of her region. All argued that these personal factors were interlinked and given meaning by broader political ideological motivations presented by the insurgency. Similarly, these women described beginning to doubt their allegiances to the Shining Path and MRTA when their personal motivations were no longer as strong or their personal priorities (for instance, in the case of the second militant, suffering the disappearance of her partner and becoming pregnant). All of the women also discussed questioning their commitment to the insurgencies when the movements became more violent or seemed hypocritical (for instance, the insurgencies' recruitment of children or witnessing the favourable living conditions of commanders). Where a rich psychosocial and ethnographic literature in Peru has documented the generational breaches and the ideological and millenarian appeal of the Shining Path, particularly for marginalized youth (Degregori 2010) and women (Cordero 1998), my interviews with female insurgents also revealed dynamics that solidify individual commitment to the insurgent groups once individuals join. Both the MRTA and Shining Path sought to indoctrinate and compromise the ability of recruits to return to civilian life. They would, for instance, attempt to reaffirm insurgents' commitment to the group through arranging intense immersion and study for new recruits and "testing" new members to commit violent acts on behalf of the movement soon after joining. These acts not only affirmed new recruits status as insurgents but they also severed their ties to their original communities.

Allowing individual narratives to emerge in public seems especially important in the Peruvian context, where in contrast to the MRTA and insurgencies elsewhere, the Shining Path was a consciously secretive movement, and refused to give press conferences during Peru's years of political violence. In areas where the Shining Path had a strong presence, notably Ayacucho, local organizations and academics frequently expressed concern that the silences surrounding the Shining Path and the motivations of its participants are dangerous for younger generations, who did not themselves experience the costs of political violence and may become more interested in its history on account of its suppressed nature.[31]

Second, the distant engagement with actors involved in the conflict has limited spaces for reintegration of ex-combatants, as a key area of peace-building (Berdal and Ucko 2010). On the political level, some civil society advocates worry that the CVR's conception of national reconciliation between state and society is "abstract", and have faulted it for failing to integrate the Shining Path.[32] Practically, both socially and economically, there has been less of a normative endorsement for combatants' reintegration. Unlike Peruvian civil society's strong activism on behalf of afectados rights and missing persons, since the CVR's cessation, mobilizing to support ex-combatants and their reintegration has been much less of a high focus area for local organizations. At present, former militants face severe stigmatization and often hide their former involvement (Friedman 2017).[33] In conversations with former Shining Path and MRTA women, all shared that their inability to speak about their pasts and reasons for enlistment contributes to their wider societal exclusion. Significantly, female combatants stated that what was most helpful to them was to be involved in socially conscious work post-violence, for instance, working with street children, but that they have only been able to do so sporadically and to varying degrees. They also cited acceptance from their families and women with similar experiences as crucial support systems and said they would have liked to testify in public. All described struggles to marry since leaving prison and the difficulties of living on the margins of society. From a gender justice perspective, there was a strong view among female informants that the social stigmatization and lack of opportunities were worse for former female Shining Path and MRTA than for their male counterparts.

Third, in terms of survivor-centered transformative justice, in indirect ways, constituencies of transitional justice are linked and it is important to think more about whether integration of combatants is important for survivor-centered justice. In affected regions, interviewees often raised the difficulty of testifying or pushing for reparations for deaths caused by non-state actors, such as the Shining Path, in regions where the Shining Path had a strong presence. In terms of everyday post-war reconstruction and opportunities, many in affected regions, such as Ayacucho, felt that the invisibility of Shining Path voices had also harmed the population as a whole. They maintained that the silence surrounding Shining Path had entrenched a view of the past in which individuals were targets or perpetrators, rather than recognizing "grey" areas, for instance, child or forced recruitment.[34] In their everyday lives, younger interviewees in Ayacucho complained about limited employment opportunities given their region's tainted association with the Shining Path.[35]

Conclusions

In recent years, scholars and practitioners have increasingly stressed the need for transformative justice. While the transformative agenda is valuable, to date, it has remained primarily normative. In this article, I used the Peruvian case study as an opportunity to examine the CVR's conscious institutional implementation of a transformative justice mandate in practice. The CVR's work provides a significant benchmark for the transformative justice agenda.

At the same time, I further argued that there are a number of key areas which transformative justice needs to address. First, as the Peruvian case makes clear, the wider contexts within which institutions are set up also shape and often constrain possible pathways and domestic reception. As is often the case, transitional justice in Peru was set up where conflict structures and identities were strong. In many ways, uneven experiences and legacies of violence and the state's military victory over the Shining Path aggravated these as state actors involved in political violence and the military remained powerful, and retained middle-class support, and had less incentive to reconcile with non-state insurgent groups.[36] Unsurprisingly, the concentration of military violence in remote parts of the country and prior marginalization of these areas had eroded political trust and social solidarity. Although the CVR provided a crucial mobilizing forum for survivors and their defenders in affected areas, it was also vulnerable to conflict-related tensions. Slow state follow up, both in relation to reparations and structural justice, and to disappearances, and criticisms surrounding its work, reinforced perceptions of victimization and marginalization. The CVR thus highlights the importance of social and political support. Where proponents of transformative justice seek to encourage processes that will facilitate social, economic, and political wide-range changes, in practice, more expansive mandates can also expose a lack of goodwill and political and social intolerance and impediments. These inevitably cause further frustration feelings of insecurity and are often harder for transitional justice processes to address.

Second, at the same time, my findings highlight unresolved tensions between micro and macro processes of conflict transformation and between constituencies of transformative justice, particularly survivors and their representatives and ex-combatants. While the CVR originally sought to contribute to both macro structural and micro transformation by providing a forum for all sides to participate, over time, CVR officials decided that the Commission should focus on the areas where it was most likely to achieve success and that resonated with broadly held societal aims and the moral and political leanings of officials within the Commission. While the Peruvian case therefore offers an important study of tensions between forms of conflict transformation, particularly in a politicized context, it is important that transformative justice does not lose sight of social learning and its affective objectives and that it thinks carefully about how to integrate conflict protagonists. Protracted conflicts are multi-layered and complex and conflict transformation will necessitate addressing both the macro and the micro drivers of insurgent participation. Where it is fundamental that transformative justice prioritizes survivors' marginalization, transformative justice must also air voices that are contentious and in disagreement and pay critical attention to the politics of visibility and invisibility in war to peace transitions.

Notes

1. In this article I use the term "survivor" or afectado (affected one in Spanish) to correspond to how many who experienced violence in Peru chose to identify themselves. These individuals and communities frequently rejected the term "victim". I only use "victim" when directly engaging with institutions of secondary literature that uses this term".
2. Some of the data from this article are drawn from my book length study, *Competing Memories: Truth and Reconciliation in Sierra Leone and Peru* (2017). The book examines how truth commissions have employed wide-ranging procedures across cases and offers a conceptualization of various levels of reconciliation and its links to transitional justice.
3. Conflict transformation is often associated with Lederach (2003, 14), who offers an expansive definition: " … creating constructive change processes that reduce violence, increase justice in direct interaction and social structures, and respond to real-life problems in human relationships." In the article I refer to conflict transformation more simply as policies that address and remedy the root causes of conflict.
4. I distinguish transitional justice as formal and informal institutions and practices to address legacies of violence during transitions from civil war or authoritarian rule from transformative justice as an agenda linking to these institutions. Transformative justice, as I understand it, is a set of normative orientations and expectations.
5. For instance, in Peru, political scientists have often focused on macro structural economic and political root causes of war, while a more ethnographically oriented and often anthropological literature has examined the micro drivers of participation in insurgency.

6. See Philpott (2012, 23–24) on implicit normative assumptions about conflict resolution in transitional justice.
7. The Sierra Leonean Truth and Reconciliation Commission had the highest participation of ex-combatants of truth commissions and separate hearings for children.
8. See CVR Working Group. See also Personal interview, Dr Salomón Lerner Febres, Lima, Peru, 10 February 2011.
9. See CVR Working Group. See also Personal interview, Dr Salomón Lerner Febres, Lima, Peru, 10 February 2011. See also personal interview, Félix Reátegui, CVR Researcher, Lima, Peru, 1 December 2011.
10. Personal interview, Rolando Ames Cobían, Lima, Peru, 7 February 2011. See also Root (2012, 85).
11. The CVR Working Group Minutes.
12. CVR Report and personal interview, Jairo Rivas, Consejo de Reperaciones, Lima, Peru, 19 December 2010.
13. See Theidon's (2000) discussion of the micro politics of reconciliation and reintegration.
14. Personal interview, José Coronel Aguirre, Ayacucho, Peru, 12 January 2011.
15. Personal interview, Tanya Molina Morote, forensic anthropologist and regional coordinator of EPAF, Ayacucho, Peru, 5 October 2010.
16. See the South African Barometer report.
17. UNSCH Law Student Focus Group, Ayacucho, Peru, 21 October 2010.
18. Focus group with widows, Cayara, Ayacucho, Peru, 13 October 2010.
19. Personal interview, Yuber Alcarón Quispe, ANFASEP official and lawyer, Ayacucho, Peru, 12 October 2010.
20. Personal interviews, Lerner and Ames.
21. For example, the CVR required insurgents to "auto-criticize" before testifying – to renounce the movement and their role in it (Friedman 2017). The CVR also characterized the Shining Path as a terrorist movement unlike the Sierra Leonean Truth and Reconciliation Commissions, for instance, which abstained from judging the legitimacy of the Revolutionary United Front.
22. Personal interviews, Coronel. Focus group with female afectados, Cayara, Peru, 13 October 2010.
23. UNSCH Anthropology Student Focus Group, Ayacucho, Peru, 21 October 2010.
24. See Martin (2016) for a discussion of everyday normalization.
25. See Ntsebeza (2000) and Hollis (2015).
26. For example, COSMA (mental health commission of Ayacucho), was established as a mental health clinic in Ayacucho in response to the CVR's recommendations for mental health reparations.
27. Personal interview, Carlos Rodrigo Infante Yupanqui, Ayacucho, Peru, 4 November 2010. Infante is a faculty member at the UNSCH and director of the journal, *Con Sentido*. His father, journalist Octavio Infante García, was murdered in the Uchuraccay massacre. See also Theidon (2004).
28. For instance, whether this was a civil war, an armed conflict, an insurgency, or terrorism and counter-terrorism.
29. Some refused to engage with the individual motivations of insurgents altogether as they saw them as illegitimate or for fear of legitimizing them.
30. On women's mobilization and the links between personal and political drivers, see Ní Aoláin (2013) and Richter-Devroe (2009).

31. In Ayacucho, university students and faculty face a heavily censored atmosphere, particularly in terms of permitted disciplines offered at universities and subjects related to the Shining Path.
32. For some victims' organizations, the CVR should have employed a Shining Path commissioner and put more emphasis on the status of ex-Shining Path prisoners and military disappearances.
33. Personal interviews, Coronel; and Pilar Coll Torrente, Lima, Peru, 3 February 2011. See also Theidon (2004).
34. See Gavilán Sánchez (2012) for an account of a former child Shining Path militant.
35. UNSCH Law and Anthropology Focus Groups and personal interview, Manuel Mayorga, UNSCH, Anthropology Department, Ayacucho, Peru, 5 November 2010.
36. In this regard, Sri Lanka is a similar recent example.

Acknowledgements

I would like to thank Denisa Kostovicova and Jim Hughes for putting together a stimulating workshop at the LSE to prepare this paper and for their invaluable feedback. I also thank the editors of *Ethnic and Racial Studies* for their support of this Special Issue. In Peru, I am very grateful for the support of Anne Carbon, Ruth Moisés Ríos, Salomón Lerner Febres and Rosemary Lerner Rizo Patron, Juana García Blásquez, Félix Reátegui, Pilar Coll Torrente, Carlos Iván Degregori, and Rolando Ames Cobián. I warmly thank the Comisión de Salud Mental de Ayacucho and El Instituto de Democracia y Derechos Humanos de la Pontificia Universidad Católica del Perú. I would additionally like to thank Benjamin Wolf, Kirsten Ainley, Chris Brown, Carmen Gayoso, Rachel Kerr, Vivienne Jabri, Jelena Obradović-Wochnik, Fionnuala Ní Aoláin, Laura Martin, Joana Quinn, and Gearoid Millar. I am also grateful for fruitful conversations and feedback from the King's College London War Crimes Research Group, a Critical Peacebuilding and Transitional Justice roundtable at the British International Studies Association Convention (2015), and a helpful panel at the International Studies Association Annual Convention (2016) for furthering my thinking on this subject.

Disclosure statement

No potential conflict of interest was reported by the author.

References

Berdal, Mats, and David Ucko. 2010. "Introduction: The Political Reintegration of Armed Groups after War." In *Reintegrating Armed Groups After Conflict: Politics, Violence and Transition*, edited by Mats Berdal and David H. Ucko, 1–9. Oxford: Routledge.

Boesten, Jelke. 2010. "Analyzing Rape Regimes at the Interface of War and Peace in Peru." *International Journal of Trnasitional Justice* 4: 110–129.

Boesten, Jelke, and Melissa Fisher. 2012. "Sexual Violence and Justice in Postconflict Peru." United States Institute of Peace Special Report: 1–12.

Boesten, Jelke, and P. Wilding. 2015. "Transformative Gender Justice: Setting an Agenda." *Women's Studies International Forum* 51: 75–80.

Cordero, Isabel Coral. 1998. "Women in War: Impact and Responses." In *Shining and Other Paths: War and Society in Peru, 1980–1995*, edited by Steve J. Stern, 345–377. Durham, NC: Duke University Press.

Cueva, Eduardo Gonzales. 2006. "The Peruvian Truth and Reconciliation Commission and the Challenge of Impunity." In *Transitional Justice in the Twenty-first Century*, edited by Naomi Roht-Arriaza. Cambridge: Cambridge University Press.

De la Cadena, Marisol. 1998. "From Race to Class: Insurgent Intellectuals *de provoncia* in Peru, 1910–1970." In *Shining and Other Paths: War and Society in Peru, 1980–1995*, edited by Steve J. Stern, 22–60. Durham, NC: Duke University Press.

Degregori, Carlos Iván. 2010. *Qué Dificil es Ser Dios: El Partido Comunista del Perú – Sendero Luminoso y el Conflicto Armado Interno en el Perú: 1980–1999*. Lima: Institute of Peruvian Studies.

Del Pino, Panciano. 1998. "Family, Culture, and '"Revolution': Everyday Life with Sendero Luminoso." In *Shining and Other Paths: War and Society in Peru, 1980–1995*, edited by Steve J. Stern, 158–192. Durham, NC: Duke University Press.

Friedman, Rebekka. 2017. *Competing Memories: Truth and Reconciliation in Sierra Leone and Peru*. Cambridge: Cambridge University Press.

Gavilán Sánchez, Lurgio. 2012. *Memorias de un soldado desconocido* [Memories of an Unknown Soldier]. Lima: Institute of Peruvian Studies.

Giles, Wenona. 2004. "Comparative Feminist Perspectives: Sri Lanka and the Post-Yugoslav States." In *Peace Work: Women, Armed Conflict and Negotiation*, edited by Radhika Coomeraswamy and Dilrukshi Fonseka, 73–95. New Delhi and Colombo: Women Unlimited and International Center for Ethnic Studies.

Gready, Paul, and Simon Robins. 2014. "From Transitional Justice to Transformative Justice: A New Agenda in Practice." *The International Journal for Transitional Justice* 8 (3): 339–361.

Heilman, Jaymie. 2010. *Before the Shining Path: Politics in Rural Ayacucho, 1895–1980*. Stanford, CA: Stanford University Press.

Hollis, Brenda. 2015. "Evaluating the Legacy of the Special Court for Sierra Leone." In *Evaluating Transitional Justice: Accountability and Peacebuilding in Post-Conflict Sierra Leone*, edited by Kirsten Ainley, Rebekka Friedman, and Christopher Mahony, 9–34. Basingstoke: Palgrave Macmillan.

Kelsall, Timothy. 2005. "Truth, Lies, Ritual: Preliminary Reflections on the TRC in Sierra Leone." *Human Rights Quarterly* 27 (2): 361–391.

Lambourne, Wendy. 2008. "Transitional Justice and Peacebuilding after Mass Violence." *International Journal of Transitional Justice* 3 (1): 28–48.

Lambourne, Wendy. 2014. "Transformative Justice, Reconciliation and Peacebuilding." In *Transitional Justice Theories: An Introduction*, edited by Susanne Buckley-Zistel, Teresa Koloma Beck, Christian Braun, and Friederike Mieth, 19–40. Abington: Routledge.

Lambourne, Wendy, and Vivianna Rodriguez Carreon. 2016. "Engendering Transitional Justice: A Transformative Approach to Building Peace and Attaining Human Rights." *Human Rights Review*. 17 (1): 71–93.

Laplante, Lisa J. 2007. "The Peruvian Truth Commission's Historical Memory Project: Empowering Truth-Tellers to Confront Truth Deniers." *Journal of Human Rights* 6: 433–452.

Laplante, Lisa J., and Kimberly Susan Theidon. 2007. "Truth with Consequences: Justice and Reparations in Post-Truth Commission Peru." *Human Rights Quarterly* 29 (1): 228–250.

La Serna, Miguel. 2012. *The Corner of the Living: Ayacucho on the Eve of the Shining Path Insurgency*. Chapel Hill, NC: University of North Carolina Press.

Lederach, John Paul. 2003. "Conflict Transformation." In *Beyond Intractability*, edited by Guy Burgess and Heidi Burgess. Boulder, CO: Conflict Information Consortium.

Martin, Laura. 2016. "Practicing Normality: An Examination of Unrecognizable Transitional Justice Institutions in Sierra Leone." *Journal of Intervention and Statebuilding* 10: 400–418.

McEvoy, Kieran, and Lorna McGregor, eds. 2008. *Transitional Justice from Below: Grassroots Activism and the Struggle for Change*. Portland, Oregon: Hart Publishing.

Millar, Gearoid. 2011. "Local Evaluations of Justice: Truth Telling in Sierra Leone: Postwar Needs and Transitional Justice." *Human Rights Review* 12: 524–529.

Millar, Gearoid, Jaïr van der Lijn, and Willemijn Verkoren. 2013. "Peacebuilding Plans and Local Reconfigurations: Frictions Between Imported Processes and Indigenous Practices." *International Peacekeeping* 20 (2): 137–143.

Milton, Cynthia E., ed. 2014. *Art from a Fractured Past: Memory and Truth-Telling in Post-Shining Path Peru*. Durham, NC: Duke University Press.

Moon, Claire. 2004. "Prelapsarian State: Forgiveness and Reconciliation in Transitional Justice." *International Journal for the Semiotics of Law Revue Internationale de Sémiotique Juridique* 17 (2): 185–197.

Ní Aoláin, Fionnuala. 2012. "Advancing Feminist Positioning in the Field of Transitional Justice." *International Journal of Transitional Justice* 6: 205–228.

Ní Aoláin, Fionnuala. 2013. "Situating Women in Counterterrorism Discourses: Undulating Masculinities and Luminal Femininities." *Boston University Law Review* 93 (3): 1085–1122.

Ntsebeza, Dumisa B. 2000. "The Uses of Truth Commissions: Lessons for the World." In *Truth v. Justice: The Morality of Truth Commissions*, edited by Robert I. Rotberg and Dennis Thompson, 158–169. Princeton, NJ: Princeton University Press.

Philpott, Daniel. 2012. *Just and Unjust Wars: An Ethic of Political Reconciliation*. Oxford: Oxford University Press.

Portocarrero, Gonzalo. 2012. *Razones de sangre: Aproximaciones a la violencia política*. Lima, Perú: Pontificia Universidad Católica del Perú.

Quinn, Joanna. 2009. "Introduction." In *Reconciliation (s): Transitional Justice in Post-Conflict Societies*, edited by Joanna Quinn, 3–17. Montreal: McGill-Queen's University Press.

Richter-Devroe, Sophie. 2009. "Here Its not about Conflict Resolution – We Can Only Resist" Palestinian Women's Activism in Conflict Resolution and Non-Violent Resistance in Women and War." In *The Middle East Transnational Perspectives*, edited by Nadje Al-Ali and Nicola Pratt, 158–190. London: Zed Books.

Robins, Simon. 2012. "Challenging the Therapeutic Ethic: A Victim-Centred Evaluation of Transitional Justice Process in Timor Leste." *International Journal of Transitional Justice* 6 (1): 83–105.

Root, Rebecca. 2012. *Transitional Justice in Peru*. New York: Palgrave Macmillan.

Shaw, Rosalind. 2005. "Rethinking TRCs: Lessons from Sierra Leone." Special Report. United States Institute of Peace.

Shaw, Rosalind, and Lars Waldorf, eds. 2010. *Localizing Transitional Justice: Interventions and Priorities after Mass Violence*. Stanford, CA: Stanford University Press.

"The CVR Report." 2004. http://www.cverdad.org.pe/ingles/pagina01.php.

Theidon, Kimberly. 2000. "'How We Learned to Kill Our Brother': Memory, Morality and Reconciliation in Peru." *Bulletin del'Institut Francais d'Etudes Andines* 29 (3): 539–554.

Theidon, Kimberly. 2004. *Entre Prójimos: El Conflicto Armado Interno y la Política de la Reconciliación en el Perú*. Lima: Instituto de Estudios Peruanos.

Theidon, Kimberly. 2006. "Justice in Transition: The Micropolitics of Reconciliation in Post-War Peru." *Journal of Conflict Resolution* 50 (3): 433–457.

Theidon, Kimberly Susan. 2013. *Intimate Enemies: Violence and Reconciliation in Peru*. Philadelphia: University of Pennsylvania Press.

United Nations. 2008. "What Is Transitional Justice? A Backgrounder." http://www.un.org/en/peacebuilding/pdf/doc_wgll/justice_times_transition/26_02_2008_background_note.pdf.

OPEN ACCESS

Looking beyond the state: transitional justice and the Kurdish issue in Turkey

Joost Jongerden

ABSTRACT

Transitional justice has been promoted as an approach to peace through a strengthening of the democratic rule of law, including a recognition of the rights of victims and the promotion of trust in legal mechanisms, to deal with legacies of violence and repression. A main critique of the transitional justice approach is that it leaves untouched the injustices underlying conflict and the structural causes of abuse. This article looks at ways in which the state in Turkey applied a transitional justice approach to the Kurdish issue, focusing on how it handled the legacy of forced migration and village evacuations from the 1990s. These state remedies to deal with forced migration ignored political dimensions and continued injustices. Against this context, it is argued that the concept of self-administration as it emerged in the course of the struggle of the Kurdish movement may be considered as a form of "do-it-yourself" transitional justice.

Introduction: placing the state at a distance

It was the 14th of July 2011, and people were walking from various directions to an open field near *Batı Kent* in Diyarbakir with the music booming from huge loudspeakers, *"Diren, ha Diyarbekir, diren! / Direnmektir sana can veren!"* ("Resist, Diyarbakir, resist! / Resistance will give you life!"). The gathering of many people, young and old, women and men, was to celebrate the anniversary of the hunger strike begun by Kemal Pir, Hayri Durmuş, Akif Yılmaz and Ali Çiçek exactly 29 years before in protest against the dehumanizing prison conditions and to show the perseverance and stubbornness of the resistance by the Kurdistan Workers Party (*Partiya Karkêren Kurdistan*, PKK).

The choice of the 14th of July for the start of the hunger strike, it is said, was not random, since it was on that day in July 1789, that the people of Paris had stormed the Bastille and brought down "humanity's jail", as, "in the millions upon millions of hearts imprisoned in servitude's dark night, liberty's first dawning rose at exactly the same moment" (Jaurès 1901). The imprisoned PKK militants had aimed at sparking a light of hope for the oppressed, primarily the Kurds, then in the darkest days of military dictatorship in Turkey. It was also on that day in 2011 that the Democratic Society Congress, an assembly of local councils, from village and neighbourhood level to city and regional level which was established in 2007, announced *democratic autonomy*, a principle for self-determination and self-administration, as its main political form. Taking the form of the establishment of assemblies – at village or neighbourhood, district, city and regional levels – this self-administration was to provide both a way to define and deal with problems people faced and also a mechanism to build trust within and among communities and develop social cohesion (Jongerden and Akkaya 2013; Knapp and Jongerden 2016). It is in this context that I will discuss the idea of self-administration as a quest by the Kurdish movement to deal with legacies of violence and degradation and relate this to debates on transitional justice, in particular those concerned with the problem of state-centred and liberal approaches and the need for local participation and agency to craft a sustainable peace in a violently divided society (Lundy and McGovern 2008).

This article will first look at ways in which the state in Turkey applied a transitional justice approach to the Kurdish issue, focusing in particular on how it handled the legacy of forced migration and village evacuations from the 1990s. I will argue that transitional justice as it appeared in Turkey is problematic for two reasons. First, it evaded the political dimension of the legacies of violence and degradation by framing forced displacement as a developmental problem and ignoring the structural causes of the conflict. An important consideration in this respect is the political architecture in which Kurds have been exposed to forced assimilation and concerted efforts to destroy their cultural identity over many decades. Since its establishment in 1923, the republican regime enacted a Turkish nationalist agenda according to which cultural difference became perceived as a national threat; Kurds were denied their existence, "to the point [...] that even the Kurds themselves began to doubt their existence" (Kisanak 2015, 206).

Second, and relatedly, Turkey's transitional justice dealt with compensation of damage as an individualized transaction. State accountability was pushed to the background by a compensation mechanism that exchanged financial payment for a renunciation of the right to litigation. Moreover, so-called compensation recovery cases turned victims of the state into debtors to the state. Consequently, legal arrangements for the compensation and reparation of injustices became a form of injustice themselves. A consequence of Turkey's apparent attempts to do justice was thus that abuses continued; indeed, the rule of law did not recognize the rights of victims and nor did it promote civic trust, but sought instead the subjugation of Kurds. Finally, I argue for the importance of collective action as a means to challenge the conditions under which injustice is (re)produced and relate this to the quest for self-administration as a "do-it-yourself" form of transitional justice, a way of dealing with injustices through "self-designation and self-gathering" (Butler 2015, 170).

The case relates to debates about a reduction of rights and justice to "a reform rhetoric which ignores the root causes of human rights violations" and how this may operate "as an effective smoke screen precluding fundamental political problems from being analysed and resolved" (Cizre 2001, 59). In particular, transitional justice approaches are said to suffer from a democratic deficit insofar as they operate top-down and, deliberately or otherwise, make voices from below unheard (Lundy and McGovern 2008, 266). Hence, it was that a public acting in concert, through the idea of self-administration, came to emerge as a way "of calling into question the inchoate and powerful dimensions of reigning notions of the political" (Butler 2015, 9) and placed the (local) agency of non-state actors at the centre of transitional justice (Lundy and McGovern 2008, 266).

To begin with, I briefly explain some of the background to the conditions that resulted in the systematic denial and degradation of Kurds and the emergence of a violent conflict and argue that the violence between the state and the PKK is not the cause of "conflict" but the expression of a situation in which modern Turkey became defined on the basis of an exclusion of Kurds as a national category and rendered them disposable. The post-1999 reforms and the emergence of return and reparation schemes functioned, in practice, as new means of subjugation, in which the state aimed to create new forms of dependency. In the final section, I turn to self-administration as a mechanism for the Kurds to re-establish and re-constitute the self socially and look at how this can be considered as a form of social justice.

Background to the conflict between Turkey and the PKK

Located in the northern Middle East, Kurdistan comprises south-eastern Turkey, western Iran, northern Iraq and parts of northern Syria. After Arabs, Persians and Turks, the Kurds are the fourth largest ethnicity in western Asia, counting a population of thirty to forty million people, the largest part of which lives in Turkey, where an estimated ten to twenty million Kurds makes up between fifteen and twenty-five per cent of the total population. The seven million Kurds in Iraq constitute approximately twenty-five per cent of the population there, while the eight million Kurds in Iran and the over two million Kurds in Syria accounting for around ten per cent of the total populations of those countries. In comparison to the neighbouring Turks, Iranian and Arabs, a sense of national belonging emerged late among the Kurds (in the course of the twentieth century) and was relatively weak (politically and military). This made the Kurds a weak actor in the post-WWI/Ottoman power play that resulted in the redrawing of the Middle Eastern political map, leaving the Kurds divided by the new borders marking out Turkey, Iran, Iraq and Syria (Jongerden and Akkaya 2016).[1] In Turkey, the emergence of Kurdish nationalism was a product of the republic's establishment as a nation state. On the one hand, this nation state was composed of a state, which feels, as the novelist Elif Şafak[2] argued, as if it needed protection against its citizens and thus constantly considered its citizens as a threat; on the other hand, it was composed of the idea of the nation, a political ideology holding that these citizens have to comply to a particular cultural identity. Together, this authoritarianism and nationalism formed a despotic compound.

Turkish nationalists, employing a metaphor from the sociologist Zygmunt Bauman, considered themselves as the gardeners of the nation, with the gardener's job being to define parts of the social habitat as part of the garden and others as weeds: "Like all other weeds, they [the others] must be segregated, contained, prevented from spreading, removed and kept outside the society boundaries; if all these means prove insufficient, they must be killed", since they are a threat to the nation state (Bauman 1989, 92). One of the great ideologues of Turkish nationalism, Ziya Gökalp, formulated the gardener's job as follows in one of his most famous poems (Jongerden 2012, 80):

> The people is like a garden,
> We are supposed to be its gardeners!
> First the bad shoots are to be cut
> And then the scion is to be grafted.

The cutting of the bad shoots was enacted in several ways. The exchange of populations, seventeen of which took place in the period 1912–24, resulted in the permanent expulsion of those considered not to be part of the new nation states – Turkey, Greece and the Balkan countries – then being established. One of these exchanges, the Greco-Turkish exchange from 1922 to 1924, involved the exchange of about 1,250,000 "Greeks" in Turkey for about 400,000 "Turks" in Greece (Lados 1932; Ari 1995). The destruction of the Armenian population, too, can be understoodd in the context of the gardening process from a multi-ethnic and multi-religious empire to the "ideal" of a homogeneous nation (Ungor 2012). The crafting of the scion consisted of a range of means to "civilize" the "not-yet": those who could, but were not yet considered part of the Turkish culture. And the Kurds in Turkey were exposed to forced assimilation and concerted efforts to destroy their cultural identity over many decades (Bruinessen 1994). The problem expresses what is referred to as the "constitutive outside" (Laclau and Mouffe 2001,127–134) or "constitutive exclusion" (Butler 2015, 4), referring to those who are considered to be outside the category of "the people" and therefore possibly subject to expulsion, assimilation and murder. Consequently, those who constitute the "outside" become "differentially exposed to injury, violence and death" (Butler 2015, 33).

It was in the context of harsh repression and cultural genocide denying the space for legal political expression that the PKK emerged, between the two military coups of 1971 and 1980 (Imset 1992; Marcus 2007; Gunes 2012; Jongerden and Akkaya 2012; Gunes and Zeydanlioglu 2013). At the time, the PKK envisaged self-determination as the right of people to decide their own destiny, conceptualized in terms of the right to separate (secede) and of independent state formation. In the 2000s, and following a (self-)critique of the character of national liberation struggles and "real existing socialism", the PKK began to question the conceptualization of independence as state/nation-state construction. This result was a redefinition of its political strategy, so that now, the PKK ties self-determination not to the establishment of a state but rather to the development of people's capacities to govern themselves (Akkaya and Jongerden 2013; Saeed 2017).

In 1984, the PKK initiated a national liberation struggle. Its strategy involved the progressive development of spatial control and counter-institutions, building up forces where the state was weakest, in the peripheral countryside, but also developing urban networks. The Turkish Armed Forces (TAF) initially focused on the defence of larger villages and towns and thus allowed the PKK to establish an extended guerrilla network throughout the Southeast, thus unintentionally contributing to the fulfilment of PKK strategy. In the mid-1990s, the TAF counter-insurgency strategy was radically changed, aiming at a contraction of the rural space afforded to the PKK and a severing of ties between the rural population and the guerrilla (Jongerden 2007, 2010; Aydin and Emrence 2015; Budak 2015).

The spatial contraction was affected through a re-ordering of rural space: a matrix of control was created through permanent and mobile checkpoints and the deployment of mobile units (alongside the existing defensive and static gendarme garrisons and also paramilitary village guards, established to fight against the PKK). Enabling the supervision and regulation of movements of people and goods, this counter-insurgency re-ordering the rural space included an emptying of the countryside; a constitutive part of the new strategy was the evacuation of large areas and the forced displacement of its inhabitants, at gun-point, which came together with the destruction of villages, burning of farmers' fields and killing of livestock. Official figures confirm that over 3,000 rural settlements were thus evacuated, mostly between 1991 and 1995, with the numbers of people displaced put at 1–3 million people (Jongerden 2007, 2010). Military, paramilitary and other counter-insurgency forces – like the Gendarmerie Intelligence and Counter-

Terrorism Unit (in practice functioning as a death squad and responsible for numerous "forced disappearances") – were protected by a formally declared state of emergency that provided a shield of immunity to members of security forces and assurances that their actions would not be scrutinized (Budak 2015, 228).

Following unilateral ceasefires in 1993 and 1995, the PKK declared another on 1 September 1998. A few weeks later, on 9 October 1998, their leader, Abdullah Ocalan, was forced to leave his base, in Syria. After travelling to Greece, Italy and Russia, Ocalan travelled to Kenya with the intention of going to South Africa. There, however, he was intercepted, abducted and brought to Turkey. In the period following Ocalan's imprisonment, the PKK not only extended its ceasefire, but also, in 1999, started to withdraw its fighters from Turkey. For its turn, the Turkish government gradually lifted the state of emergency, until it was finally ended in the two remaining provinces, Diyarbakir and Şırnak, in November 2002 (Budak 2015, 230). In the years that followed, indirect and direct talks between the state and the PKK took place, notwithstanding the occasional flaring up of hostilities. In 2015, however, the Turkish government declared an end to the peace process and bombed PKK camps in Iraqi Kurdistan, leading to blanket curfews and full-fledged urban warfare in the southeast of Turkey where the younger activists in particular, many the children of the rural people displaced in the 1990s, had placed defensive barricades across the streets and claimed autonomy from the state.

Reform, return and reparation

Earlier, a gradual lifting and termination of the state of emergency had developed through a period of legal reforms that started in 1999. A tripartite periodization can be made of Turkey's reform agenda, distinguishing the "golden years" (1999–2006), a "slowing down" (2007–13) and a "backsliding" (2013–) (Müftüler-Baç 2016). Turkey's agenda for reform cannot really be said ever to have stemmed from a political will to come to terms with its "Kurdish issue", however. On the one hand, the reform agenda was related to the Turkish candidacy for EU membership (in 1999) and the opening of accession negotiations (in 2005), while, on the other hand, it was related to the struggle for power between the Islamist and neoliberal Justice and Development Party (*Adelet ve Kalkınma Partisi*, AKP), elected to power in 2002, and the secular and statist Kemalist elite. Although the AKP government was regarded internationally as a force for democratization in Turkey, its initial struggle with the nationalist elite should not be confused with a liberal pluralism, since it was rather motivated by a struggle for power (Bahcheli and Noel 2011, 104; Cinar 2011, 22). Importantly, the reform agenda generally was essentially apolitical in its formulation: "the AKP framed its policies in a technocratic way:

defending them with reference to the European Union, and not based on a deepening of the awareness that the political system in Turkey truly needed radical reforms" (Cinar 2011, 121).

The abolition of the state of emergency (in 2002) and of the death penalty[3] (2004), but also the granting of limited rights of mother-tongue education and broadcasting (2002), were initially welcomed as fragile first steps towards a possible paradigm shift of the state in respect of the Kurdish issue, one in which the security (military) approach could finally be replaced by a political approach. However, statements by AKP leaders were contradictory, swinging back and forth between mild-toned and reconciliatory to hard-line and bombastic, and a long-awaited "democratization package", announced in September 2013, came as a disappointment. In addition to freedoms like the lifting of a ban on headscarves in public institutions, the package did allow for Kurdish language education at private schools, enabled villages to return to their Kurdish names, backtracking on the old Republican Turkification programme and lifted the ban on non-Turkish alphabet letters Q, W and X, which are used in Kurdish but not Turkish; however, it made no direct reference to the Kurds or the Kurdish issue, did not indicate more extensive language reforms to come for mother-tongue (Kurdish language) education, failed to touch on the matter of changes to the Turkish Penal Code, in particular the anti-terror laws, under which thousands of Kurdish activists had been imprisoned, and did not lower the ten per cent electoral threshold. Fundamentally, the so-called democratization package was perceived as comprising just a few offerings, and without any suggestion of a future strategy for change to promote a genuine conflict resolution. In fact, the actual reforms passed by the AKP aimed primarily at extending its span of control. This had become quite clear with measures such as the judicial reform of 2014, which increased the control of the Minister of Justice over the judiciary, the exact opposite of a long-awaited move towards a more independent and impartial judiciary (Müftüler-Baç 2016, 19), and other reforms that eroded freedom of expression and the freedom of assembly.[4]

In the context of reconciliation, the drafting of a new constitution was considered an urgent task. For a settlement of the Kurdish issue in Turkey, three major changes in the constitution, a product of the 1989 military coup, were thought to be necessary:

> first, recognition and safeguarding of education in Kurdish as a mother tongue; second, amendment of the definition of citizenship based on the "Turkish" ethnic identity and its replacement with a constitutional citizenship that stands at an equal distance to all ethnic identities; and third, the empowerment of local administration. (Larrabee and Tol 2011, 150)

The drafting of a new constitution was a way to deal with the creation of Kurds as a constitutive "outside" or "exclusion" (Laclau and Mouffe 2001, 127–134;

Butler 2015, 4) therefore, through the abolition of the equation of citizenship with ethnicity and introduction of a notion of the civil and through affording people a stronger say in their own affairs, by empowering local government. The new constitution failed to address these concerns (Larrabee and Tol 2011, 150) Kurdish voices were silenced (Gunter 2013), eventually resulting in a Kurdish boycott of the constitutional referendum in September 2010.

A consequence of this failure to address Kurdish concerns was recognized as a major concern, and it was thought that "Turkey could face increasing domestic instability and violence" (Larrabee and Tol 2011, 143), a prediction that was to come true. In 2015 and 2016, blanket curfews were imposed on major Kurdish cities, enforced by tens of thousands of security personnel from different agencies (regular army, special police, state intelligence, etc.) and accompanied by the deployment of shadowy special forces, such as the "Lions of Allah Teams" (*Eseddulah Timleri*), along with heavy shelling destroying residential areas, sniper fire preventing people from getting to hospital or burying their dead, and a litany of other such rights' infringements, extending the use of rape as a weapon of terror and massacre by burning alive. Simultaneously, political opposition was suppressed and legal organizations engaged in a struggle for the "right to have rights" (Kesby 2012) were hampered, restricted and closed down, their members investigated, detained, imprisoned and even killed; MPs have been stripped of their immunity and the parliamentary party leaders arrested, municipality offices raided and their elected officials replaced by AKP trustees. The attempt to create a political space has been blocked, and on the journey to peace, the government took a violent exit.

At that time, back in 2002, one of the most pressing social problems in Turkey had been that of forced displacement and return, a transitional justice test-case for how to deal with the legacies of past violence. The issue of return had entered the political agenda in 1995, shortly after the peak in village evacuation and forced displacement. Implicitly at least, it was recognized that the depopulation of the countryside was an anomaly and return inescapable, though return was made conditional on the ability of the army to provide security. In 2001, under the responsibility of the Office of the Prime Minister, a master plan for return was drafted. The plan acknowledged that the evacuation and displacement had inflicted great pains and sorrows, yet gave no word on responsibility, and, moreover, evaluated the situation as an opportunity for the state to create a more "rational" and "vital" settlement structure. Dispersed and unproductive settlement units were to be changed into settlements units of sufficient size and potential. Therefore, it was argued that the issue was not merely one of "return" but also the creation of conditions in which the "forced migrants" could become more productive, both for themselves and for "their country".

The plan employed a narrative in which the rural (one might add "ethnic") cleansing was transformed from an *act* of involuntary exclusion – both geographic and socio-economic – into a *context* that provided opportunities for the state creation of something new. The aim of the plan was neither the restoration of property nor reparation of possessions for those whose houses and assets had been destroyed, but rather the more exalted, supra-individual objective of "rehabilitation" of "the region" (Jongerden 2007, 109). In the context of this plan, the rehabilitation did not refer to that of the displaced, but to the treatment of perceived disabilities in settlement structure, those that hampered effective administrative control and the imposition of state power. Although the government failed to facilitate a return, displaced villagers have, nevertheless, been re-migrating by their own means since 1999, and in spite of various obstacles (e.g. lack of state provision of otherwise state-provided amenities, such as water, electricity and primary-school transport services). This return was a multifaceted process leading to a new settlement structure (Jongerden 2007, 220, 280); importantly, however, it has showed how, even in the face of tremendous difficulties, people are able to self-organize their own lives.

Meanwhile, in the absence of domestic remedies for compensation for the hundreds of thousands of families and millions, even, of people who had lost their property and livelihoods, the lawyers for displaced villagers took cases to the European Court of Human Rights (ECtHR). In a landmark ruling on 29 June 2004, the ECtHR identified a structural problem with how the Turkish state had dealt with the forced displacement and called upon the government to develop a sustainable solution for those who had suffered material and non-material damage. Essentially, the court concluded that policies to facilitate return had failed and, as Kurban and Gulalp (2013, 168) noted, stressed that "effective legal remedy" required "not only the payment of compensation for the pecuniary and non-pecuniary damages of victims, but also the identification and punishment of perpetrators who committed human rights violations".[5]

Turkey was thus faced with judgements of responsibility regarding its prosecution of the war with the PKK and treatment of its own Kurdish population in addition to the payment of levels of compensation set in Strasburg (along with ongoing legal fees); with some 1,500 cases already pending, a domestic legal remedy could effectively cut off the road to the ECtHR and head off the worst of the rulings, from both a political and economic perspective (Kurban 2012, 14; Budak 2015, 233). As a result, the ECtHR ruling prompted speedy passage of the "Law on Compensation for Losses Resulting from Terrorism and the Fight against Terrorism" in Ankara, which was accepted by parliament on 17 July 2004 and came into effect on 27 July. Under this law, individuals who had suffered damage and loss as a result of "terrorist activities" or "activities as a result of the fight against terrorism" were entitled to compensation

(Budak 2015, 232). The law was supposedly intended to contribute to reinforcing trust in the state, creating cohesion between citizens and the state, and contributing to social peace – but the preamble to the law also referred to supporting the struggle against terrorism and the successes obtained by the security forces and Turkey's EU candidacy and agreements made in the context of the accession process, as well as the simple need to reduce the number of cases brought to the ECtHR. Thus, the 2014 Law on Compensation was clearly not designed to come to terms with forced migration and the Kurdish issue, but rather to block the road to justice at the ECtHR for the victims. In response to the new law, the ECtHR rejected pending cases and "reduced the notion of 'effective remedy' to compensation, overlooking the victims" demands for truth and justice and enabling Turkey to continue to commit "gross violations with impunity" (Kurban 2016, 731).

Crucially, although the domestic compensation law allowed for the state to compensate citizens for damage and loss suffered, this did not imply a political recognition of responsibility (Kurban 2012). In fact, the law enabled the state to redefine the results of its policy of forced displacement in terms of responsibilities to individuals with whom it entered into an economic agreement; it separated the question of compensation for damage and loss from that of political and social responsibility, producing, in effect, victims without perpetrators. This was not in accordance with the ECtHR ruling, but calibrated rather to the EU reform agenda. The EU reform agenda had a bias towards the future and did not involve accountability for past crimes, such as requiring the identification and prosecution of those responsible for human rights' violations (Budak 2015, 230).

From a quantitative perspective, the instalment of a domestic mechanism to deal with forced migration looks impressive. According to the information of the Ministry of Internal Affairs, a total of 366,782 claims had been filed up until 9 June 2015, with 342,954 concluded, 183,139 being accepted by the commissions and 159,635 rejected. A total of almost 3.4 billion Turkish Lira (TL) had been paid as compensation, at an average of 18,558 TL per claim (about 6,200 Euros).[6] But there is also criticism, with doubts about the fairness of damage assessments and concerns about exclusionary rules. Human Rights Watch (2006) has stated that the government failed to provide fair compensation to the mainly Kurdish villagers displaced in the military's counter-insurgency campaign. It also reported several injustices in the practices of the damage assessment commissions. These have included the manipulation of house prices to reduce property values by calculating house values on the basis of values for cowsheds – the commissions arbitrarily reduced valuations by placing a ceiling on the maximum compensation for damage to houses, outhouses and barns; and the value of land holdings was underestimated, stock being excluded and compensation or assistance already received exaggerated (Human Rights Watch 2006, 20–29). Further to these, the lack of transparency, the nature of the evidence required and the high number of rejections (forty-three per cent of concluded cases) were also considered problematic (Kurban 2012; Budak 2015, 234). In its *Roadmap for a Solution to the Kurdish Question*, the Turkish NGO TESEV (Turkish Economic and Social Studies Foundation) called upon the establishment of an administrative appeal mechanism "to inspect the decisions of the damage assessment commissions, especially the refusals" (TESEV 2008, 10). Moreover, "Adding insult to injury, in some areas villagers themselves [were] obliged to finance the operation of the provincial damage assessment commissions", expenses that were "substantial" (Human Rights Watch 2006, 20).

In addition to a lack of fairness, six rules that were applied resulted in the exclusion of compensation. The first one was the single person rule, which disqualified persons who ran a single household at the time of displacement. This also implied that people who had married using a customary religious marriage arrangement and did not have a civil marriage were excluded from compensation. The second was that people with children born outside the village after 1987 were considered to be economic migrants and not victims of forced displacement and therefore did not receive compensation. The third exclusionary rule was that all those displaced prior to 19 July 1987 were treated as economic migrants. Fourth was the "closure of conflict rule", implying that losses resulting from inaccessibility of the village and land after 1999 were excluded from compensation (Human Rights Watch 2006, 29–32). Fifth was that non-pecuniary damage was excluded from compensation, and the sixth rule excluded from compensation all those convicted under the anti-terror law (Budak 2015, 233).

Repair and compensation as subjugation

The issue of repair and compensation has been more than one of shortcomings, failings or imperfections. In *Haunted by Debt*, Zerrin Özlem Biner argues that the state has used "legal devices to transform reparative justice mechanisms into debt-producing mechanisms that create new compulsory bonds between the state and Kurdish citizens" (2016, 1). Legally, the damage commissions proposed "friendly settlements", with those entering into them accepting "the legal closure of their files with respect to the injuries that they suffered under the emergency rule between 1987 and 2004", the period covered by the compensation law, and thereby renouncing all rights to any further litigation (Biner 2016). The settlement has functioned as an exchange of money for the right of the displaced to initiate any legal procedures related to their case that may have led to a trial. Given that these were mostly impoverished people placed in a precarious situation as a result of the displacement and appropriation of rights, this may be considered as abusive.

In Turkey's dealing with the past, there have been not only the "friendly settlements" but also "compensation recovery cases", including those cases in which compensation was paid to members of security forces for injuries and losses. The costs for these compensations are recovered from third parties, who are held accountable for the loss and injury. Once identity is established, the third party is required to reimburse the state with the amount of the compensation paid to the security officer (with interest and court expenses). If the third party is deceased, the state claims the amount from his/her family, who is held responsible for the debt on the basis of Inheritance Law. Biner (2016, 4) claims that while the compensation law's friendly settlement erases the accountability of the state by exchanging money for a renunciation of the right to litigation, "the compensation recovery cases create an unmovable and permanent relation between the state and families of the dead militant as the inheritors of punishment in the form of debt". In the context of the compensation law and friendly settlement, no local government officials or members of the security forces "were imprisoned for violent acts that caused the destruction of the environment and lives of Kurdish citizens" (Biner 2016, 4). The families of local government officials and security forces were not hold "responsible for the compensation paid to the Kurdish citizens who applied for and received compensation in exchange of the loss that they incurred during the conflict"; yet Kurdish citizens *were* held responsible for the acts of relatives and held liable for the recovery of compensation paid.

> As the rule of inheritance became the key component of this forced contract, its renunciation became the only clear path to escape the obligation of this bond. In other words, the erasure of the legal debt was conditioned on the parent's renunciation of their bond with their child. The debtor-creditor relationship would be voided through the legal dissolution of the parent-child relationship. The state was offering another opportunity for closure by forcing the families to disown their children, which would in turn mean disowning their connections to themselves. (Biner 2016, 5)

The "compensation recovery cases" thus became the application of symbolic violence, in which victims either entered into a debtor relation with the state or had to renounce the bonds with their children.

Transitional justice beyond the state

With the process of rehabilitation, and repair and compensation, we have seen how (i) the issue of forced migration was disentangled from the Kurdish issue and re-established as a technical problem of (rural) development (Ayata and Yükseker 2005; Jongerden 2007), and how (ii) injustices and violations inflicted on a group were transformed into individualized cases of compensation under the disguise of a "friendly settlement" to preclude litigation and subjugate through the mechanism of debt (Biner 2016). Simultaneously, repressive measures were and continue to be employed in response to the expression of Kurdish identity and the quest for proper civil rights and citizenship motivated by what was and still is regarded as an existential threat to the Republic, and it was in this context that various incidents created the occasion for the state to denounce the Kurdish movement as a whole and discontinue so-called peace process purportedly aimed at resolving the issue.

This seems to be the reverse of a transitional justice approach, referring to the application of the rule of law in transition processes from authoritarian to democratic regimes, and which, in recent years, has emerged as a widely favoured way of addressing legacies of violence and violations in the context of armed conflicts. Yet even the more usual transitional justice approach, it is argued, inherently suffers from a democratic deficit. What is at stake is the issue of agency, or who initiates and controls change (Lundy and McGovern 2008, 273, 275). In this context, the importance of an emancipatory approach, of social struggles that challenge the conditions under which repression is reproduced and collective action to overcome this, places agency at the centre of transitional justice. This constitutes transitional justice less in legal terms than in social practices and "the ability of local people to define local obstacles or problems, conceptualise, initiate, design and implement programs to address these problems" (Lundy and McGovern 2008, 281). There is a need to think outside the legalistic and state-oriented box, and, rather than privileging state agencies, international institutions, law and legal expertise, focus on popular programmes through which collective action and the raising of consciousness, especially a moral consciousness – "consciencisation" – becomes the means through which people confront the condition of oppression and abuse (Lundy and McGovern 2008, 280, 292). This is why concerns such as return and compensation in relation to the Kurdish issue in Turkey should be dealt with as a socio-political issue.

At the heart of the political issue is the demarcation between those who are considered the people and those who are considered a dangerous and disposable population (Butler 2015, 4); ultimately, this results in a questioning of the very foundation of the state itself. The inquiry into the constitutive exclusion is an act of saying and an act of doing that both exposes the exclusion but also challenges it. Following Butler (2015, 11), we may say that the possibility of establishing people as people, as citizens, is dependent on (i) the capacity to speak and to be heard and (ii) the capacity to appear, to become visible and to be seen by others. So, democratic struggle is not only about the possibility of using language for the formulation of alternatives; it is also about the possibility of assembling for a self-expression in the public domain, and, relatedly, the right to appear and be visible, again, publically (Butler 2015). Indeed, this is fundamentally, since without appearance and voice, how can any communication about alternatives even begin? Thus, Merrifield (2014) refers to the need for places of encounter, for places where people who have been silenced – the "shadow citizenry" – can appear and bring into focus the politically induced conditions of their exclusion.

One of the responses of the Kurdish movement to the intransigence of state power was the development and declaration of self-administration. This was a way in which the Kurdish movement attempted to re-establish itself as a political movement, in which people tried to shape and organize the physical and social infrastructures of their lives. In other words, self-administration was developed as a way to act politically in a situation of structural oppression. In 2011 and 2012, the Kurdish movement started a campaign around a Kurdish language slogan, "I am here" (*Ez li vir im*). Gülten Kışanak, then co-chair of the party and in 2014 elected as Mayor of Diyarbakir, stated:

> When we initiated this campaign we thought of the following. This system, this state, the mentality of the AKP imposes surrender on us, it wishes to strike fear in us through violence and repression. They wish to intimidate and scare everyone. If that is the case then we must show them that we are not scared. If that is the case then we all must say "I am here", I am right in front before you and I continue to resist. (2015, 212)

The key to these actions as expressions of the principle of self-administration lies, in the words of Butler (2015, 58), "in the acting, laying claim to the power one requires … [to] secure the conditions of existence". This can be linked to what is referred to as in debates on transitional justice as the ability of people to define obstacles or problems and then to act on these (Lundy and McGovern 2008, 281). Self-administration, or democratic autonomy as it is referred to in the Kurdish movement, is people acting in concert, and calling into question reigning and violent notions of the political (Butler 2015, 9). It placed the (local) agency of non-state actors at the centre of transitional justice (Lundy and McGovern 2008, 266). As such, this relates to the creation of a form of justice beyond the state (Jongerden and Akkaya 2013; Mauer and Staal 2015; Yarkin 2015).

Self-administration had been already practised for several years since the mid-2000s at a developmental level, sometimes under huge duress (Casier, Jongerden, and Walker 2011). By the end of 2015, the dimension of self-defence came to the fore, when youngsters started to dig ditches as barricades in response to threats, security operations and eventually the full-fledged urban war we have seen in several cities in the southeast of Turkey, particularly in Diyarbakir (the Sur district), Cizre (Cudi, Nur and Yafes), Nusaybin and Şırnak but also in other cities, notably, Silopi, Silvan and Yüksekova. The basic level of self-administration is the neighbourhood council, a local participatory (non-representative) government structure. The main activities in which the councils were engaged before the state military interventions in 2015 and 2016 were oriented towards education, social safety and poverty and could be described under the headings of "mediation" and "community development". Regarding their educational work, the councils organized courses for the youth (in music, theatre, drawing, etc.) and provided information and instruction on, among other things, gender equality and women's rights. A neighbourhood council in the city of Diyarbakır, where many forced migrants settled, was involved in the establishment of the first school at which Kurdish was the language of instruction (the Ferzad Kemanger Primary School in the Bağlar neighbourhood), and, in doing so, engaged in a form of direct action that went beyond just demanding the right to education in Kurdish from the state to actually realizing it. Such activities are to be regarded as countering the social and cultural deprivation effects of a repressive state regime. One could say that this has nothing to do with transitional justice, and, indeed, it is not directly concerned with "law" even, but all these activities have to be understood in the context of decades of denial and degradation. Indeed, this is how people re-establish themselves as citizens, and collectively deal with legacies of violence and degradation.

Final remarks

Transitional justice is considered a successful way of dealing with legacies of violence and repression through the strengthening of democratic rule of law. Crucially, transitional justice is thought to promote trust in legal mechanisms and a recognition of the rights of victims of violence and abuses. Yet an important critique of this approach is that it leaves untouched injustices underlying conflict and (thus) the structural causes of abuse. This has been discussed here by looking at the ways in which the state in Turkey applied its transitional justice to the Kurdish issue, focusing on how it dealt with the legacy of forced migration and village evacuations from the 1990s, when some 3,000 rural settlements were forcedly evacuated and burned. I have argued that the so-called rehabilitation programme was not concerned with the social re-establishment of the disrupted lives of the displaced villagers but with the treatment of perceived shortcomings in human geography, namely, a dispersed settlement structure that supposedly hampered effective administrative control and the imposition of state power. Moreover, the rehabilitation programme was framed as a development imperative, disentangling the issue of forced migration from the Republic's Kurdish issue and re-establishing it as a technical problem of (rural) development. In this process, as contextualized by the Law on Compensation, injustices and violations inflicted on Kurds as a group were transformed into individualized cases of compensation, which, under the disguise of a "friendly settlement", precluded litigation and yet further oppressed through a mechanism of debt. Thus, both rehabilitation and compensation have effectively functioned as instruments of subjugation and control of the victims of violence and abuses, enabling impunity for perpetrators and providing a legalistic smoke screen allowing structural problems to go unanalysed, unspoken in the normative/hegemonic public discourse and thus unrecognized. It was in this context that I discussed the attempt to create assemblies for local self-administration as fundamental to the recovery of a sense of humanity (Harvey 2014, 272). This is "do-it-yourself" transitional justice, a way in which, against a background of denial and degradation, a sense of self and community is being re-established.

Notes

1. See for a discussion of Kurdish nationalism (Bruinessen 1978; Olson 1989; Jwaideh 2006; Gunes 2012).
2. See the interview with Elif Şafak in Der Spiegel, http://www.spiegel.de/international/world/turkish-author-elif-shafak-on-society-under-erdogan-a-1066223.html.
3. For the Kurdish movement this was a key-issue, since it feared that Turkey would sentence Ocalan to death.
4. See https://freedomhouse.org/report/freedom-press/2015/turkey and https://www.hrw.org/report/2014/09/29/turkeys-human-rights-rollback/recommendations-reform.
5. See the case of Dogan and Others v. Turkey http://www.refworld.org/pdfid/414d86ab4.pdf
6. http://www.illeridaresi.gov.tr/5233-sayili-kanun-uygulanmasi-istatistikleri.

Disclosure statement

No potential conflict of interest was reported by the author.

References

Akkaya, A. H., and J. Jongerden. 2013. "Confederalism and Autonomy in Turkey: The Kurdistan Workers' Party and the Reinvention of Democracy." In *The Kurdish Question in Turkey: New Perspectives on Violence, Representation and Reconciliation*, edited by C. Gunes and W. Zeydanlioglu, 186–204. London: Routlede.

Ari, K. 1995. *Büyük Mübadele Türkiye'ye Zorunlu Göç 1923–1925*. Istanbul: Tarih Vakfi Yurt Yayinlari.

Ayata, B., and D. Yükseker. 2005. "A Belated Awakening: National and International Responses to the Internal Displacement of Kurds in Turkey." *New Perspectives on Turkey* 32: 5–42.

Aydin, A., and C. Emrence. 2015. *Zones of Rebellion, Kurdish Insurgents and the Turkish State*. Ithaca: Cornell University Press.

Bahcheli, T., and S. Noel. 2011. "The Justice and Development Party and the Kurdish Question." In *Nationalisms and Politics in Turkey: Political Islam, Kemalism and the Kurdish Issue*, edited by M. Casier and J. Jongerden, 101–120. London: Routledge.

Bauman, Z. 1989. *Modernity and the Holocaust*. Cambridge: Polity Press.

Biner, Z. O. 2016. "Haunted by Debt: Calculating the Cost of Loss and Violence in Turkey." *Theory & Event* 19 (1): 1–6.

Bruinessen, M. V. 1978. *Agha, Shaikh and State: On the Social and Political Organization of Kurdistan*. Utrecht: Proefschrift.

Bruinessen, M. V. 1994. "Genocide in Kurdistan? The Suppression of the Dersim Rebellion in Turkey (1937–38) and the Chemical War Against the Iraqi Kurds (1988)." In *Conceptual and Historical Dimensions of Genocide*, edited by G. J. Andreopoulus, 141–170. Philadelphia: University of Pennsylvania Press.

Budak, Y. 2015. "Dealing with the Past: Transitional Justice, Ongoing Conflict and the Kurdish Issue in Turkey." *International Journal of Transitional Justice* 9: 219–238.

Butler, J. 2015. *Notes Towards a Performative Theory of Assembly*. Cambridge: Harvard University Press.

Casier, M., J. Jongerden, and N. Walker. 2011. "Fruitless Attempts? The Kurdish Initiative and Containment of the Kurdish Movement in Turkey." *New Perspectives on Turkey* 44: 103–127.

Cinar, M. 2011. "Turkey's Present Ancien Regime and the Justice and Development Party." In *Nationalisms and Politics in Turkey: Political Islam, Kemalism and the Kurdish Issue*, edited by M. Casier and J. Jongerden, 11–27. London: Routledge.

Cizre, U. 2001. "The Truth and Fiction About (Turkey's) Human Rights Politics." *Human Rights Review* 3 (1): 55–77.

Gunes, C. 2012. *The Kurdish National Movement in Turkey: From Protest to Resistance*. London: Routledge.

Gunes, C., and W. Zeydanlioglu. 2013. *The Kurdish Question in Turkey: New Perspectives on Violence, Representation and Reconciliation*. London: Routlede.

Gunter, M. 2013. "Reopening Turkey's Closed Kurdish Opening?" *Middle East Policy* 20 (2): 88–98.

Harvey, D. 2014. *Seventen Contradictions and the End of Capitalism*. Oxford: Oxford University Press.

Human Rights Watch. 2006. *Unjust, Restrictive, and Inconsistent: The Impact of Turkey's Compensation Law with Respect to Internally Displaced People*. New York: Human Rights Watch.

Imset, I. G. 1992. *The PKK: A Report on Seperatist Violence in Turkey*. Ankara: Turkish Daily News.

Jaurès, J. 1901. "History of the French Revolution." https://www.marxists.org/archive/jaures/1901/history/july-14.htm.

Jongerden, J. 2007. *The Settlement Issue in Turkey and the Kurds: an Analysis of Spatial Policies, Modernity and War*. Leiden & Boston: Brill.

Jongerden, J. 2010. "Village Evacuation and Reconstruction in Kurdistan." *Etudes Rurales* (186): 77–100.

Jongerden, J. 2012. "Elite Encounters of a Violent Kind: Milli Ibrahim Pasa, Ziya Gökalp and Political Struggle in Diyarbekir at the end of the 20th Century." In *Social Relations in Ottoman Diyarbekir, 1870–1915*, edited by J. Jongerden and J. Verheij, 55–84. Leiden: Brill.

Jongerden, J., and A. H. Akkaya. 2012. "The Kurdistan Workers Party and a New Left in Turkey: Analysis of the Revolutionary Movement in Turkey Through the PKK's Memorial Text on Haki Karer." *European Journal of Turkish Studies* (14).

Jongerden, J., and A. H. Akkaya. 2013. "Democratic Confederalism as a Kurdish Spring: the PKK and the Quest for Radical Democracy." In *The Kurdish Spring: Geopolitical Changes and the Kurds*, edited by M. Ahmet and M. Gunter, 163–185. Costa Mesa: Mazda.

Jongerden, J., and A. H. Akkaya. 2016. "Kurds and the PKK." In *The Wiley Blackwell Encyclopedia of Race, Ethnicity, and Nationalism*, edited by J. Stone, R. M. Dennis, P. S. Rizova, A. D. Smith and X. Hou. London: Wiley Blackwell.

Jwaideh, W. 2006. *The Kurdish National Movement: Its Origins and Development*. New York: Syracuse University Press.

Kesby, A. 2012. *The Right to Have Rights: Citizenship, Humanity, and International Law*. Oxford: Oxford University Press.

Kışanak, G. 2015. *Democratic Politics as an Alternative in Turkey*. Cologne: Network for an Alternative Quest.

Knapp, M., and J. Jongerden. 2016. "Communal Democracy: The Social Contract and Confederalism in Rojava." *Comparative Islamic Studies* 10 (1): 87–109.

Kurban, D. 2012. *Reperations and Displacement in Turkey: Lessons Learned from the Compensation Law*. Brookings Institute.

Kurban, D. 2016. "Forsaking Individual Justice: The Implications of the European Court of Human Rights' Pilot Judgment Procedure for Victims of Gross and Systematic Violations." *Human Rights Law Review* 16 (4): 731–769.

Kurban, D., and H. Gulalp. 2013. "A Complicated Affair: Turkey's Kurds and the European Court of Human Rights." In *The European Court of Human Rights: Implementing Strasbourg's Judgments on Domestic Policy*, edited by D. Anagnostou, 166–187. Edinburh: Edinburgh University Press.

Laclau, E., and C. Mouffe. 2001. *Hegemony and Socialist Strategy: Towards a Radical Democratic Politics*. London: Verso.

Lados, S. P. 1932. *The Exchange of Minorities: Bulgaria, Greece, and Turkey*. New York: MacMillan Company.

Larrabee, F. S., and G. Tol. 2011. "Turkey's Kurdish Challenge." *Survival: Global Politics and Strategy* 54 (4): 143–152.

Lundy, P., and M. McGovern. 2008. "Whose Justice: Rethinking Transitional Justice from the Borrom up." *Jorunal of Law and Society* 35 (2): 265–292.

Marcus, A. 2007. *Blood and Belief: the PKK and the Kurdish Fight for Independence*. New York & London: New York University Press.

Mauer, R. in der and J. Staal, eds. 2015. *Stateless Democracy*. Utrecht: BAK.

Merrifield, A. 2014. "The Shadow Citizenry." Open Security.

Müftüler-Baç, M. 2016. *Judicial Reform in Turkey and the EU's Political Conditionality: (Mis)Fit Between Domestic Preferences and EU Demands*. Berlin: Freie Universität Berlin.

Olson, R. 1989. *The Emergence of Kurdish Nationalism and the Sheikh Said Rebellion, 1880–1925*. Austin: University of Texas Press.

Saeed, S. 2017. *Kurdish Politics in Turkey: From the PKK to the KCK*. London: Routledge.

TESEV. 2008. *Roadmap for a Solution to the Kurdish Question, Policy proposals from the Region for the Government Istanbul*, TESEV.

Ungor, U. U. 2012. "Disastrous Decade: Armenians and Kurds in the Young Turk Era, 1915–25." In *Social Relations in Ottoman Diyarbekir, 1870–1915*, edited by J. Jongerden and J. Verheij, 267–295. Leiden: Brill.

Yarkin, G. 2015. "The Ideological Transformation of the PKK Regarding the Political Economy of the Kurdish Region in Turkey." *Kurdish Studies* 3 (1): 26–46.

Towards transitional justice? Black reparations and the end of mass incarceration

Desmond S. King and Jennifer M. Page

ABSTRACT
There are many commonalities between the goals of transitional justice and domestic redress movements. We look at the movement for reparations for enslavement and Jim Crow in the United States as an example of a domestic reparations movement, and argue for the usefulness of the concept of transitional justice. We are particularly interested in showing that a future democratic transition – the end of mass incarceration – could animate a renewed push for reparations and a formal investigation into America's legacy of racial injustice.

Domestic reparations movements – which consist of citizens pressuring their own governments for acknowledgment, accountability, and symbolic and material redress – share many common aims with transitional justice. As with domestic reparations movements, transitional justice seeks to directly address past abuses, and rails against the tendency in politics to "forget and move on" (Crocker 1998, 495). Neither transitional justice practitioners nor domestic reparations activists tend to see standalone apologies as enough; concrete actions must be taken to demonstrate accountability for the past.

It is perhaps surprising that, in spite of overlaps such as these, domestic reparations movements have not made greater use of the concept of transitional justice in framing their case for acknowledgment and redress. In this article, we look at the movement for reparations for enslavement and Jim Crow in the United States – sometimes called the "black reparations movement" (Darby 2010) – as an example of a domestic reparations movement that could reasonably frame its case in terms of transitional justice.[1]

The essay proceeds as follows. In section one, we discuss the theory of transitional justice and how it can be understood as applicable to continuous political regimes. In section two, we discuss the black reparations movement in the United States. Section three draws a contrast between remedial justice and transitional justice. Finally, section four considers the end of mass incarceration as a future transitional moment that could spur the payment of reparations and a formal investigation into America's legacy of racial injustice.

Contextualizing transitional justice

First used in 1991, the terminology of "transitional justice" was proposed by Ruti Teitel as a way of thinking about then-recent transitions to democracy in Latin America and the dissolution of the Soviet Union. Teitel's aim was, in her own words, to "account for the self-conscious construction of a distinctive conception of justice associated with periods of radical political change following past oppressive rule" (Teitel 2014, 3). Transitional justice was conceived in order to think through a unique set of practical challenges faced by post-conflict societies: How to deal with those who carried out atrocities on behalf of the previous regime? Punishment or impunity? What about colluders? What is owed to the victims?

Instruments typically associated with transitional justice include truth commissions, reparations, and criminal prosecutions. As Jon Elster (2004) argues, though the language of transitional justice is recent, its particular challenges and methods are ancient, going back to the days of Athenian democracy. It is thus not anachronistic to think about what transitional justice may have required following times of political upheaval and formal regime change before the late twentieth century.

Times of political upheaval and formal regime change are not necessarily the same, however. On one view of transitional justice, it is reserved for the most extraordinary of domestic political events: when an oppressive government is toppled through war or revolution, and a new democratic regime claims the right to rule. Understood thusly, transitional justice is a time-limited set of practices designed to close the books on the previous political era (see Williams and Nagy 2012, 20–21). Yet the question arises, is transitional justice relevant to continuous domestic political constitutions? Is it a formal regime change that triggers transitional justice measures, or is it the presence of atrocities?

These questions came up recently when the United States Department of State issued a white paper advocating truth commissions and other forms of transitional justice for societies with legacies of "large-scale and often systematic atrocities" (US Department of State 2016). In the *New York Times*, Anand Giridharadas writes about contacting the State Department to see whether the white paper was intended to apply to the domestic United

States, particularly with regard to its legacy of enslavement and segregation. The spokesperson's initial reply was evasive, and to Giridharadas' subsequent question as to whether "the United States in fact fits the description of a country transitioning out of conflict", the State Department responded: "I won't have anything further for you" (Giridharadas 2016). As Giridharadas' framing of the matter suggests, there is rhetorical and moral power in using the language of transitional justice in the context of the United States. Doing so invites comparison between the US and other "emerging" democracies, and implicitly challenges the longstanding tendency to think of the US as an "established" democracy – indeed, as one of the oldest in the world.

That the United States is a country that has leveraged "large-scale and often systematic atrocities" on its black population – and therefore is a country to which transitional justice is relevant – is argued for by Andrew Valls (2003). As Valls reasons, there have been at least two periods in US history that fit our standard understanding of democratic regime transitions. The first occurred during the Reconstruction period, following upon the upheaval of the Civil War and the transition from the atrocities of chattel slavery to the democratizing Thirteenth and Fourteenth Amendments (Valls 2003; see also Teitel 2000, 152–157). The second transition took place during the Civil Rights era. Marked by the passage of the Civil Rights Act (1964) and the Voting Rights Act (1965), this transition saw the end of Jim Crow and the abuses inherent in "Black Codes", enforced by the lynch mob. As Valls writes:

> In both cases the state … enforced racial subordination and permitted private citizens to violate the human rights of members of the subordinated class with impunity. In both cases, equal protection of the law and equal political representation were denied. In both cases, the state and society at large then underwent a transformation in which governmental policy shifted to no longer practicing the systematic violation of basic human rights of its racially subordinated populations … . (Valls 2003, 61)

Valls argues that without satisfying minimum levels of transitional justice, democratic transitions may remain incomplete. During the US's two major transitions, the basic mechanisms of transitional justice – prosecuting individuals who committed atrocities, setting the historical record straight about the abuses that occurred, and paying redress to the victims – were neglected.

Since the Reconstruction period, African Americans have pushed for the United States Government to pay reparations for enslavement and segregation. The language of transitional justice has never been explicitly employed as central to the black reparations movement, though this movement was active in the 1990s and beyond. Yet the idea of incomplete transitional justice has untapped potential in making the case for reparations. Let us turn to the black reparations movement.

Black reparations in the United States: judicial vs. legislative strategies

In the United States, reparations activists have pushed for redress for freedmen and women, and later on for the descendants of the enslaved, both in the courts and by legislative means. In this section, we provide a brief overview of the activities of the multi-generation black reparations movement through the lens of these two strategies.

The judicial route

How African Americans have used the courts to challenge unjust laws and political formations is well-known. Less familiar is the use of the courts as a means of seeking reparations. During Reconstruction and beyond, groups of freedpersons pressured the government to provide monetary relief to the formerly enslaved. The most prominent of these groups, the National Ex-Slave Mutual Relief, Bounty, and Pension Association, employed the clever tactic of suing the government for the amount that it had collected in taxes on cotton. *Johnson v. McAdoo* was heard by the Supreme Court in 1917, but in a short opinion, the majority justices affirmed the lower court's ruling that sovereign immunity – i.e. the common law principle that a political subject cannot sue the government without the latter's consent – barred the case (Berry 2005).

In more recent times, members of a group called the National Coalition of Blacks for Reparations in America (N'COBRA), founded in 1988 by Imari Obadele and Adjoa Aiyetoro, have pursued reparations in the courts (Berry 2005, 244). The 1995 case *Cato v. United States* sought reparations to slave descendants for the

> forced, ancestral indoctrination into a foreign society; kidnapping of ancestors from Africa; forced labor; breakup of families; removal of traditional values; deprivations of freedom; and imposition of oppression, intimidation, miseducation and lack of information about various aspects of their indigenous character,

as well as an official apology. In litigated reparations cases, an expired statute of limitations is often an insurmountable barrier, but the *Cato* plaintiffs argued that no statute of limitations should apply based on the continuing violations doctrine: "African Americans are still subjected to the badges and indicia of slavery". The 9th Circuit justices did not dispute this claim per se, but found that sovereign immunity barred the case, as it had for its 1917 predecessor (Aiyetoro 2001).

The plaintiffs' argument that they faced a continuous violation of their rights created a new obstacle: the standing doctrine (Aiyetoro 2001). According to the standing doctrine, the basis for challenging the government must be that the repeated enforcement of an unconstitutional law would bring about a foreseeable future injury to the plaintiff. This means a current law or government practice must be causally linked to a *particular* injury which the *plaintiff herself* is in danger of experiencing; standing prevents a plaintiff from pursuing relief for others without their knowledge. The court found that *Cato* was unable to surmount this requirement: "Cato proceeds on a generalized, class-based grievance", and did not name a "concrete, personal injury that is not abstract and that is fairly traceable to the government conduct that she challenges as unconstitutional". This not only applied to the claim for monetary redress, but also to Cato's seeking an apology, ruled the court.

In addition to *Cato*, N'COBRA affiliates have pursued redress against companies that used slave labour, illegally sold insurance policies on the lives of the enslaved, and accepted the latter as collateral on loans. The opinions in these cases underscore the mismatch between the motivating ambitions of the lawsuits and the narrow legal standards used by courts. "There is no way to determine that a given black American today is worse off by a specific, calculable sum of money (or monetized emotional harm) as a result of the conduct of one or more of the defendants", ruled the court in the consolidated case *In re African American Slave Descendants Litigation* (2006). It went on to equate the case to a hypothetical one in which a descendant of a fallen Union soldier sues present-day gun manufacturers whose historical predecessors illegally sold munitions to the Confederacy.

In spite of outcomes like this, it makes sense why the claimants would have wanted to pursue reparations judicially. Pessimism that white public opinion would ever favour Congressional legislation for reparations is understandable, and rolling the dice for an activist liberal judge would seem to be a better bet. But it is nevertheless a time-honoured lawyerly custom to try to bypass the unruly masses, whose indoctrinated ideologies and self-serving beliefs impede progress, in order to secure social change through the courts (Unger 1996). Indeed, N'COBRA co-founder Adjoa Aiyetoro and Deadria Farmer-Paellmann, organizer and lead plaintiff in the corporate redress lawsuits, are both law professors.

The strategy of pursuing reparations through the courts has a parallel in post-Civil Rights era workplace affirmative action and school desegregation efforts. Both affirmative action and school desegregation were remedial social policies based in judicial mandates, rather than in legislation. Affirmative action began as an administrative invention, and expanded under the oversight of judges in its heyday (King and Smith 2011; Skrentny 1996). It is significant that debate over affirmative action was heated, and white opposition strong, with critics charging "reverse racism". School desegregation, like affirmative action, came from above, for the most part mandated by federal courts. Again, there was significant opposition. White students resisted integration by harassing black newcomers with racist slurs and forms of physical violence (see, e.g. Beals 1994/2007, chap. 7), and parents were quick to move their children to new school districts or enrol them in private school (Clotfelter 2004).

Given the high stakes, the course of action taken by the courts – "legislating from the bench" though it may have been – was reasonable (cf. Brooks 1996, 104–108). At issue was the second-class citizenship of African Americans, and if the government had waited for a strong contingency of whites to favour race-conscious remedial policies, the danger was that whites would never come around. Yet a bill up for debate in Congress would have provided an opportunity for anti-affirmative action and anti-integration whites to publicly air their positions.[2] When public debate emerges in anticipation of a major legislative decision, rather than as a response to a judicial ruling that has been handed down, the outcome is more likely to be seen and accepted as legitimate by those who disagree with it (Waldron 2006).

The position that decisions of great moral importance should be determined by the legislature is known as the "political question doctrine", a common subject in American debates over judicial review. The appellate justices invoked the political question doctrine explicitly in *In re African American Slave Descendants Litigation*, citing prior cases which "simply exceeded judicial capabilities".

The legislative route

The driving force behind contemporary slavery reparations lawsuits has been a fundamental concern with justice, regardless of white acceptance of the cause (Ogletree 2004, 14). But it would be a missed opportunity if reparations were paid, and afterwards there were no differences in racial power relations. In this regard, legislative redress – the other major strategy pursued by the black reparations movement – has natural potential. H.R. 40 is a bill that Representative John Conyers, who is black, has introduced every Congressional session since 1989, proposing to set up a committee to study proposals for reparations.[3] Its title a reference to the failed post-Civil War promise of "forty acres and a mule" to freedpersons, the bill has never been taken seriously enough to make it out of committee. As Representative Conyers emphasizes, the bill is moderate in that it is fundamentally a study bill: "We study the water, the air. We can't even study the issue? This bill does not authorize one red cent to anyone" (Coates 2014).

Compared to a court-ordered reparations payment, legislative redress has a better chance of being seen as the outcome of a debate over which the American public has some, if not total, ownership (Westley 1998). Of course, it is not likely that this debate would be wholly salutary. Japanese Americans were successful in obtaining internment reparations through Congress (after a failed attempt in the courts) in spite of having inspired the formation of anti-redress organizations like "Americans for Historical Accuracy" (Henry 2003). A recent poll has shown a spike in support among millennials for black reparations (Holland 2016), and this piece of information alone has triggered scorn from the right. "Young people are spoon-fed garbage from academia and the media that somehow blacks are under the boot of a racially biased system, an idea that is totally anti-intellectual", as one web commentator wrote (Girdusky 2016). If H.R. 40's passage were imminent, we might expect a flurry of pointed opposition, and even increases in activity among white supremacist groups, confederate flag displays, and hate incidents. At the same time, backlash is expected given the bill's overall message – indeed, it bears out the urgency of the message – *viz.*, a historical legacy that includes enslavement and Jim Crow is still with us today.

The black reparations movement is not monolithic, but support for H.R. 40 is wide-ranging. N'COBRA backs H.R. 40, as does the NAACP, which "strongly supports" the bill (McCoy 2014).[4] In addition, there have been forays into a deliberate campaign to build greater support for the proposal, combining the efforts of individual groups dedicated to the cause of black reparations and other pro-reparations community organizations. N'COBRA has held numerous reparations events; Chicago Alderman Dorothy Tillman hosted multiple conferences on the topic; and a 2004 National Reparations Congress in Compton, California drew representatives from 50 organizations. Yet these efforts have not resulted in the broad mainstream support, even among black people, that Clarence Munford once conceived of as necessary – albeit before the dawn of the present Black Lives Matter movement:

> Reparations slogans and buzzwords must become household words across black America. We must put our issues and topics on every African American lip. Thereby we may hope to regenerate the mass black liberation movement that has languished in suspended animation since the 1970s. (Munford 2007, 447; see also Howard-Hassmann 2004)

In this vein, Manning Marable (2004, 4) considers "convincing black people, not whites, that we can actually win" to be "the greatest challenge" of black reparations. Perhaps this is overstated. In spite of the uptick in millennial support, whites are staunchly opposed to reparations. A 2004 study found that 96 per cent of whites were against black reparations (Dawson and Popoff 2004). The same 2016 poll that broke down support for reparations by age found that 81 per cent of whites were opposed to reparations – an improvement, but far from majority support. Munford, however, did not think that *majority* white support was needed to create the political pressure to pass a reparations bill. "A coalition between a black America *united* for reparations and an antiracist white minority rallying in support of black reparations can prevail over mass white opposition", he argued (Munford 2007, 451).

At the present moment, of course, much of the mobilization around racial injustice has centred on police violence and overly harsh penal policies. However, a transitional moment in this policy arena could provide a window of opportunity for the reparations movement. If the "New Jim Crow" system of mass incarceration was dismantled, and sweeping reforms passed in the areas of law enforcement and criminal justice, black reparations advocates and activists could make the case that the racial history of post-Civil Rights era incarceration policies, a racialized war on drugs, and so on, are the contemporary manifestations of anti-blackness in America, and that tangible reparations are owed. Indeed, the groundwork for this is already laid out in the contemporary Black Lives Matter movement: One of the six pillars of the umbrella group "The Movement for Black Lives" is reparations ("Platform" 2017).

A renewed push for reparations in the US, as we argue, would most likely be successful in a transitional moment, and would moreover benefit from the language and moral logic of transitional justice. Before making this argument in full, it is necessary to turn to an all-important distinction between transitional justice and remedial justice.

Transitional vs. remedial justice

The scale of black–white inequality in the US is daunting (King 2014). Instead of the wealth gap diminishing over time, it is becoming more substantial: results based on an analysis of the Panel Survey of Income Dynamics show that in the 23 years prior to 2007, the wealth gap between African American and white households increased by $75,000, from $20,000 to $95,000 (Shapiro, Tatjana, and Osoro 2013). Durable inequalities are also present in income, not just wealth. Considering the per capita income differential between white and African American workers in 1968, john powell (2007, 42) calculates that at the present pace of change, "it would take blacks 580 years" to close the gap. A Federal Reserve study moreover finds that African Americans are much less the beneficiaries of upward income mobility, and more likely to move downward than whites. Using two sets of intergenerational data, Mazumder (2014, 8) finds that "more than 50 per cent of blacks who start in the bottom quintile in the parent generation remain there in the child generation, but only 26 per cent of whites remain in the bottom quintile in both generations".

Statistics like these seem to bolster the claim that African Americans are owed reparations for intergenerationally transmitted inequalities that show no sign of abating on their own. The point of reparations, so it seems, would be to overcome economic inequalities tracking racial lines.

Here a distinction between what is sometimes called *corrective* or *remedial justice* and *transitional justice* is relevant. Remedial justice consists of policies and programmes designed to remedy the harmful effects of past injustice. Transitional justice, by contrast, is more focused on the causes that gave rise to the harmful effects, particularly rights violations, abuses of power, and atrocities. Because of its focus on causes, transitional justice is more interested in identifying perpetrators (even if amnesty is ultimately preferred to retribution), whereas remedial justice repairs harms without necessarily placing blame. This is not to say that transitional justice is only concerned with blame and unconcerned with repairing harms. But, for the transitional justice practitioner, coming to terms with past abuses and repairing harms go hand-in-hand.

The methods of transitional justice and remedial justice can and do overlap: monetary redress, land restitution, and programmes designed to correct particular inequalities are associated with both. However, the spirit in which such measures are undertaken varies significantly depending on whether a transitional or remedial justice standpoint is adopted. Consider affirmative action in the US. Though affirmative action emerged during a transitional moment, on the heels of the Civil Rights movement, it was quintessentially a remedial justice programme. As Owen Fiss, a Yale law professor and prominent white affirmative action advocate, describes the dilemmas that the policy fell into:

> For rejected white applicants, there is the frustration of desire, of not being able to attend particular schools or to obtain specific jobs. In addition, these applicants suffer a hurt that blacks know all too well – the hurt that comes from being judged disfavorably on a criterion unrelated to individual merit and over which they have no control. These grievances are indeed genuine; they are wrongs never to be forgotten and never to be trivialized ... In an imperfect world, a great transformation cannot be achieved without pain and sacrifice, without even a measure of injustice. Surely, this must be the great lesson of the Civil War. (Fiss 1997, 38)

Remarkably, Fiss is claiming that a white student with test scores equivalent or higher than her successful black counterpart who winds up at a lower-ranked university experiences a wrong "never to be forgotten and never to be trivialized". He calls attention to her "pain", her "sacrifice", the "injustice" – a sort of noble martyrdom which apparently warrants comparison to the Civil War's Union soldiers. But this formulation dangerously undervalues the sacrifices of those born into racial domination. Ironically, Fiss seems to be in the peculiar position of advocating that we forget *these* sacrifices – he explicitly rejects that affirmative action should have a backward-looking justification – while wanting us to never forget the sacrifices made by whites so that blacks may be equal.

Understood thusly, there is little difference between remedial justice, aiming to repair harm without tracing harm's origin or placing blame, and distributive justice, which determines how to allocate goods fairly. Whether

African Americans are given a "racial preference" in hiring and university admissions because of the *harm* of being disproportionately underrepresented or because of the *unfair allocation* implied in their disproportionate representation, the end result is the same. Efforts are made to increase numbers without reference to past injustices as the reason for the disparity. Here an observation made by Derrick Bell (1979, 8) rings true: the very language in which debates on the matter are conducted – affirmative action, preferential treatment – "sounds in *noblesse oblige*", suggesting "the giving of charity rather than the granting of relief".

We hypothesize – though without fully exploring the claim here – that during the major transitional moments in US history, programmes undertaken to advance the material and social equality of black Americans have been enacted under the banners of remedial and distributive justice, with little to no attention paid to racial inequality's origins. In addition to affirmative action, such programmes include school desegregation and, in the postbellum period, the Freedmen's Bureau.[5]

By contrast, advocates of black reparations have always been intensely focused on enslavement and segregation as the sources of intergenerationally transmitted harms, and on coming to terms with America's past as essential to any programme of monetary redress. Certainly, this is the whole point of Representative Conyer's H.R. 40 proposal. Yet because of their translatability into familiar policies, and their seeming to expeditiously address race-based material inequalities, (merely) remedial policies may be tempting.

Consider the publication of Ta-Nehisi Coates' 15,000-word essay, "The Case for Reparations" in the June 2014 issue of the *Atlantic* – an event which, if briefly, triggered widespread public debate about the "compounding moral debts" owed to black Americans. Debunking the myth of American innocence, and calling for a full examination of the abuses wrought by enslavement and segregation, were Coates' chief aims. But Coates also devoted a portion of the essay to examining West Germany's payment of monetary redress to Israel following the Holocaust. Reparations, in other words, could not just take the form of collective soul-searching. The debt would have to be paid off.

Coates' essay inspired many responses, with some commentators arguing that the proposal of material reparations was not so unrealistic. *Slate* journalist Jamelle Bouie contrasted direct cash payments to a more palatable "policy approach":

> Instead of cash, the federal government would implement an agenda to tackle racial inequality at its roots. This agenda would focus on major areas of concern: housing, criminal justice, education, and income inequality. As for the policies themselves, they don't require a ton of imagination. To break the ghettos and reduce the hyper-segregation of black life, the federal government would aggressively enforce the Fair Housing Act, with attacks on housing and

> lending discrimination, and punishment for communities that exclude low-income residents with exclusionary zoning. (Bouie 2014)

Bouie's response went on to discuss improving education and criminal justice reform as other important aspects of "policy reparations".

Bouie makes clear that he shares Coates' belief in the importance of undertaking a critical examination of the racist foundations of the American republic. But one can easily imagine a programme of "policy reparations" being implemented in a way that is completely ahistorical, for remedial and distributive justice reasons.

A deliberate programme of transitional justice, however, eschews the methods of ahistorical remedial justice. The difference between transitional justice's focus on rights violations and abuses (that may give rise to unjust inequalities) and remedial justice's focus on unjust inequalities (that may be caused by rights violations and abuses) is important. A form of transitional justice that fails to attend to past wrongdoing can be criticized as not properly being transitional justice.

To be clear, our aim here is not to make a normative argument about why the methods of transitional justice might be preferable to remedial justice, or why past injustices should be confronted. Again, it is to show that there is common ground between the aims of domestic reparations movements and transitional justice, and to argue for the usefulness of transitional justice to the domestic movements. Suffice it to say, looking at the way the black reparations movement frames its goals – e.g. "to heal the wounds of centuries of disdainful, brutal and inhumane treatment that the international community acknowledges as a crime against humanity" (Aiyetoro 2001, 474) – it seems clear that at issue is both unjust causes and harmful effects, and not just the latter on their own. As such, the movement has a greater affinity with transitional than with remedial justice.

Moreover, given the general complacency of many Americans, especially white Americans, regarding durable material inequalities between blacks and whites, it may only be during a "transitional" political moment that the claim to reparations has a chance of success. The end of mass incarceration holds promise to be such a transitional moment.

The end of mass incarceration: a time for reparations?

The US has the highest incarceration rate worldwide (Alexander 2012; Travis et al. 2014). This was not always the case. During the 1950s, the US's incarceration rate was comparable to other advanced industrial nations. Carceral expansion originated in the crime policies of the 1960s, and proliferated dramatically in the 1970s. These days, Americans are incarcerated at a rate five to ten times higher than their counterparts in other advanced industrial nations (Travis et al. 2014).[6]

The significance of carceral expansion's origins in the 1960s is deeply tied to race. As Vesla Weaver (2007) argues, increasingly punitive crime policy originated as a proactive response by white elites to the gains of the Civil Rights movement. "Mass imprisonment", a term first defined by sociologist David Garland, is a trait of criminal justice systems wherein "it ceases to be the incarceration of individual offenders and becomes the systematic imprisonment of whole groups of the population" (Garland 2001, 2). Michelle Alexander (2012, 6) points out that the percentage of the black population behind bars is higher in the contemporary US than in South Africa during apartheid. Young black men are incarcerated at such high rates that sociologists have come to consider prison a stage in the "life course" (Pettit and Western 2004. At any given point in time, 44 per cent of black women and 32 per cent of black men have a family member in prison (Lee et al. 2015).

In recent years, the US's approach to incarceration has been viewed with increasing critical scrutiny. In fact, ending mass incarceration is an issue that has received bipartisan political support. The non-partisan Brennan Center for Justice recently published a book featuring essays from prominent Democrats and Republicans all arguing for the imperative of criminal justice reform (Chettiar and Waldman 2015). It is not inconceivable, at least in the future, that Congress could pass sweeping criminal justice reforms effectively dismantling mass incarceration.[7]

If this were to happen, one thing is almost certain: the end of mass incarceration would not be an *ex gratia* act by political elites. Already the contemporary Black Lives Matter movement has brought much greater visibility to mass incarceration (Harris 2015), and draws comparisons with previous generations of Civil Rights activists (Porter 2016). If legislation is passed that is to mass incarceration what the Civil Rights Act of 1964 was to Jim Crow, this would likely be the result of dedicated, sustained grassroots pressure.

In light of this, recall the point that Black Lives Matter activists have embraced the earlier work of the black reparations movement, incorporating reparations into their formal platform. The end of mass incarceration would bear a significance that could justify a renewed push for reparations. In the black radical tradition, the racial epochs of American history are often understood as a chronology of enslavement, segregation, and mass incarceration (Davis 2016a), with each recalling the ghosts of previous epochs. The title of Michelle Alexander's bestseller on mass incarceration, "The New Jim Crow", references this "historical sequence of 'peculiar institutions'" (Wacquant 2001, 95). The end of the first two epochs saw remedial policies – the Freedmen's Bureau following the end of slavery, school desegregation and affirmative action following the end of segregation – but not transitional justice. The end of mass incarceration, signifying a major democratic transition, presents an opportunity to do better.

We envision a national programme of transitional justice inaugurated by Congressional legislation, either H.R. 40 or a successor bill. Like the injustices at issue in many post-conflict contexts, mass incarceration is a multifaceted, multi-layered state-sponsored injustice enabled by widespread societal participation. The federal government is a responsible party for its part in mass incarceration, but also plays the role of a moral "respondeat superior" (1) as the highest level of government in a highly complex system in which past and present actors at the federal, state, county, and municipal levels are complicit parties; and (2) insofar as it represents ordinary citizens whose attitudes towards and actions around crime and punishment have contributed to a political climate enabling mass incarceration.[8] Accordingly, the federal government should oversee a programme of transitional justice, unequivocally taking responsibility for contributions to mass incarceration at the federal level. But, it should also encourage lower-level governments, government officials, and members of society to reflect on and take responsibility for their actions and attitudes, and to join in as co-participants in the transitional justice process.

In the remainder of this section, we discuss different dimensions of transitional justice, and how they could be adapted to the context of mass incarceration in the United States.

Creating a public record

In most democratic transitions, the need arises to create an institutionalized public record that is able to counter revisionist claims and to show that public officials are committed to understanding and accepting the truth of past abuses, regardless of how damaging to a country's self-understanding or reputation. The end of mass incarceration would be no exception. Public hearings could be set up nationwide to collect testimony from individuals unjustly incarcerated due to draconian "three strikes" laws and mandatory minimum sentences (see Alexander 2012); who were subject to lengthy pre-trial detentions because they could not afford bail (see Subramanian et al. 2015); who pled guilty to spurious charges to escape pre-trial detention (see Heaton, Mayson, and Stevenson 2017), or because subject to "third degree" practices or other harsh interrogation tactics (see Skolnick and Fyfe 1994, chap. 3); and so on. Testimony could also be collected from family and community members of the incarcerated, as well as from prison guards, police officers, lawyers, judges, and others. Because carceral expansion has affected persons of all races, testimony on the "victim" side would not be limited to African Americans. However, one of the central goals of the hearings would be to collect testimonies that specifically speak to the theme of black humanity – in keeping with the spirit of the Black Lives Matter movement (Harris 2015) – and that contextualize mass incarceration as part of a historical legacy that includes enslavement and segregation.

Would these public hearings be understood as part of a "truth commission"? A "truth *and reconciliation*" commission? The form is important. However, it also should be a matter of public debate and ownership. If Americans were to self-consciously embark upon a national project of transitional justice in the wake of mass incarceration, they would have look to other countries for examples of each approach, and decide which model or models to emulate.[9]

Reparations

Boris Bittker's early 1970s work *The Case for Black Reparations* was the first book on black reparations hailing from the legal academy. Bittker's proposal was to pay monetary redress to individual African Americans who attended segregated schools (Bittker 1973). A long debate has ensued about whether reparations should in fact be paid to individuals, or should go to African Americans as a group – a "Reparations Superfund" administered by black trustees (Berry 2014).

A future national project of transitional justice should include reparations. In the spirit of Bittker's post-Civil Rights era proposal, reparations could be paid to unjustly incarcerated people. Alternatively, a Reparations Superfund could be used to fund projects in disadvantaged black neighbourhoods that mass incarceration has hit the hardest. There have also been other reparations proposals, like the idea of "Baby Bonds" (Hamilton and Darity 2010). We do not take a stand in favour of a particular proposal, but stress that it is not only the general public's input that should be sought. Amighetti and Nuti (2015) have argued that, in deciding what form reparations should take, government officials should bring in stakeholders for a process of deliberation. A deliberative forum could be held bringing together African Americans from all over the country to give their input, or the public hearings could be used to collect testimony on the question of what kind of reparations are owed.

Tailored measures

A national programme of transitional justice should also include "tailored measures" (Page 2015). Though not usually formally considered as part of the transitional justice toolkit, this is in keeping with the arguments of transitional justice scholars who point out that transitional justice is localized in practice (Williams and Nagy 2012). There may be measures that serve transitional justice aims – helping victims heal, cultivating trust, creating paths to reconciliation, and so on – that are only discernable by attending to the particular circumstances giving rise to a transitional justice response.

For example, in Chicago in the 1970s and 1980s, police commander Jon Burge subjected over one hundred African American men to torture in order to extract confessions (Taylor 2015). The subsequent grassroots reparations campaign culminated in 2015, when the city of Chicago passed a reparations ordinance allocating an apology, a memorial, monetary redress, including police torture in Chicago public school curricula, free college education for the torture survivors and their kin, and a counseling centre for the torture survivors. The latter two elements are the tailored measures, addressing the fact that the torture victims were imprisoned on illegally obtained, often false confessions. Like many formerly incarcerated people, the men tended to struggle with finding stable work upon reentry, and expressed interest in receiving educational support and access to a career centre. Now up and running (Eltagouri 2017), the Chicago Torture Justice Center could serve as a prototype for one kind of tailored measure appropriate to transitional justice in the wake of mass incarceration.

Accountability

A final category of transitional justice, "accountability", creates difficulties in the context of transitional justice for mass incarceration. Many organizers dedicated to ending mass incarceration are restorative justice activists; others identify more specifically as prison abolitionists. Transitional justice often involves criminal prosecution and punishment for government and military officials who committed atrocities, but this would hardly seem appropriate in the context under consideration. Alternative forms of accountability – perhaps restorative justice, perhaps other alternatives to incarceration that may emerge in the future – should be considered for those who have leveraged criminal justice-related abuses under colour of law.

Conclusion

In the past few years, there have been at least two hopeful moments for black reparations advocates and activists. The first was the publication of Ta-Nehisi Coates' "The Case for Reparations" and the largely positive reception given to the essay. The second was a 2016 report issued by the United Nations' Working Group of Experts on People of African Descent. "Despite substantial changes since the end of the enforcement of Jim Crow and the fight for civil rights", the report stated, "a systemic ideology of racism ensuring the domination of one group over another continues to impact negatively on the civil, political, economic, social and cultural rights of African Americans today" ("Report" 2016, 4). Among the Working Group's proposals were comprehensive reparations ("Report" 2016, 20). This received mention in many news outlets, though not inspiring nearly the same level of commentary as Coates' piece.

That a major American newsmagazine was willing to devote almost an entire edition to the topic, and that a group housed at the United Nations chose to spend time and political capital on the subject, suggests that reparations to African Americans are not a fringe idea. And yet, it seems hard to imagine a moment any time soon in which, as Clarence Munford envisioned, a united black majority and a strong contingent of antiracist whites and other people of colour would come together, rallying around reparations. As we have argued in this essay, there are strong affinities between the goals of transitional justice and domestic reparations movements. A major democratic transition, such as the end of mass incarceration no doubt represents, would provide an opening for the language and moral logic of transitional justice. This would be an opportunity not only to push for monetary redress, but also for a public inquiry into American racial history's most recent epoch and the ones preceding it.

Notes

1. In keeping with the editorial policies of *Ethnic and Racial Studies*, we use lower-case initial letters for "black/blacks" and "white/whites". The argument of this paper does not hinge on a distinction between the designations "black" and "African American"; accordingly, we use both terms.
2. Note that numerous congressional hearings did permit critics to vent their spleen against these policies and to blame the Labor Department for affirmative action schemes likes the Philadelphia Plan (Skrentny 1996).
3. N.B., In 1989, the bill was called H.R. 3745.
4. The United Nations' Working Group of Experts on People of African Descent also endorses H.R. 40 ("Report" 2016, 20).
5. It is true that symbolic reparative measures have been undertaken at various point, such as designating February "Black History Month" and issuing Congressional apologies for slavery and lynching (see also Valls 2003, 67). But these have not been part of a broader program to *interrogate* the past as a means of trying to *repair* the past.
6. This is in spite of there being similar levels of crime in the United States and other advanced industrial nations.
7. Because it is not the focus of this essay, we do not go into detail about what policies the end of mass incarceration would consist of. But naturally, this is a topic that others have written about (see, e.g. Austin and Eisen 2016). N.B., It is also possible for mass incarceration to be dismantled incrementally, a scenario that would not seem as conductive to our vision of a national program of transitional justice.
8. See Page 2015 for more on the "moral 'respondeat superior'". How responsibility for mass incarceration should be understood is an issue much larger than the present analysis can satisfactorily discuss, but to be clear, on our understanding,

it is not necessary to think that that there was a grand blueprint for mass incarceration that individual actors carried out. Mass incarceration, in our view, developed more organically, at multiple sites and in response to multiple factors. On normative accounts of responsibility (e.g. Pettit 2007), state actors and institutions can reasonably be understood as contributing to the state authorization of injustice, while leaving room for the causal role played by broader social structures and public attitudes.

9. Ifill (2003) proposes a truth and reconciliation commission for lynching, going into much more detail than we do here. Davis (2016b) discusses restorative justice as a basis for a truth and reconciliation commission for violence against African Americans; see also Valls 2003. Stevenson (2017) advocates transitional justice and emphasizes truth-telling.

Acknowledgements

Many thanks to the anonymous referees and to Jessica Simes for providing helpful feedback.

Disclosure statement

No potential conflict of interest was reported by the authors.

ORCID

Jennifer M. Page http://orcid.org/0000-0002-7326-6243

References

Aiyetoro, Adjoa. 2001. "Formulating Reparations Litigation Through the Eyes of the Movement." *NYU Annual Survey of American Law* 58: 457–474.

Alexander, Michelle. 2012. *The New Jim Crow*. New York: The New Press.

Amighetti, Sara, and Alasia Nuti. 2015. "Towards a Shared Redress: Achieving Historical Justice Through Democratic Deliberation." *Journal of Political Philosophy* 23 (4): 385–405.

Austin, James, and Lauren-Brooke Eisen. 2016. *How Many Americans Are Unnecessarily Incarcerated?* New York: Brennan Center for Justice. https://www.brennancenter.org/sites/default/files/publications/Unnecessarily_Incarcerated_0.pdf.

Beals, Melba Pattillo. 1994/2007. *Warriors Don't Cry*. New York: Simon Pulse.

Bell Jr., Derrick A. 1979. "Bakke, Minority Admissions, and the Usual Price of Racial Remedies." *California Law Review* 67 (1): 3–19.

Berry, Mary Frances. 2005. *My Face Is Black Is True: Callie House and the Struggle for Ex-slave Reparations*. New York: Alfred A. Knopf.

Berry, Mary Frances. 2014. "We Need a 'Reparations Superfund'." *New York Times*, June 9. http://www.nytimes.com/roomfordebate/2014/06/08/are-reparations-due-to-african-americans/we-need-a-reparations-superfund.

Bittker, Boris. 1973. *The Case for Black Reparations*. Boston, MA: Beacon Press.

Bouie, Jamelle. 2014. "Reparations Are Owed: Here Are a Few Ways to Pay the Bill." *Slate*, May 22. http://www.slate.com/articles/news_and_politics/politics/2014/05/

reparations_should_be_paid_to_black_americans_here_is_how_america_should.html.

Brooks, Roy L. 1996. *Integration or Separation?* Cambridge, MA: Harvard University Press.

Cato v. United States. 70 F.3d 1103 (9th Cir. 1995).

Chettiar, Inimai, and Michael Waldman, eds. 2015. *Solutions: American Leaders Speak Out on Criminal Justice*. New York: Brennan Center for Justice.

Clotfelter, Charles T. 2004. *After "Brown": The Rise and Retreat of School Desegregation*. Princeton: Princeton University Press.

Coates, Ta-Nehisi. 2014. "The Case for Reparations." *Atlantic*, June. http://www.theatlantic.com/magazine/archive/2014/06/the-case-for-reparations/361631/.

Crocker, David. 1998. "Transitional Justice and International Civil Society." *Constellations (Oxford, England)* 5 (4): 492–517.

Darby, Derrick. 2010. "Reparations and Racial Inequality." *Philosophy Compass* 5 (1): 55–66.

Davis, Angela J. 2016a. *Freedom Is a Constant Struggle*. Chicago, IL: Haymarket Books.

Davis, Fania. 2016b. "This Country Needs a Truth and Reconciliation Process on Violence Against African Americans – Right Now." *YES! Magazine*, July 8. http://www.yesmagazine.org/peace-justice/this-country-needs-a-truth-and-reconciliation-process-on-violence-against-african-americans.

Dawson, Michael, and Rovana Popoff. 2004. "Reparations: Justice and Greed in Black and White." *Du Bois Review* 1: 47–91.

Elster, Jon. 2004. *Closing the Books: Transitional Justice in Historical Perspective*. Cambridge: Cambridge University Press.

Eltagouri, Marwa. 2017. "Chicago's New Center for Police-torture Victims Is First of Its Kind in US." *Chicago Tribune*, May 27. http://www.chicagotribune.com/news/local/breaking/ct-burge-torture-justice-center-met-20170526-story.html.

Fiss, Owen M. 1997. "Affirmative Action as a Strategy of Justice." *Philosophy & Public Policy* 17: 37–38.

Garland, David, ed. 2001. *Mass Imprisonment*. London: SAGE Publications.

Girdusky, Ryan. 2016. "Millennials Open to the Idea of Slavery Reparations: Thank Academia?" *Red Alert Politics*. May 12. http://redalertpolitics.com/2016/05/12/millennials-open-idea-slavery-reparations-thank-academia/.

Giridharadas, Anand. 2016. "Turning the Call for Racial Reckonings Back on the U.S." *New York Times*, July 18. https://www.nytimes.com/2016/07/19/us/truth-reconciliation-commission-slavery.html.

Hamilton, Darrick, and William Darity Jr. 2010. "Can 'Baby Bonds' Eliminate the Racial Wealth Gap in Putative Post-Racial America?" *Review of Black Political Economy* 37: 207–216.

Harris, Fredrick. 2015. "The Next Civil Rights Movement?" *Dissent*. https://www.dissentmagazine.org/article/black-lives-matter-new-civil-rights-movement-fredrick-harris.

Heaton, Paul, Sandra Mayson, and Megan Stevenson. 2017. "The Downstream Consequences of Misdemeanor Pretrial Detention." *Stanford Law Review* 69 (3): 711–794.

Henry, Charles P. 2003. "The Politics of Racial Reparations." *Journal of Black Studies* 34 (2): 131–152.

Holland, Jess. 2016. "Older Whites Overwhelmingly Against Reparations for Slavery, But Millennials Are Not as Opposed." *US News & World Report*. May 11. https://www.

usnews.com/news/politics/articles/2016-05-11/poll-millennials-more-open-to-idea-of-slavery-reparations.

Howard-Hassmann, Rhoda. 2004. "Getting to Reparations: Japanese Americans and African Americans." *Social Forces* 83: 823–840.

Ifill, Sherrilyn. 2003. "Creating a Truth and Reconciliation Commission for Lynching." *Law & Inequality* 21: 263–311.

In re African American Slave Descendants, 471 F.3d 754 (7th Cir. 2006).

Johnson v. McAdoo. 244 U.S. 643 (1917).

King, Desmond S. 2014. "America's Civil Rights State: Amelioration, Stagnation or Failure?" In *Developments in American Politics*, 7th ed., edited by Gillian Peele, Christopher J. Bailey, Bruce Caine, and B. Guy Peters, 263–283. London: Palgrave Macmillan.

King, Desmond S., and Rogers M. Smith. 2011. *Still a House Divided*. Princeton: Princeton University Press.

Lee, Hedwig, Tyler McCormick, Margaret T. Hicken, and Christopher Wildeman. 2015. "Racial Inequalities in Connectedness to Imprisoned Individuals in the United States." *Du Bois Review* 12 (2): 269–282.

Marable, Manning. 2004. "In Defense of Black Reparations." *Freedom and Justice Crier*. http://www.neym.org/sites/default/files/Issue13.summer2004.pdf.

Mazumder, Bhashkar. 2014. *Black–White Differences in Intergenerational Economic Mobility in the United States*. Chicago: Chicago Federal Reserve Board. https://www.chicagofed.org/~/media/publications/economic-perspectives/2014/1q2014-part1-mazumder-pdf.pdf.

McCoy, Brian. 2014. "Renewed Call for Reparations." *NAACP*, May 30. http://www.naacp.org/blog/entry/renewed-call-for-reparations.

Munford, C. J. 2007. "Reparations: Strategic Considerations for Black Americans." In *Redress for Historical Injustices in the United States*, edited by Michael T. Martin and Marilyn Yaquinto, 447–451. Durham: Duke University Press.

Ogletree Jr., Charles. 2004. "Tulsa Reparations: The Survivors' Story." *Boston College Third World Law Journal* 24: 13–30.

Page, Jennifer M. 2015. "Reparations and State Accountability." PhD diss., Harvard University.

Pettit, Becky, and Bruce Western. 2004. "Mass Imprisonment and the Life Course: Race and Class Inequality in US Incarceration." *American Sociological Review* 69 (2): 151–169.

Pettit, Philip. 2007. "Responsibility Incorporated." *Ethics* 117 (2): 171–201.

"Platform." 2017. The Movement for Black Lives. https://policy.m4bl.org/platform/.

Porter, Nicole. 2016. "Unfinished Project of Civil Rights in the Era of Mass Incarceration and the Movement for Black Lives." *Wake Forest Journal of Law and Policy* 6 (1): 1–34.

powell, john a. 2007. "Structural Racism and Spatial Jim Crow." In *The Black Metropolis in the 21st Century: Race, Power, and Politics of Place*, edited by Robert D. Bullard, 41–65. Lanham, MD: Rowman & Littlefield.

"Report of the Working Group of Experts on People of African Descent on Its Mission to the United States of America." 2016. United Nations Human Rights Council. https://documents-dds-ny.un.org/doc/UNDOC/GEN/G16/183/30/PDF/G1618330.pdf.

Shapiro, Thomas, Tatjana Meschede, and Sam Osoro. 2013. "The Roots of the Widening Racial Wealth Gap." Institute on Assets and Social Policy Research and Policy Brief. http://www.naacpldf.org/files/case_issue/Shapiro%20racialwealthgapbrief.pdf.

Skolnick, Jerome, and James Fyfe. 1994. *Above the Law*. New York: Free Press.

Skrentny, John David. 1996. *The Ironies of Affirmative Action*. Chicago: University of Chicago Press.

Stevenson, Bryan. 2017. "The Presumption of Guilt: The Legacy of America's History of Racial Injustice." In *Policing the Black Man: Arrest, Prosecution, and Imprisonment*, edited by Angela J. Davis, 3–30. New York: Pantheon Books.

Subramanian, Ram, Ruth Delaney, Stephen Roberts, Nancy Fishman, and Peggy McGarry. 2015. "Incarceration's Front Door." Vera Institute of Justice. https://jpo.wrlc.org/bitstream/handle/11204/3988/Vera%20Report%20-%20Misuse%20of%20Jails%20-%202015.pdf.

Taylor, G. Flint. 2015. "Reparations Won." *Police Misconduct and Civil Rights Law Report* 11: 1–10.

Teitel, Ruti. 2000. *Transitional Justice*. Oxford: Oxford University Press.

Teitel, Ruti. 2014. *Globalizing Transitional Justice*. Oxford: Oxford University Press.

"Transitional Justice Initiative: Truth Commissions." 2016. Washington, DC: United States Department of State. https://www.state.gov/documents/organization/257772.pdf.

Travis, Jeremy, Bruce Western, and Steve Redburn, eds. 2014. *The Growth of Incarceration in the United States*. Washington, DC: National Academies Press.

Unger, Roberto Mangabeira. 1996. *What Should Legal Analysis Become?* London: Verso.

Valls, Andrew. 2003. "Racial Justice as Transitional Justice." *Polity* 36 (1): 53–71.

Wacquant, Loic. 2001. "Deadly Symbiosis: When Ghetto and Prison Meet and Mesh." *Punishment & Society* 3 (1): 95–133.

Waldron, Jeremy. 2006. "The Core of the Case Against Judicial Review." *Yale Law Journal* 115 (6) 1346–1406.

Weaver, Vesla M. 2007. "Frontlash: Race and the Development of Punitive Crime Policy." *Studies in American Political Development* 21 (2): 230–265.

Westley, Robert. 1998. "Many Billions Gone: Is It Time to Reconsider the Case for Black Reparations." *Boston College Third World Law Journal* 19: 429–476.

Williams, Melissa, and Rosemary Nagy. 2012. "Introduction." *Nomos LI: Transitional Justice*: 1–30.

Race, reconciliation, and justice in Australia: from denial to acknowledgment

Mark McMillan and Sophie Rigney

ABSTRACT

The harm perpetrated by the state of Australia against it Indigenous peoples has been structured, prolonged, and driven by race. In this paper, we conceptualize this harm and how it has been denied (and particularly how race has affected this harm and its denial). Although transitional justice literature has not traditionally been applied to an established democracy like Australia, we demonstrate why it is appropriate to apply transitional justice practices to the relationship between the Australian state and Indigenous peoples, and what transitional justice practices might provide in the Australian case. In particular, we argue that a transitional justice framework may allow Indigenous voices to name the harm inflicted on them, and position the state as acknowledging the harm that they have perpetrated – bringing a fundamentally new relationship between the state and Indigenous peoples.

Since the arrival of the British to what is now Australia in 1788, a great deal of harm been perpetrated against Australia's Indigenous peoples. Race has been a major driver of this harm: it has been used to justify the infliction of harm (for example, the removal of Indigenous children from their families on the basis of their race), and it has been used to structure the relationship between the Australian state and Indigenous peoples in a way that has allowed harm to be perpetrated (e.g. the insertion of the Race power in the Australian Constitution in 1901). Not only has this harm occurred, but it has been repeatedly denied by the Australian state. In this article, we examine the infliction of harm and its denial by the state of Australia. We argue that the prolonged and structured violence perpetrated by the state against Indigenous peoples requires a transitional justice framework to facilitate healing. The existing transitional justice literature has only recently turned to the Australian context, in part because an established democracy like Australia has not been traditionally seen as a "paradigmatic" case for transitional justice mechanisms. In order to establish why transitional justice might be appropriate in the Australian context, we commence this article by offering a novel understanding of how Australian political history has been constructed around the denial of racialized harm. We set out three key phases of the harm that has occurred, its denial, and its connection to race: Australia's progression from colony to nation and its relationship with the colonizing power; Australia's modern history of state institutions refusing to acknowledge the type and scale of harms; and the reconciliation movement as a political gesture rather than a healing move.

In the next part of the article, we examine why and how a transitional justice framework for Australia could permit greater realization of justice for Indigenous peoples. Numerous authors have pointed out the challenges of transitional justice in settler-colonial societies (see Nagy 2012; Henry 2015; Edmonds 2016). We acknowledge these problems, but argue that transitional justice has several characteristics which might make it useful in the Australian context. Unlike the Australian reconciliation policy, transitional justice places the state properly at the centre of any question of redress, and allows race to have a place in the construction of what healing might look like. These aspects are integral to the idea that transitional justice might allow a more fulsome healing to occur. We further argue that, in order to avoid the possible problems of transitional justice, such a framework should have at least two features: it must be structured with Indigenous voices naming the harm they have survived and the healing that is appropriate, and it must involve a full acknowledgment of the harm by the Australian state. This paper therefore makes three contributions: it sets out a novel history of race relations in Australia and the way the Australian state has denied the harm inflicted on Indigenous peoples; it offers a suggestion as to why transitional justice might be appropriate in Australia; and it makes normative proposals for how transitional justice should operate in Australia.

We write, together, as a form of a dialogue between Indigenous and non-Indigenous legal scholars. We have written previously about the utility of our coming together in this way, to provide a viewpoint from both an Indigenous and non-Indigenous perspective (McMillan and Rigney 2016). This article is an example of how we consider reconciliation dialogue can be optimally undertaken: with both Indigenous and non-Indigenous people talking openly, listening properly, and taking responsibility for their heritages and their current and future engagements. It is important for non-Indigenous peoples to have solidarity with Indigenous justice claims against the state, and also to take responsibility for their roles and position in the ongoing violence of settler-colonialism. However, this article focuses on the relationship between Indigenous Australians and the state of Australia, as the entity that has been responsible for much harm and that should now be responsible for acknowledging that harm and being involved with healing mechanisms.

Transitional justice: a framework for understanding race and historic injustices in established democracies?

Transitional justice can be defined as "the full range of processes and mechanisms associated with a society's attempt to come to terms with a legacy of large-scale past abuses, in order to achieve accountability, serve justice and achieve reconciliation" (United Nations 2004). Applying transitional justice mechanisms in Australia – an established democracy with a Constitution and stable governance, which has not experienced declared war on its territory – may appear contentious. The "transition" of transitional justice has typically referred to one of two "paradigmatic" cases: societies emerging from conflict, or moving from an old (authoritarian) regime to a new (democratic) one. Traditionally, transitional justice has been conceived of as involving a moment of rupture in a society (see Balint, Evans, and McMillan 2014). Transitional justice is "intimately tied with particular conceptions of democracy" (Ní Aoláin and Campbell 2005, 173). Established democracies have not traditionally been seen as requiring the mechanisms of transitional justice.

Yet democratic states can still perpetrate harm on a segment of their populations. As Ní Aoláin and Campbell point out, there can be cases of "conflicted democracies", where there is "prolonged, structured, communal, political violence, even where the political structures could broadly be considered 'democratic'" (Ní Aoláin and Campbell 2005, 174). We argue that Australia is an example of a democratic state, whose white structures of governance have inflicted such "prolonged, structured, communal, political violence" upon Indigenous Australians. A "conflicted democracy" has both a "deep seated and sharp division in the body politic, whether on ethnic, racial, religious, class, or ideological grounds", and actual or threatened "significant political violence" (Ní Aoláin and Campbell 2005, 176). We argue that both these conditions are met in the context of the Australian state and Indigenous Australians.

In response to this acknowledgement that established democracies may inflict harm upon their population, there has been some recent work that has considered the utility of employing transitional justice mechanisms in established democracies (Winter 2014). As Winter notes, while cases of paradigmatic change "makes it easier to distinguish transitional justice institutions [...] the context of established democracies requires more precision" (Winter 2013, 231). In such a context, human rights violations might be considered "systemic" (and therefore in need of a response) when such wrongdoing "is embedded in state policy" (Winter 2013). In these cases, state wrongdoing is not "deviant" or in breach of the accepted standards, but rather "the regime of citizen-state relations is itself perverse" (Winter 2013). Winter's analysis centres on the legitimacy of the state, and he argues that transitional justice can operate to "resolve the burden" which rests upon the legitimacy of the state as a result of the state's wrongdoing. In this article, we are less concerned with the state's legitimacy, than with the ongoing relationship between the state and Indigenous peoples. Nonetheless, Winter's work is important for conceptualizing the possibility of using transitional justice to ensure redress in cases of systemic harm committed by an established, democratic state.

Recent literature applying transitional justice to the relationship of a settler-colonial state and an Indigenous population has primarily focused on the Canadian experience. This literature has emerged particularly from Canada's recent Indian Residential Schools Truth and Reconciliation Commission (see James 2012; Nagy 2012; Nagy 2013). Australia and Canada share many similarities: both are former British colonies and are now settler-colonies with an Indigenous population. However, there are also significant differences regarding how the state interacts with Indigenous peoples. In particular, Canada has both a treaty framework and a human rights framework to regulate this relationship, while Australia has neither of these. This difference is due, in part, to the different histories of Canada and Australia, and particularly their different historical relationships with Great Britain: the British entered into treaties with Indigenous peoples in Canada, but in Australia they invoked the doctrine of *terra nullius*, or "land belonging to no-one" This allowed the British to claim the territory, as it was considered to exist without a state exercising sovereignty over it. The presence or absence of treaty and human rights frameworks is particularly relevant to state recognition of Indigenous people, their sovereignty, and the potential for the state to inflict harm. Treaties suggest a mutual recognition between the state and Indigenous peoples, and a human rights framework acknowledges that the state may wrongly engage in human rights violations against Indigenous people, and seeks to remedy any such violations. The absence of these two frameworks in Australia means that the relationship between the state and Indigenous peoples is profoundly different from the Canadian case.[1] For Australia's Indigenous people, the United Nations *Declaration on the Rights of Indigenous Peoples* is the main vehicle to regulate the relationship between Indigenous people and the state (Davis 2008, 470), and in the absence of domestic provisions, Australia's Indigenous peoples are compelled to use this international framework.[2] In this way, the emerging transitional justice literature on Canada is helpful for the Australian context, but only in part. The Australian story is sufficiently different to require its own conceptualizations. However, the application of transitional justice to the relationship between the Australian state and Indigenous Australians is a new field of scholarship, emerging only very recently (Balint, Evans, and McMillan 2014; Henry 2015). We seek to build upon this literature by reiterating the importance of black voices in building a transitional justice framework for Australia, and the importance of race in conversations of harm and healing.

However, transitional justice can be undertaken in ways that can undermine Indigenous justice claims. With its emphasis on the state, transitional justice can operate to silence or deny the justice claims of minorities and

> peoples' who make claims against the state. The emphasis of transitional justice on state-building has been matched with an "excessive individualism and false universalism, which may at times mask or obscure power relations within that discourse and which dominates "the imaginative space of emancipation". (Henry 2015, 207)

This individualism has been reflected in the frequent focus of transitional justice on individual restoration, rather than on forms of Indigenous healing (Nagy 2012, 60), which tend to be more communal and political. In these ways, transitional justice is not *always* or *necessarily* able to bring improved justice outcomes for Indigenous peoples. These potential failures must be overcome. In this article, we suggest ways in which transitional justice might be structured, to overcome some of these issues.

Identifying the harm done to indigenous populations in Australia

In this section of this article, we outline the key moments of harm in the Australian context, and demonstrate the ongoing denial of harm that has occurred. This can be conceptualized as falling into three phases: first, the emergence of Australia as a nation-state and the denial of conflict ("it is not us"); second, the unwillingness of the state to account for the type and scale of harm inflicted on Indigenous peoples ("that which cannot be named"); and third, reconciliation as a political discourse rather than one of justice. At each point, we attempt to acknowledge the complexity of the Australian situation, with its multiple and overlapping spheres of responsibility for harm – in particular, the relationship between the UK of Great Britain and Northern Ireland and the state of Australia. We do this by tracking the shifts in the entity that perpetrated the harms against Indigenous peoples in Australia. These timelines are not clearly demarcated: they circle in and around each other, and together constitute a history of Australia's race relations.

In setting out the three phases of harm and its denial in Australia, we demonstrate how race has been utilized by white structures of state to perpetrate – and then deny – the harm. Race has been built into the institutions and apparatuses of the Australian state. It was not until 1967 that the Australian Constitution was amended to allow Indigenous people to be counted in the population of Australia, and as we explain below, race has been placed into the Australian Constitution. There have only ever been eight members of federal parliament who were or are Indigenous, and of that number, four are incumbent at the time of writing this article in 2017. It is these white institutions of state that have engaged in a steadfast denial of the conflicts with Indigenous Australians and the harm inflicted on them.

(1) "It is not us": the denial of conflict

The territory now known as Australia has over 200 separate Indigenous communities, who lived with the land prior to British arrival, and have never ceded their sovereignty of this land. From the start of British settlement in 1788, "prolonged, structured, communal, political violence" has been inflicted on Indigenous Australians. This has included the use of force, armed hostilities, massacres, the removal of children, and dispossession of land (see Reynolds 2001; Creative Spirits 2016). However, the emergence of the Australian state independent from the colonial power, Great Britain, has obscured which entity must be accountable for past harms to Indigenous populations. At different points since the arrival of the British settlers, Australia has been a colonial outpost, a collection of colonies, a federation of states and territories, a dominion, and a member of the Realm of the Commonwealth with a British head of state. This multitude of political configurations, along with a complicated relationship with the colonial power, has permitted a space of plausible deniability for taking responsibility for the harms committed against Indigenous people. The state of Australia can deny their past responsibility, and at the same moment, Great Britain can deny any ongoing responsibility.

Race has been critical to the formation of the Australian nation-state, and particularly the transition of Australia from colony to nation (Moreton-Robinson 2007, 86–87). It was through "the intersection between race and property" that the legal fiction of *terra nullius* was permitted to be invoked by the British Crown, in order to justify British settlement (Moreton-Robinson 2007). Race, therefore, has always been integral to the encounters that have occurred between Indigenous peoples and settlers – and integral to the harms that have been inflicted on Indigenous peoples. The incorrect application of *terra nullius* permitted the acquisition of Indigenous lands for the British, and ensured that the Australian legal system was established upon incorrect assumptions about Australia's Indigenous peoples. One justification for *terra nullius* was that Indigenous peoples were technically not people of sufficient evolution on a scale of civilization (*Mabo v Queensland (No 2)*), and therefore it was not possible to be in conflict with them. These incorrect assumptions continued for nearly 200 years: it was only in 1992 that the doctrine of *terra nullius* was recognized by the Australian High Court as a legal fiction (*Mabo v Queensland (No 2)*). While this finding meant that there was no legal justification for the removal of land, by 1992 settler-colonialism was too advanced to fully return the lands to their traditional owners, and a complicated system of Native Title law emerged in Australia. This application of *terra nullius* was therefore integral to the claim made by the state of Australia, that it was not responsible for the harms done by the colonial state to the Indigenous peoples.

Prior to the federation of Australia, the colonies retained the sovereign powers to deal with Aborigines. This structure was facilitated by Great Britain, which allowed these self-governing powers to the individual colonies. During the 1880s and 1890s, each colony implemented their own versions of apartheid legislation that sought to minimize or "breed" out Aborigines – thereby using race to justify the infliction of harm (see, e.g. *Aboriginal Protection Act* 1869 (Vic)). The stated objective of the colonies in denying the Commonwealth the capacity to legislate for Aborigines was on the basis that it was their function to "smooth the pillow of the dying breed" (Human Rights and Equal Opportunity Commission 1997). These policies were intended to ensure the demise of the Indigenous populations in Australia (Human Rights and Equal Opportunity Commission 1997).

During the negotiations between the colonies and Great Britain to create the federation of Australia in 1901, Aboriginal peoples were denied a place within the new federal entity. Instead, the "race power" was drafted to specifically ensure that the federation of Australia would be denied the capacity to legislate for Aborigines (*Australian Constitution 1900*, s 51 (xxvi)). The "race power" originally read that the federal parliament possessed the ability to make laws with respect to "the people of any race, *other than the aboriginal race in any State*, for whom it is deemed necessary to make special laws" (*Constitution of Australia 1900*). Because of the structure of the Australian *Constitution*, which vests power in the states of Australia to make law in instances where there is no explicit federal power to do so, the capacity to legislate with respect to Aboriginal people remained with the states of Australia. In this way, race would be used to structure the relationship of the state to a segment of its population – its Indigenous peoples – so as to deny federal responsibility and vest that responsibility with the newly formed states. The "race power" would subsequently be amended in 1967 to permit the federal government to draft "special laws" for Indigenous people (see McMillan and Clark 2015). However, this change served to further embed race into the *Constitution* of the state of Australia, and thus into how the state interacts with Indigenous peoples.

Australia's progression to nation-state was complex, and it is not obvious when Australia officially became a nation-state. Between 1901 and 1926 the Commonwealth of Australia was a federal framework for the states. In 1926 with the enactment of the Balfour Declarations, Australia became a dominion within the Empire. In 1931 the UK parliament enacted the Statute of Westminster, which declared the dominions to be "autonomous Communities within the British Empire", equal in status and "united one to another by a common allegiance to the Crown" (Bennett 2004). In 1942, the Statute of

Westminster was adopted by Australia and back-dated to 3 September 1939. However Australia was not legally independent from the UK until 1986, when the *Australia Acts* cut off any appeals from Australian courts to the Privy Council. Australia remains a member of the Realm of the Commonwealth, and today still retains the Monarch of the UK as the Australian Head of State. British involvement in the "internal" affairs of Australia has continued.

This relationship between the UK and Australia has meant that both entities can plausibly deny their involvement in, or responsibility for, the harms that were committed. White Australian institutions have been able to argue that it was the colonies and ultimately the colonial power that was responsible, while the UK rarely features in any discussion about Indigenous and non-Indigenous relationships in Australia, and is reticent to engage in any such conversations (Lawson 2014). As will be demonstrated in the next section, the Australian state has continued to actively deny the harms that occurred and their continued ramifications on Indigenous peoples today.

(2) That which cannot be named: the denial of genocide

The space for denial that has been permitted by Australia's complex history of nationhood and its relationship with the colonial power, has been opened further through a steadfast refusal to name the degree and type of harm inflicted. In particular, Australian institutions of state have refused to name the harm as genocide. Genocide – a term linked with state based or state sanctioned atrocities – has been debated ferociously in Australia since the 1970s (Tatz 2011). Under the *Convention on the Prevention and Punishment of the Crime of Genocide* (1948), "genocide" is defined as undertaking particular acts, "with intent to destroy, in whole or in part, a national, ethnical, racial or religious group, as such". These acts include killing and "forcibly transferring children of the group to another group". However, it was Australia's ratification of this Convention in 1948, which first forewarns of the difficulties of the concept to be applied in Australia. During the parliamentary debates at this time, several members of parliament stated that genocide as an "act of state" would be unimaginable to occur or apply in the Australian context (see Tatz 2011, who makes reference to two parliamentarians speaking in the Commonwealth Parliament in 1948).

Genocide has continued to be denied in the Australian context. Official mechanisms of state that have tried to raise the issue of genocide against the Indigenous populations have been discouraged. To the extent that such mechanisms have occurred at all, they have been piecemeal and limited. For example, legal proceedings and processes have been unwilling to describe any such instances of harm as genocide (see *Kruger v Commonwealth* 1997). During the twentieth century, there were 118 government investigations into Indigenous Affairs (Tatz 1998, 2). Of these, the most "powerful and critical" investigation was the National Inquiry into the "Separation of Aboriginal and Torres Strait Islander Children from Their Families" (Tatz 1998). As will be demonstrated below, however, whilst this Inquiry might have been "the most critical", it still failed to adequately name the harm done – and this failure actually further facilitated the space for denial.

This Inquiry into the "Stolen Generations" was established in 1995. The report of the Inquiry – entitled *Bringing Them Home* – was tabled in the Australian parliament in 1997 (Human Rights and Equal Opportunity Commission 1997). This report examined the question of whether the removals of children amounted to genocide, and found that the policy of forcible removal of Indigenous children "could properly be labelled 'genocidal' in breach of binding international law from at least 11 December 1946" (Human Rights and Equal Opportunity Commission 1997, 239). This declaration is an important acknowledgement of the harm caused by policy and practice of removing children from their families. On first impression, this statement appears to recognize that this practice amounted to genocide. Certainly, this is how some scholars have read this statement (see Gunstone 2016). However, the particular wording invoked – that the practice *could* be labelled genocidal, rather than *is* properly labelled genocidal – in fact leaves a large degree of uncertainty and equivocation. This softer language permits a space for some to contest the idea that this practice was genocidal. This framing of the genocide issue is further complicated and made particularly egregious because the original draft of the *Bringing Them Home* report is understood to have included a particular recommendation that genocide be a finding of the Inquiry. However, this recommendation did not appear in the final report (Human Rights and Equal Opportunity Commission 1997), and instead was replaced with this more ambiguous language. What remains is not a finding of genocide having occurred, or a finding that government policy in fact amounted to genocide. Instead, this is a finding that allows some to argue that the removal of children from their families was not genocide. Indeed, this is what then occurred, including at the highest levels of the state. By not articulating the harm unequivocally as genocide (but rather as "could be labelled 'genocidal'"), *Bringing Them Home* actually facilitated this denial.

Australia has actively been involved in "culture wars" since the mid-1990s. The "culture wars" has included debates about how history should be understood and taught, particularly the history of violence perpetrated against Indigenous peoples and whether this was genocide. Some historical accounts are being recast to genuinely reflect the magnitude of harms by the colonial apparatus against Indigenous peoples (see Reynolds 1982; Curthoys and Docker 2001; Ryan 2012). However, others have advocated a perspective that either denies or minimizes the harms. In particular, some have argued that the scale of harm has been exaggerated (see e.g. Windschuttle 2002; Windschuttle 2009). It is not only in academic argument that the harms have been denied or minimized: this has also been a hallmark of the Australian state institutions.

One example of this use of scale to deny the harm done to Indigenous peoples was the claim by the Federal Minister for Indigenous Affairs in 1996, that the Stolen Generations was not a "generation" at all – because only ten per cent of children that potentially could have been removed from their families, were in fact removed (Herron 2000). This statement ignores the fact that all Aboriginal children considered to be "half caste" or "less" *could* be removed. Playing with numbers cannot change the genocidal intention behind the removal of children, nor the effect that has had (intergenerationally) on all Indigenous people. Being Indigenous meant that you could be taken away from your family. Indigenous people have had to live with this, as their truth, from 1886. As a result, large numbers of people could not identify as Indigenous. The trauma of this continues today. That the Federal Minister for Indigenous Affairs was able to engage so readily in this denial of harm – in his official capacity as the Minister responsible for interactions between Indigenous peoples and the state – demonstrates the connections between the state, and the active denial of harm and responsibility for harm done by the state to Indigenous peoples.

The *Bringing Them Home* report made several recommendations that can be understood as further transitional justice mechanisms: apologies, the provision of reparations, and self-determination. The report recommended that all Australian Parliaments "officially acknowledge" previous "laws, policies and practices" of removal, and that they "negotiate with the Aboriginal and Torres Strait Islander Commission a form of words for official apologies" (Human Rights and Equal Opportunity Commission 1997, recommendation 5a). From this, two things are particularly clear: first, that acknowledgement of harm is required, and second, that it is for Indigenous peoples to name the harm that occurred and the healing that is acceptable to them (as we discuss further, below). However, it was not for another decade that the federal Australian parliament undertook this apology. In the intervening years, Australia continued to deny the scale and type of harm – as well as denying Indigenous self-determination and sovereignty. Even more egregiously, this denial was conducted under the banner of "reconciliation". The next section of this paper examines how the state of Australia has engaged in "reconciliation" as a political discourse rather than a justice discourse.[3]

(3) Reconciliation as a political discourse of private relationships

To the degree that the Australian state has engaged in questions of harm and healing, it has done so through a model of "reconciliation". This policy has lacked definitional clarity (see Short 2008, 39–41). However, the Australian government has defined reconciliation as being "about unity and respect between Aboriginal and Torres Strait Islanders and non-Indigenous Australians. It is about respect for Aboriginal and Torres Strait Islander heritage and valuing justice and equity for all Australians" (Australian Government 2015). As a policy of the Australian government, "reconciliation" is forward-looking, does not adequately acknowledge the harms of the state, and does not allow the capacity for Indigenous peoples to seek justice through reconciliation post conflict.

The reconciliation policy commenced in 1991, with the establishment of the Council for Aboriginal Reconciliation (later Reconciliation Australia). The preamble for the *Council for Aboriginal Reconciliation Act* 1991, which established this Council, states that "to date, there has been no formal process of reconciliation between Aborigines and Torres Strait Islanders and other Australians". As Henry points out, the Australian reconciliation movement is

> premised on a vision of formal equality ("equity for all Australians") located within a restorative justice paradigm that seeks to unite all Australians. In this conceptualization, the state does not feature as a reconciling party but rather serves as the behind-the-scenes facilitator of reconciliation. (Henry 2015, 204)

The state *supports* reconciliation, rather than participating in it – this passive role allows the state to gain legitimacy, by making invisible the state's role as the cause of harm to Indigenous people. Reconciliation is individualized and the emphasis is on private relationships, rather than on the state and how the state relates to communities that it has inflicted harm upon. Ultimately, the reconciliation policy has allowed a denial of the harms perpetrated by the state, and therefore has been used to "bolster the legitimacy, authenticity and stability" of the Australian state (Henry 2015). The reconciliation process is hence best understood as a stage in the colonial project rather than a genuine attempt at atonement (Short 2008). In particular, the reconciliation policy has dismissed Indigenous claims to sovereignty and nationhood (see Short 2008; Henry 2015). This is a further reiteration of the denial of harm, as it does not permit a acknowledgment that cultures, ways of knowing law, and governance systems were attacked in the colonial process. It also reinforces white supremacy over territory, and ignores black understandings of the harm that was done, and what is required for healing. Reconciliation has been conducted on "white" terms.

The response to the *Bringing Them Home* report is a particular example of how "reconciliation" has been conducted as a politically controlled discourse, in a way that denied the justice sought by Indigenous peoples and that denied their sovereignty. Prior to the tabling of the *Bringing Them Home* report, a new conservative government headed by Prime Minister John Howard was elected in 1996. The Howard government rejected the recommendations for apology, reparations, and Indigenous rights on the basis that such actions "premised [reconciliation] solely on a sense of national guilt and shame" (Howard 1997).

In 1999, Howard made a *Motion of Reconciliation* to the federal parliament. In part, this motion stated that the parliament recognizes "the achievements of the Australian nation" and that it "recognises the importance of understanding the shared history of indigenous and non-indigenous Australians and the need to acknowledge openly the wrongs and injustices of Australia's past" (Howard 1999). It continued with the acknowledgement "that the mistreatment of many indigenous Australians over a significant period represents the most blemished chapter in our national history" and that the parliament "expresses its deep and sincere regret that indigenous Australians suffered injustices under the practices of past generations, and for the hurt and trauma that many indigenous people continue to feel as a consequence of those practices" (Howard 1999). Finally, it ends with the statement that parliament "believes that we, having achieved so much as a nation, can now move forward together for the benefit of all Australians" (Howard 1999).

This *Motion* has been criticized for its expression of "regret" rather than an apology. Further, the mention of "mistreatment" in this motion significantly understates the harm inflicted on Indigenous peoples (see Gunstone 2016) and is, clearly, a long way from an acknowledgement of genocide. Although Howard consulted with the only Indigenous member of parliament at that time, there were a great number of Indigenous people who felt that this motion was deeply insufficient. Indigenous conceptions of harm and healing had not been prioritized. Finally, the emphasis of this motion on the nationhood of Australia and "the achievements of the Australian nation" explicitly uses reconciliation as a nation-building exercise for the Australian state, further denying Indigenous sovereignties.

In 2007, following the election of a new government, prime minister Kevin Rudd made a formal apology to the Stolen Generations, in federal parliament. The repeated invocation of the words "we say sorry" made this apology particularly powerful, and the apology was "generally well received by Indigenous and non-Indigenous peoples" (Gunstone 2016, 308). However, the Rudd apology again refused to acknowledge the practices of removing children as genocide. As Short has noted, in this sense "the apology failed to describe the harm inflicted accurately and in the terms favoured by many of the victims" (Short 2012, 299).

At the time of writing, in 2017, the recommendations from *Bringing Them Home* still have not been implemented in full. In particular, reparations have not been offered by the federal government; and the recommendations for "self-determination" have not been implemented. The major political discourse in relation to Indigenous Australians and the state is focused on Constitutional amendment to "recognize" Indigenous Australians in the *Constitution*. Unlike some state governments (in Victoria and South Australia), the federal government has no plans to enter into treaty negotiations with Indigenous communities. Meanwhile, attempts to "close the gap" between Indigenous and non-Indigenous wellbeing indicators have stalled: in 2017, it was announced that targets to improve life expectancy and reduce infant mortality rates for Indigenous Australians would not be met (The Guardian 2017). In these ways, structural and political harms are continuing.

The possibility of justice: naming the harm

It is therefore clear that there has been a disavowal of the nature and type of harm in white Australian narratives and institutions of state, and also a disavowal of Indigenous conceptions of healing. Reconciliation, rather than being a mechanism for healing, has been employed by the state as a mechanism for the state's legitimation – a form of "hijacking" of supposedly healing mechanisms, for political motives (see Subotic 2009). In this way, both harm and healing have been "whitewashed" in Australia. There is a disjuncture between, on the one hand, reconciliation as a project; and on the other hand, reconciliation as an attribute of transitional justice discourse and practice.

Given the failures of the reconciliation movement, and the failures of state processes to adequately name the harm (let alone offer any redress), a more appropriate approach may be transitional justice. Henry has similarly argued that transitional justice is a "more useful conceptual framework to examine past historical injustices in established democracies" (Henry 2015, 205). Henry has suggested a transitional justice model for Australia based on acknowledgement of harm, reparation "through innovative justice mechanisms", and an acknowledgment of "differing and competing political perspectives of both injustice and justice" (Henry 2015).

As discussed above, transitional justice does have many potential problems. However, it is our argument that transitional justice has two particular characteristics that the reconciliation policy has not demonstrated: it centralizes the role of the state, and it allows black voices to articulate the harm done and the healing that is possible. However, these are *possibilities* and not *certainties* for the use of transitional justice, and we therefore make the normative argument that these aspects be enforced in any transitional justice framework. Any such framework must be structured with Indigenous voices naming the harm they have survived, and must involve a full acknowledgment of the harm by the state. We now turn to these arguments.

First, transitional justice brings an understanding of the state having perpetrated harms on a section of its population – and that the state that is responsible for the provision of redress. The state is therefore placed as a core entity in the infliction of harm and the responsibility for healing. As Henry points out, transitional justice "has the potential to draw critical attention to the role and harms of the state, rather than presenting it in either neutral or beneficial terms" (Henry 2015). This is a key strength of applying transitional justice literature to established democracies, because such states might otherwise refuse to acknowledge the harm they have caused, or that they can be integral to ensuring healing. As we have shown, the reconciliation movement in Australia has been criticized because it minimized the role of the state as an active participant in the reconciliation process. Transitional justice, however, emphasizes the state and its responsibility – while at the same time, transitional justice permits the voices of victims to have an integral part in naming the harm and conceptualizing the healing. Although the state is highlighted, it is not the sole focus of transitional justice.

Secondly, just as race has operated as a factor in the infliction of harm, race can also be central to practices of healing. In particular, race is an important aspect of why the reconciliation movement in Australia has been limited, and why transitional justice could be a more appropriate model for addressing historical and ongoing injustices inflicted on Indigenous peoples by the state. In particular, transitional justice may be able to centralize black voices in articulating the harm and healing, and thus to support Indigenous conceptions of justice. As Kieran McAvoy and Lorna McGregor have argued, communities must have input into transitional justice mechanisms appropriate for their community: this is transitional justice "from below" (McAvoy and McGregor 2008). In the Australian context, we argue that community-driven transitional justice must centre an Indigenous framing of harm and healing, with Indigenous communities setting out what type of redress they want – and from whom. The over two hundred separate Indigenous communities in Australia may have different experiences of harm, and different expectations of what constitutes healing. Understanding this multiplicity must be a first step in any transitional justice framework for Australia. There are, however, some apparent commonalities between Indigenous communities, and these form a useful place to start an examination of what transitional justice might look like. It follows from what we have set out above that it is necessary to have an act of acknowledgment of the responsibility for, and the scale of, the harm done. Acknowledgment is the opposite of the denial we have outlined above. Such denial has only served to further reinforce the harm: to refuse to acknowledge the stories of harm, or to minimize the scale of the harm, is fundamentally re-traumatizing.

While both the *Bringing Them Home* report and the apology to the Stolen Generations can be understood as moments of transitional justice (see Balint, Evans, and McMillan 2014; Henry 2015) and indeed as moments of acknowledgment of harm, these moments have been piecemeal and have not been undertaken as part of a transitional justice framework. They have not definitively named the violence as genocide. Moreover, they also both address just one aspect of violence – the removal of children from their families –

while other violence has gone unacknowledged. Future transitional justice mechanisms should address the multiplicities of harm inflicted on Indigenous peoples, in a holistic manner. Such mechanisms should also consider the continued structural injustices inflicted by the settler-colonial state. Both the harms inflicted by Great Britain (and its colonies), and by the state of Australia, should be considered. This is not a small project, and if the history we have set out above is any guide, it may prove to be politically unpalatable to white Australia. Nonetheless, it is a crucial project if Australia is to account for its historical injustices.

Arguably, the closest that Australia has come to such a moment of acknowledgment of the harm inflicted on Indigenous peoples was the then-Prime Minister Paul Keating's "Redfern" speech, which acknowledged:

> it begins, I think, with that act of recognition. Recognition that it was we who did the dispossessing. We took the traditional lands and smashed the traditional way of life. We brought the diseases. The alcohol. We committed the murders. We took the children from their mothers. We practiced discrimination and exclusion. (Keating 1992)

Keating was correct that healing must begin with a proper, complete act of recognition of harm and who was responsible for it. For this reason, the Redfern speech remains a powerful moment of and the Australian state, represented by the prime minister, acknowledging some responsibility for past injustices. However, this speech did not go as far as constituting an apology for that harm. Keating stated that he did not believe guilt was something that white Australia should feel (Keating 1992). Further, the Redfern speech centred the state of Australia, rather than Indigenous sovereignties, with Keating's assertion that Aboriginal Australians "helped build this nation" (Keating 1992). Although the Redfern speech was an important moment of acknowledgment of harm, it is also an example of how this was done in a manner which did not engage with Indigenous wishes. This moment can be transcended.

A transitional justice framework for Australia might include a Truth and Reconciliation Commission with a mandate to address all the harm perpetrated against Indigenous Australians (not only the removal of children). This would rectify the problem that the National Inquiry into the Stolen Generations only focused on one aspect of harm, rather than the other complex patterns of violence that were committed as part of settler-colonialism, but that have never been fully investigated as part of a Commission of Inquiry. Further, full reparations for the Stolen Generations, and reparations for other forms of harm, should also be implemented. Finally, a new legal relationship between the state and Indigenous peoples, which recognizes the sovereignty of those peoples – a treaty – should be negotiated. In this way, transitional justice would be undertaken in a way that prioritizes Indigenous sovereignties. This would be fundamentally different from the reconciliation policy, which denied Indigenous sovereignties. This, then, is a political implication of allowing black voices in the construction of healing, and of placing the state at the centre of questions of redress. However, all these mechanisms must be conceptualized and undertaken in a way that allows Indigenous peoples to name the healing processes that are most meaningful.

Conclusion

The Australian state has denied the harms committed against Indigenous peoples, and at the basis of this denial has been race. White Australian institutions of state have actively created a narrative that has denied responsibility for harm, and white Australian institutions of law and state have further reinforced this narrative through denying to name the harm done as genocide. Finally, reconciliation policies have been driven by white Australian institutions of politics, in order to bolster their own position and deny Indigenous understandings of harm, healing, and sovereignty. In light of all this, we call for a renewed framework, based in a transitional justice conceptual model, to better align Indigenous and non-Indigenous ways of relating.

We have demonstrated that although transitional justice has not traditionally been associated with established democracies, increasingly it is understood that that transitional justice is necessary in states – including democracies – that have systemic wrongdoings embedded in state policy. This has been the case in settler-colonial states such as Australia, but the application of transitional justice to Australia is only now emerging. Without a treaty framework, the Australian story is different from that of other established democracies that have started to employ transitional justice frameworks for understanding the relationship between the settler-colonial state and Indigenous peoples. The Australian context necessitates its own examination of how transitional justice can be operationalized. In addition, the Australian state is now a party to the *United Nations Declaration on the Rights of Indigenous Peoples*, which – in the absence of a treaty with Indigenous peoples – is the main mechanism for Indigenous peoples to seek justice. This *Declaration* requires states to provide effective redress for acts of harm (article 8(2), *Declaration on the Rights of Indigenous Peoples* 2007). In light of this obligation in the *Declaration* – and the emergent scholarship that properly situates transitional justice within established democracies – now is an appropriate moment to use transitional justice frames to understand the relationship between white history and black sovereignty. As we have argued, in order to actually encourage improved justice outcomes for Indigenous Australians, a model of transitional justice for Australia must prioritize Indigenous understandings of harm and healing, in order to ensure that the state undertakes an appropriate acknowledgment of harms caused and the continuing existence of Indigenous sovereignties.

Notes

1. Similarly, in New Zealand a treaty governs the relationship between the state and Indigenous peoples. The literature on transitional justice in New Zealand (see Winter 2014) is of some assistance, but not precisely on point for Australia.
2. Other relevant international human rights documents include the International Covenant on Civil and Political Rights, the International Covenant on Economic, Social and Cultural Rights, and the International Covenant on the Elimination of all forms of Racial Discrimination.
3. When we discuss a "political discourse" as being problematic in this article, we are referring particularly to the way that the reconciliation policy of the Australian state has been undertaken in a political mode – involving the legitimizing of state behavior, rather than a mode of atonement. We do not mean to suggest that all politics are inherently negative; indeed, it is also a political act to engage in transitional justice.

Disclosure statement

No potential conflict of interest was reported by the authors.

ORCID

Sophie Rigney http://orcid.org/0000-0001-6247-2159

References

Australian Constitution. 1900.

Australian Government. 2015. "Reconciliation." Accessed May 4 2015. http://www.australia.gov.au/about-australia/australian-story/reconciliation.

Balint, Jennifer, Julie Evans, and Nesam McMillan. 2014. "Rethinking Transitional Justice, Redressing Indigenous Harm: A New Conceptual Approach." *International Journal of Transitional Justice* 8: 194–216. doi:10.1093/ijtj/iju004.

Bennett, Scott. 2004. "Australia's Constitutional Milestones" Accessed August 27, 2004. http://www.aph.gov.au/About_Parliament/Parliamentary_Departments/Parliamentary_Library/Publications_Archive/online/Milestones.

Creative Spirits. 2016. "Aboriginal History Timeline (1770–1899)." Accessed May 27, 2016. http://www.creativespirits.info/aboriginalculture/history/aboriginal-history-timeline-1770-1899#axzz47IEPai00.

Curthoys, Ann, and John Docker. 2001. "Introduction – Genocide: Definitions, Questions, Settler-Colonies." *Aboriginal History* 25 (1): 1–15.

Davis, Megan. 2008. "Indigenous Struggles in Standard-setting: The United Nations Declaration on the Rights of Indigenous Peoples." *Melbourne Journal of International Law* 9 (2): 439–471.

Edmonds, Penelope. 2016. *Settler Colonialism and (Re)conciliation: Frontier Violence, Affective Performances, and Imaginative Refoundings*. Hampshire: Palgrave Macmillan.

The Guardian. 2017. "Closing the Gap Report Shows Life Expectancy and Child Mortality Targets Are Not Being Met." Accessed February 14, 2017. https://www.theguardian.com/australia-news/2017/feb/14/closing-the-gap-report-shows-life-expectancy-and-child-mortality-targets-are-not-being-met.

Gunstone, Andrew. 2016. "Reconciliation, Reparations and Rights: Indigenous Australians and the Stolen Generations." In *Handbook of Indigenous Peoples' Rights*, edited by Corinne Lennox and Damien Short, 301–312. Abingdon: Routledge.

Henry, Nicole. 2015. "From Reconciliation to Transitional Justice: The Contours of Redress Politics in Established Democracies." *International Journal of Transitional Justice* 9: 199–218.

Herron, John. 2000. "A Generation Was Not Stolen." The Sydney Morning Herald, April 4, 15.

Howard, John. 1997. "Transcript of the Prime Minister the Hon John Howard MP Opening Address to the Australian Reconciliation Convention." Accessed May 26, 1997. https://pmtranscripts.dpmc.gov.au/release/transcript-10361.

Howard, John. 1999. "Transcript of the Prime Minister the Hon John Howard MP Motion of Reconciliation." Accessed August 26, 1999. http://parlinfo.aph.gov.au/parlInfo/search/display/display.w3p;query=(Id:media/pressrel/23e06);rec=0.

Human Rights and Equal Opportunity Commission. 1997. *Bringing Them Home: National Inquiry into the Separation of Aboriginal and Torres Strait Islander Children from Their Families*. Sydney: Commonwealth of Australia.

James, Matt. 2012. "A Carnival of Truth? Knowledge, Ignorance and the Canadian Truth and Reconciliation Commission." *International Journal of Transitional Justice* 6: 182–204.

Keating, Paul. 1992. "Redfern Speech (Year for the World's Indigenous Peoples) – Delivered in Redfern Park by Prime Minister Paul Keating." Accessed 10 December 1992.

Kruger v Commonwealth. 1997. 190 CLR 1.

Lawson, Tom. 2014. *The Last Man: A British Genocide in Tasmania*. London: I.B. Tauris.

McMillan, Mark, and Martin Clark. 2015. "Making Sense of Indigeneity, Aboriginality and Identity: Race as a Constitutional Conundrum Since 1983." *Griffith Law Review* 24 (1): 106–126.

McAvoy, Kieran, and Lorna McGregor. 2008. *Transitional Justice from Below: Grassroots Activism and the Struggle for Change*. Oxford: Hart.

McMillan, Mark, and Sophie Rigney. 2016. "The Place of the First Peoples in the International Sphere: A Logical Starting Point for the Demand for Justice by First Peoples." *Melbourne University Law Review* 39 (3): 981–1002.

Moreton-Robinson, Aileen. 2007. *Sovereign Subjects: Indigenous Sovereignty Matters*. Sydney: Allen & Unwin.

Nagy, Rosemary. 2012. "Truth, Reconciliation and Settler Denial: Specifying the Canada–South Africa Analogy." *Human Rights Review* 13 (3): 349–367.

Nagy, Rosemary. 2013. "The Scope and Bounds of Transitional Justice and the Canadian Truth and Reconciliation Commission." *International Journal of Transitional Justice* 7: 52–73.

Ní Aoláin, Fionnuala, and Colm Campbell. 2005. "The Paradox of Transition in Conflicted Democracies" Human Rights Quarterly Mabo v Queensland (No 2) (1992) 175 CLR 1.

Reynolds, Henry. 1982. *The Other Side of the Frontier. Aboriginal Resistance to the European Invasion of Australia*. Melbourne: Penguin.

Reynolds, Henry. 2001. *An Indelible Stain? The Question of Genocide in Australia's History*. Melbourne: Viking.

Ryan, Lyndall. 2012. *Tasmanian Aborigines: A History Since 1803*. Sydney: Allen & Unwin.

Short, Damien. 2008. *Reconciliation and Colonial Power: Indigenous Rights in Australia*. Abingdon: Routledge.

Short, Damien. 2012. "When Sorry Isn't Good Enough: Official Remembrance and Reconciliation in Australia." *Memory Studies* 5 (3): 292–304.

Subotic, Jelena. 2009. *Hijacked Justice: Dealing with the Past in the Balkans*. Ithaca: Cornell University Press.

Tatz, Colin. 1998. "The Reconciliation 'Bargain'." *Melbourne Journal of Politics* 25: 1–8.

Tatz, Colin. 2011. "Genocide in Australia: By Accident or Design?" Indigenous Human Rights and History 1 (1). https://www.monash.edu/__data/assets/pdf_file/0020/141554/tatz-essay.pdf.

UN General Assembly. 1948, December 9. *Convention on the Prevention and Punishment of the Crime of Genocide*. United Nations, Treaty Series, Vol. 78, p. 277.

United Nations. 2004. "The Rule of Law and Transitional Justice in Conflict and Post-conflict Societies, UN Doc S/2004/616." Accessed August 23, 2004 [8].

United Nations. Declaration on the Rights of Indigenous Peoples, GA Res 61/295, UN GAOR, 61st sess, 107th plen mtg, Supp No 49, UN Doc A/RES/61/295. Accessed September 13, 2007.

Windschuttle, Keith. 2002. *The Fabrication of Aboriginal History: Volume One: Van Diemen's Land 1803–1847*. Sydney: Macleay Press.

Windschuttle, Keith. 2009. *The Fabrication of Aboriginal History: Volume Three: The Stolen Generations 1881–2008*. Sydney: Macleay Press.

Winter, Stephen. 2013. "Towards a Unified Theory of Transitional Justice." *International Journal of Transitional Justice* 7: 224–244.

Winter, Stephen. 2014. *Transitional Justice in Established Democracies: A Political Theory*. Basingstoke: Palgrave Macmillan.

Index

Note: Boldface page numbers refer to tables & page numbers followed by "n" denote endnotes.

For Product Safety Concerns and Information please contact our EU representative GPSR@taylorandfrancis.com
Taylor & Francis Verlag GmbH, Kaufingerstraße 24, 80331 München, Germany

www.ingramcontent.com/pod-product-compliance
Ingram Content Group UK Ltd.
Pitfield, Milton Keynes, MK11 3LW, UK
UKHW011017180926
475701UK00004B/785
* 9 7 8 0 3 6 7 5 8 4 3 7 5 *